World Stage Press

Verse from the Village

THESE PAGES SPEAK

THESE PAGES SPEAK

You Tube

Creative Writing Course Reader

Edited by

HIRAM CHARLES SIMS

World Stage Press
Verse from the Village

World Stage Press
Verse from the Village

Copy Edit by Marilyn Forrest
Layout Design by Nadia Hunter Bey
Cover Design by Lorraine Butler

This book is dedicated to the students at The Los Angeles Film School. These are the poems and stories you loved most.

acknowledgements

I'd like to thank my beautiful wife, Charisse Sims for supporting me during the compilation of this work. I'd also like to thank Nadia Hunter Bay and Tanya Ko for the invaluable editorial assistance they gave during this project.

Most importantly, I would like to thank every author who contributed something to this text.

To enjoy each author's performance of their work, please downloan any QR Code Reader App on your phone, or enter the title and author into a youtube search window.

CONTENTS

PREFACE

Every time a student takes out their cell phone in my class, it makes me sick to my stomach. I endeavor to design each class's curriculum so that each minute is just as captivating as the last. I use an array of multi-media, countless group exercises, introspective writing prompts--I even stand on the table and perform. I do all this for the purpose of creating an engaging lesson that will keep them focused, so when I see them dig through their purse or pocket and extract the bane of my professional existence, it makes my blood boil. The message I received in a silent, finger scrolling scream was that this class is boring. What you are saying is boring. What you are reading is boring. You are boring, and I would rather scroll through old text messages than listen to you. One day, my student Marcus was typing something on his phone while I was going over an essay prompt. It took me a good twenty minutes to complete the explanation, and when I asked the students to begin brainstorming, he was still neck-deep in his iPhone. Forgetting momentarily that he was an adult, I walked over to him enraged, prepared to snatch his phone and put it in my desk like he was a 6th grader. I said, "Marcus, I asked you to write your outline. What are you doing?" He turned the screen toward me and said, "I'm writing my essay." I took the phone and read this amazing introduction paragraph, filled with academic sources he also found on his phone, and I realized I was a caveman in a digital age.

As all teachers know, technology is rapidly changing the way that we teach classes. SMART classrooms, filled with computers, projectors, and sound systems, have given us the option to digitize our lessons, allowing us to integrate multi-media in a manner never before experienced in a school. This, of course, is no revelation to anyone who has taken a class in the last 10 years. But what has changed is the way we read and consume literature. The advent of YouTube and Vimeo has given us unprecedented access to the author's actual voice. I have always enjoyed reading poetry and fiction, but I fell in love with creative writing when I realized that I was reading a remnant of a **live** experience. When I began visiting poetry lounges and fiction readings in Los Angeles, I realized that authors were performing everything I was reading. I also discovered that some of the rhythms and cadences (with which I was reading their work on my own) were wrong. None more evident as my favorite poem *We Real Cool*, by Gwendolyn Brooks. I had been reading that poem to students for years, but when I googled her biography and came upon an audio clip of her reading it, I discovered my rhythm was totally off.

When we have the power, rhythm, and cadence of the original author's voice, we have a treasure that turns the literary experience into something more personal and provocative. We hear the original inflection and emotion with which each author intended their work to be heard or experienced. To hear the tone and nuance of the author's voice while I am reading their work has always been my favorite way to consume literature, and it has become the favorite method of my own creative writing students. Nearly every single literary device example in this book can be found on YouTube, read by the original author.

The purpose of this text is for creation, and individualized recreation. Often times as students, we are asked to look at a model, examine the model, and recreate our own individualized version of the archetype. In my 8th grade Algebra textbook, the first page of each chapter described the lesson, showed me a problem, solved the problem, then asked me to complete 50 sample problems.   This textbook is no different. The goal is for you to understand the lesson (or literary device) through the visual examination of the model poem or story, then create your own. We must see the construction of iambic pentameter in order to recreate it. We must see the format of story dialogue in order to reconstruct it. The beauty of this text is that now, you can hear it as you examine the form.

Use your phone. Fashion it now as a tool by which you will gain unprecedented access to this amazing contemporary literature. When you discover something you love, search the web for more of their outstanding work. These pages speak, if you are willing to listen.

Hiram Sims

RHYTHM

noun \ˈri-thəm\

: a regular, repeated pattern of sounds or movements
a :an ordered <u>recurrent</u> alternation of strong and weak elements in the flow of sound and silence in speech
b:the group of instruments in a band supplying the rhythm — called also *rhythm section*

Trochee: A stressed syllable, followed by an unstressed one
Iamb: An unstressed syllable followed by a stressed one, as in *to-DAY*

In literature, rhythm is the pattern of stressed and unstressed beats. Rhythm is most commonly found in poetry, though it is also present in some works of drama and prose. The rhythm of a poem can be analyzed through the number of lines in a verse, the number of syllables in the line, and the arrangement of syllables based on whether they are long or short, accented or unaccented. All poetry can be understood in the context of rhythm. If poetry can be contextualizd as an equation, an idea married to a rhythm equals a poem (rhythm + idea = poem). Some poets find a classic or contemporary rhytm first, then pour their idea into the rhythm. Other poets prefer the inverse. Within this chapter are iambic poems, trochaic poems, chorus poems, list poems, free verse and some spoken word styles. The one thing to remember above all else is that if you have no rhythm, you have no poem.

MY ARSENAL
Glen Fitch

I like to stack them tall or end-to-end,
but then I dread I'll find some dud I've penned.
Each syllable feels heavy in my hand,
a sharp, slick sound to pierce and then expand.
Like shrapnel multi-meanings pack each shell.
A shot with match-grade words set to propel
incendiary sentences. I use
the slightly fraying phrases as a fuse.
And oh, the satisfaction, oh the fun
to set with care then hide the trip-wire pun,
or plant an ode or sonnet meadow with
no hint of hidden mines of symbol, myth.
Believe me, no offense meant on my part,
but every bullet's aiming at your heart.

WHAT I WILL
Suheir Hammad

I will not dance to your war
drum. I will
not lend my soul nor
my bones to your war
drum. I will
not dance to your
beating. I know that beat.
It is lifeless. I know
intimately that skin
you are hitting. It
was alive once
hunted stolen
stretched. I will
not dance to your drummed
up war. I will not pop
spin beak for you. I
will not hate for you or
even hate you. I will
not kill for you. Especially
I will not die
for you. I will not mourn
the dead with murder nor
suicide. I will not side
with you nor dance to bombs
because everyone else is
dancing. Everyone can be
wrong. Life is a right, not
collateral or casual. I
will not forget where
I come from. I
will craft my own drum. Gather my beloved

near and our chanting
will be dancing. Our
humming will be drumming. I
will not be played. I
will not lend my name
nor my rhythm to your
beat. I will dance
and resist and dance and
persist and dance. This heartbeat is louder than
death. Your war drum ain't
louder than this breath.

TO MY FAVORITE 17-YEAR-OLD HIGH SCHOOL GIRL
Billy Collins

Do you realize that if you had started
 building the Parthenon
on the day you were born,
you would be all done in only one more year?
Of course, you couldn't have done that all alone.
So never mind; you're fine just being yourself.
You're loved for just being you.

But did you know that at your age
Judy Garland was pulling down 150,000 dollars a picture,
Joan of Arc was leading the French army to victory
and Blaise Pascal had cleaned up his room
— no wait, I mean he had invented the calculator?
Of course, there will be time for all that later in your life,
after you come out of your room and begin to blossom,
or at least pick up all your socks.

For some reason I keep remembering that
Lady Jane Grey was queen of England
when she was only 15.
But then she was beheaded,
so never mind her as a role model.
A few centuries later, when he was your age,
Franz Schubert was doing the dishes for his family,
but that did not keep him from composing two
symphonies,
four operas and two complete masses as a youngster.
But of course, that was in Austria at the height of Romantic
lyricism,
not here in the suburbs of Cleveland.

Frankly, who cares if Annie Oakley was a crack shot at 15
or if Maria Callas debuted as Tosca at 17?
We think you're special just being you —
playing with your food and staring into space.
By the way, I lied about Schubert doing the dishes,
but that doesn't mean he never helped out around the
house.

WHAT SHALL THEY SAY IN MY DEMISE?
Hiram Sims

What Shall they say in my demise?
Shall trumpet roar, and drummers blare
the country's pain upon their snare?
Shall roses pour into the wind
to mark my legendary end?
Shall mourners line the city streets
to watch my coffin's dark retreat?
When banners fill these western skies,
What shall they say in my demise?

How shall they weep upon my fall?
Will mothers scream and daughters wale?
Will Widows moan beneath their veil?
Will Fathers curse and brothers sob
amidst the sullen, angry mob?
Will preachers pray to understand
 the brittle, fragile life of man?
Shall tears consume a million eyes?
What shall they say in my demise?

What utterance will grace their lips?
Shall friends recant my noble deeds
while Catholics rub their rosary beads?
Will politicians all condone
the grace I wielded from my throne?
Shall glory and brilliance exclaim
from every mouth that speaks my name?
"Another Vain King shuts his eyes"
Are words they'll spew in my demise!

DO NOT GO GENTLE INTO THAT GOOD NIGHT
Dylan Thomas

Do not go gentle into that good night,
Old age should burn and rave at close of day;
Rage, rage against the dying of the light.

Though wise men at their end know dark is right,
Because their words had forked no lightning they
Do not go gentle into that good night.

Good men, the last wave by, crying how bright
Their frail deeds might have danced in a green bay,
Rage, rage against the dying of the light.

Wild men who caught and sang the sun in flight,
And learn, too late, they grieved it on its way,
Do not go gentle into that good night.

Grave men, near death, who see with blinding sight
Blind eyes could blaze like meteors and be gay,
Rage, rage against the dying of the light.

And you, my father, there on the sad height,
Curse, bless, me now with your fierce tears, I pray.
Do not go gentle into that good night.
Rage, rage against the dying of the light.

LESS IS MORE
Kuahmel

Less broken homes, more fathers together with mothers
Less niggas, more brothers
Less bitches, more civilized queens
More good-mannered youth, less snotball teens
More living within means, less fakin' it till ya make it
Less ending up broke, homeless, hungry, and naked
Less slackers, more achievers above average
Less jailbirds, more college graduates
Less penitentiary chances, more calculated risks
Less materialism, more materialists
Less check cashing places, more money banked
Less ungrateful behavior, more praise and thanks
Less entertainers, more educators
Consume less now, leave more for later
Less monopolies, more competition,
More variety
Makes way less of a bland society
Addition by subtraction
Less is more
Quality over quantity
Less is more
When you know the law of cause and effect
Significant change is in store
Less is more
Less can't, more can. Less won't, more will
Less relying on youth and talent, more skill
Less religion, more free thinking
Less cheap soda pop, more water drinking
More live foods, less dead meat
More well-adjusted children when less dads are deadbeats
More activity, less obesity
More fast food has been less of a good look recently

Less vacant lots, more parks and houses
More nice scenery for me when less chicks wear blouses
Less prisons and jails, more hospitals and schools
More geniuses, less damn fools
Less gang bangin', more organized action
More unity, less factionin'
Less littering, more keeping the hood beautiful
Which in turn makes the hood more suitable
Addition by subtraction
Less is more
Quality over quantity
Less is more
Eliminate the root of the problem
Plant the seed of solution at the core
Less is more
More politeness, less vulgarity
Less confusion blurring things, more clarity
More protecting and serving, less excessive force
More marrying at the right time, less divorce
More good sex at home, less cheating
The more listening, the less need for repeating
Less gluttony, more moderation
More art, more science, less mindless entertainment
More lucrative careers, less turning to crime
Less gassing boogerwolves, more bagging dimes
Less clutter and hoarding, more organizing
Less gas guzzlers on the road with more downsizing
More biofuels, less petroleum complications
More respect for borders, less oppressor occupation
More productivity with less substance dependency
We'd progress much more with less of these bad
tendencies

YOU MAKE LOVE LIKE A PINBALL MACHINE

Cynthia Alessandra Briano

The focus, the rolling of silver, the   lopsided bunt,
Love, it is not   the thumbed jab of the lever
that keeps   the mercury rolling, nor

the spasmkick of knee
that retrieves those lost balls, still

I ring my encouragement, ring
'cause it doesn't even matter that I'm
always   kinda   off to the side,

a slanted   amusement device
you roll down   with a   bump.
Even when   all your springs are exhausted, I

whirr and   blink at the
score I pretend not to keep,

the it'll-do buzz
the little-point pong

the spiral
spring of laughter
and

woop
at the

occasional

thousand-point

ping.

AFTER (excerpt)
Carolina Rivera

It is after the assassination of Archbishop Monseñor Oscar Arnulfo Romero.

It is after the end of the rainy season, the end of October.

It is after the school year ends.

It is after the American nuns are raped, shot and buried at the side of a road, out of sight of the airport.

It is after the massacre of students at the Universidad de El Salvador, who were bombed and burned alive in the tunnels they themselves had dug under the university to hide weaponry from the military, tunnels where they thought they might hide, too.

It is after the first guerilla uprising. It is soon after the government's decision to have the death squads leave body parts in neighborhoods, to create fear and intimidation.

It is after our Papá loses his job forever as a master builder, because he refuses to leave the workers' union.

It is after he is swallowed up by the daily drinking he cannot stop.

It is after the first Christmas the family spends without our three oldest boys.

It is after our parents force them to flee to Mexico because they are politically involved, because there is no way for young men to avoid being conscripted from the streets, because there is no work here, and because our father and mother cannot feed us all.

It is after our father says to the eldest, "Take this money. Tomorrow we wake up at four in the morning. We are leaving. I am dropping you at the border of Guatemala and Chiapas." He says, "God go with you. Don't forget us." A few months, then a year later he repeats the same scene with my second oldest and then my third oldest brothers. We get up early and give each brother a hug. Each time our mother's attempts to weep quietly, but it is too hard for her. The wrinkles around our father's eyes grow more obvious, deeper each time the ritual is repeated.

It is after my father and uncle spend a whole day going from the jail in Santa Ana to the prison in San Salvador, looking for cousins who had been taken away the night before because some *orejas* say these young men from the countryside are with the guerilleros.

It is after our father and uncle return to Santa Ana that next day to be told that clear plastic bags, with tops carefully tied with plastic-coated wire have been found discarded on the street in Santa Ana. The bags contain the disassembled bodies of two young males.

It is after our uncle identifies his sons from their gold dental work and a ring left on a finger.

It is after I fall in love with a guerillero. He says, "Let's meet at the *Parque Libertad* tomorrow at eight a.m. Then I will take you to a house where other compañeros and I are hiding." Orlando wants to hold me in his arms. I take his hand and give it a squeeze to say yes. When we arrive at the house the next day, not in the morning but at dusk, I see the house has no electricity, no water. He says, "We are careful to enter and exit unnoticed, at night only, for a few days at a time. Then we move on to another secret location." There are only a few blankets on the tile floor. "Sit down and don't open any windows," he whispers to me after we climb through a back window. "And don't go into the other room." He smiles at me. "There's a very fat man, a very strange person living there."

As he walks towards the bathroom, I notice the open door to the other room. I've been told not to, but I go in and find the floor covered with Spanish newspapers from

31

1930 to 1935. There are boxes of books, medals and antique bullets on shelves. There are pictures of military men from that era on the walls. Everything in the room is related to the civil war in Spain. I feel strange as I think of Spain, and then of Europe and its subsequent holocaust.

An arm reaches around my waist, and I let out a short scream. "I told you not to come over here!" Orlando smiles, grows serious as he holds his index finger to my lips.

"Shhh... We are only here for a few days to do a special task and then we will go to another place. Who knows where?" he hugs me, kisses me so hard that I feel I am disappearing into him in that dark room.

It is after my friend Alba's family found her body on San Francisco Street in the neighborhood of Jardines de Guadalupe. Her breasts had been hacked off and a stick was shoved into her vagina. The death squads liked to dump bodies in this quiet stretch of neighborhood where children take short cuts to and from school.

It is after my sister Estela starts having visions of evil shadows at the window and takes to her bed for six months. I spend hours and hours at her bedside consoling her.

It is after my father comes home very drunk from a day's search for a job that doesn't exist. He breaks the television, all the light bulbs in the house and then some furniture. With our mother we hide from him under the beds until he passes out. Then, we tie him to the side of his wooden bed until the next morning.

It is after the guerillas' final offensive. I say goodbye to Orlando and never see him again.

It is after I finish my high school studies and my mother makes me a white cotton jumpsuit for the graduation ceremony, but I am not able to wear it because I spill coffee on it at breakfast. "Damn it, girl! Just because you don't like it doesn't mean you have to do that." My mother starts crying. I wear an old pair of my brother's pants and a boy's shirt. At graduation, the Director of the Ministry of Education says, "I am very happy to honor our successful art students, who, with such great effort, have completed their secondary education." Certificates are passed out to each of us, and we are asked to pose for a picture. In the class photo there are 5 other girls in dresses and I look like a boy, with a big smile. One of the girls is pregnant. I roll up my certificate and stick it in my pants pocket. The graduation party is at one of the boys' homes. His mother is cooking a pig to celebrate.

It is after I find myself looking for a job on the streets of San Salvador, and instead of finding a job, I have men stopping their cars to ask me if I want to hop in. From a distance, I yell, "Pig! Hijos de puta!" and I feel better.

It is after one of my former teachers asks me to join a guerrilla movement.

(Continued)

X-TREEM
Queen Socks

they say opposites attract
is this true
because it's you
it's you that separate me from the rest of the world
and ironically you complete me
so to say opposites attract
seems to be a bit extreme
but if this is true
then I start to say extreme things
Like
you are the oil to my water
the dumb to my smarter
the sunshine to my rain
you are the cure to my pain
and everything you touch I claim
you take me to my extremes
or I can be extreme and use two things that are the same
Like
you are the wet to my water
or the smart to my smarter
the hot to my sunshine
or the cure that cures no pain yet seems to make
everything feel better
but if opposites really attract
then I might say things that don't make sence
Like
you are the hot water that Makes my sunshine wet!
or around you I make a dummy look smarter because I
forget......
or your pain is better than your cure because it's more
X-treem

do you understand what kind of love I mean?
I mean the type of love that makes yo momma sing
old negro spirituals and church hymns
on the front porch with her friends and them
My God
you are the cloud that produces my rain
the bad word that's used in vain
and when I feel that I have nothing else in this world to gain
you are the truth that keeps me sane
you are the dark in my coffee
the light when the world is to dark around for me to see
that you are what I want to be
'cause who can love me as much as you but me

when my money is funny
you are the bee to my honey
the flavor in my tea
you are my red eyes when I get no sleep
you are what keeps me meek
you complete me
Like
sugar to kool-aid
A smile to a bad day
the words when I am stuck but I have something to say
a good night sleep to my next day
a mothers nursing nipple to a newborn baby
the answers to my maybe
the answers to my questions
the punishments to my lesson
the sins to my confession

My God
you complete me
taking me to my extremes
you are the supper to my natural

35

the pick to my afro
you are the water when my bath is full
you are the bark to my tree and my dog
the brick to my basket ball and my wall
you are the air to my plane and my breath
and because of you I just plain breath air
now I'm an air head
floating on cloud 9
hoping it will bring me closer to you
you are the done to my through
but everyone seems to have one just like you
but theirs is a little different
and in this case that makes a lot of since
because you are...

MY GOD!!!!

COLLOQUIALISM

noun \ -ˈlō-kwē-ə-ˌli-zəm\
: a word or phrase that is used mostly in informal speech *b* : a local or regional dialect expression

Vernacular

adjective \və(r)-ˈna-kyə-lər\
: of, relating to, or using the language of ordinary speech rather than formal writing: of or relating to the common style of a particular time, place, or group

The word "colloquialism" comes from the Latin *colloquium*, which means a "conference" or "conversation." As a literary device, colloquialism refers to the usage of informal or everyday language in literature. Colloquialisms are generally geographic in nature, in that a colloquial expression often belongs to a regional or local <u>dialect</u>. They can be words, phrases, or aphorisms (see below for examples). Native speakers of a language understand and use colloquialisms without realizing it, while non-native speakers may find colloquial expressions hard to translate. This is because many colloquialisms are not literal usages of words, but instead idiomatic or metaphorical sayings. Colloquialism is similar to slang, but the definition of colloquialism has some key differences as described below. In our attempt to capture the sound of a character or voice, we must endeavor to bend the language to reflect the time and region of the speaker. Keep in mind that writing in dialect is a conscious choice-- the writer knows both formal and informal English, and is choosing the informal.

WHEN MALINDY SINGS
Paul Laurence Dunbar

G'way an' quit dat noise, Miss Lucy--
Put dat music book away;
What's de use to keep on tryin'?
Ef you practise twell you're gray,
You cain't sta't no notes a-flyin'
Lak de ones dat rants and rings
F'om de kitchen to de big woods
When Malindy sings.

You ain't got de nachel o'gans
Fu' to make de soun' come right,
You ain't got de tu'ns an' twistin's
Fu' to make it sweet an' light.
Tell you one thing now, Miss Lucy,
An' I 'm tellin' you fu' true,
When hit comes to raal right singin',
'T ain't no easy thing to do.

Easy 'nough fu' folks to hollah,
Lookin' at de lines an' dots,
When dey ain't no one kin sence it,
An' de chune comes in, in spots;
But fu' real malojous music,
Dat jes' strikes yo' hea't and clings,
Jes' you stan' an' listen wif me
When Malindy sings.

Ain't you nevah hyeahd Malindy?
Blessed soul, tek up de cross!
Look hyeah, ain't you jokin', honey?
Well, you don't know whut you los'.

Y' ought to hyeah dat gal a-wa'blin',
Robins, la'ks, an' all dem things,
Heish dey moufs an' hides dey face.
When Malindy sings.

Fiddlin' man jes' stop his fiddlin',
Lay his fiddle on de she'f;
Mockin'-bird quit tryin' to whistle,
'Cause he jes' so shamed hisse'f.
Folks a-playin' on de banjo
Draps dey fingahs on de strings--
Bless yo' soul--fu'gits to move 'em,
When Malindy sings.

She jes' spreads huh mouf and hollahs,
"Come to Jesus," twell you hyeah
Sinnahs' tremblin' steps and voices,
Timid-lak a-drawin' neah;
Den she tu'ns to "Rock of Ages,"
Simply to de cross she clings,
An' you fin' yo' teahs a-drappin'
When Malindy sings.

Who dat says dat humble praises
Wif de Master nevah counts?
Heish yo' mouf, I hyeah dat music,
Ez hit rises up an' mounts--
Floatin' by de hills an' valleys,
Way above dis buryin' sod,
Ez hit makes its way in glory
To de very gates of God!

Oh, hit's sweetah dan de music
Of an edicated band;
An' hit's dearah dan de battle's
Song o' triumph in de lan'.

It seems holier dan evenin'
When de solemn chu'ch bell rings,
Ez I sit an' ca'mly listen
While Malindy sings.

Towsah, stop dat ba'kin', hyeah me!
Mandy, mek dat chile keep still;
Don't you hyeah de echoes callin'
F'om de valley to de hill?
Let me listen, I can hyeah it,
Th'oo de bresh of angel's wings,
Sof' an' sweet, "Swing Low,
Sweet Chariot,"
Ez Malindy sings.

THE BOY AND THE BAYONET
Paul Laurence Dunbar

To Hannah and "Little Sister," as to Bud, all of the remainder of the drill was a misery. The one interest they had had in it failed, and not even the dropping of his gun by one of Company "E" when on the march, halting in line, could raise their spirits. The little girl tried to be brave, but when it was all over she was glad to hurry out before the crowd got started and to hasten away home. Once there and her tears flowed freely; she hid her face in her mother's dress, and sobbed as if her heart would break.

"Don't cry, Baby! don't cry, Lammie, dis ain't da las' time da wah goin' to be a drill. Bud'll have a chance anotha time and den he'll show 'em somethin'; bless you, I spec' he'll be a captain." But this consolation of philosophy was nothing to "Little Sister." It was so terrible to her, this failure of Bud's. She couldn't blame him, she couldn't blame anyone else, and she had not yet learned to lay all such unfathomed catastrophes at the door of fate. What to her was the thought of another day; what did it matter to her whether he was a captain or a private? She didn't even know the meaning of the words, but "Little Sister," from the time she knew Bud was a private, knew that that was much better than being captain or any of those other things with a long name, so that settled it.

Her mother finally set about getting the supper, while "Little Sister" drooped disconsolately in her own little splint-bottomed chair. She sat there weeping silently until she heard the sound of Bud's step, then she sprang up and ran away to hide. She didn't dare to face him with tears in her eyes. Bud came in without a word and sat down in the dark front room.

"Dat you, Bud?" asked his mother.

"Yassum."

"Bettah come now, supper's puty 'nigh ready."

"I don' want no supper."

"You bettah come on, Bud, I reckon you mighty tired."

He did not reply, but just then a pair of thin arms were put around his neck and a soft cheek was placed close to his own.

"Come on, Buddie," whispered "Little Sister," "Mammy an' me know you didn't mean to do it, an' we don' keer."

Bud threw his arms around his little sister and held her tightly.

"It's only you an' ma I care about," he said, "though I am sorry I spoiled the company's drill; they say "B" would have won anyway on account of our bad firing, but I did want you and ma to be proud."

"We is proud," she whispered, "we's mos' prouder dan if you'd won," and pretty soon she led him by the hand out to supper.

Hannah did all she could to cheer the boy and to encourage him to hope for next year, but he had little to say in reply, and went to bed early.

In the morning, though it neared school time, Bud lingered around and seemed in no disposition to get ready to go.

"Bettah git ready fer school," said Hannah cheerily to him.

"I don't believe I want to go any more," Bud replied.

"Not go any more? Why ain't you shamed to talk that way! O' cose you a goin' to school."

"I'm ashamed to show my face to the boys."

"What you say about de boys? De boys ain't a-goin' to give you no edgication when you need it."

42

"Oh, I don't want to go, ma; you don't know how I feel."

"I'm kinder sorry I let you go into dat company," said Hannah musingly; "'cause it was de teachin' I wanted you to git, not de prancin' and steppin'; but I did t'ink it would make mo' of a man of you, an' it ain't. Yo' pappy was a po' man, ha'd wo'kin', an' he wasn't high-toned neither, but from the time I first see him to the day of his death I nevah seen him back down because he was afeared of anything," and Hannah turned to her work.

"Little Sister" went up to Bud and slipped her hand in his. "You ain't a-goin' to back down, is you, Buddie?" she said.

"No," said Bud stoutly, as he braced his shoulders, "I'm a-goin'."

But no persuasion could make him wear his uniform.

The boys were a little cold to him, and some were brutal. But most of them recognised the fact that what had happened to Tom Harris might have happened to any one of them. Besides, since the percentage had been shown, it was found that "B" had outpointed them in many ways, and so their loss was not due to the one grave error. Bud's heart sank when he dropped into his seat in the Assembly Hall to find seated on the platform one of the blue-coated officers who had acted as judge the day before. After the opening exercises were over he was called upon to address the school. He spoke readily and pleasantly, laying especial stress upon the value of discipline; toward the end of his address he said: "I suppose Company 'A' is heaping accusations upon the head of the young man who dropped his bayonet yesterday." Tom could have died. "It was most regrettable," the officer continued, "but to me the most significant thing at the drill was the conduct of that cadet afterward. I saw the whole proceeding; I saw that he did not pause for an instant, that he did not even turn his head, and it appeared to me as one of the finest bits of self-control I had ever seen in any youth; had he forgotten himself for a moment and stopped, however quickly, to secure the weapon, the next line would have been interfered with and your whole movement thrown into confusion." There were a half hundred eyes glancing furtively at Bud, and the light began to dawn in his face. "This boy has shown what discipline means, and I for one want to shake hands with him, if he is here."

When he had concluded the Principal called Bud forward, and the boys, even his detractors, cheered as the officer took his hand.

"Why are you not in uniform, sir?" he asked.

"I was ashamed to wear it after yesterday," was the reply.

"Don't be ashamed to wear your uniform," the officer said to him, and Bud could have fallen on his knees and thanked him.

There were no more jeers from his comrades now, and when he related it all at home that evening there were two more happy hearts in that South Washington cottage.

"I told you we was more prouder dan if you'd won," said "Little Sister."

"An' what did I tell you 'bout backin' out?" asked his mother.

Bud was too happy and too busy to answer; he was brushing his uniform.

THE ADVENTURES OF HUCKLEBERRY FINN
Mark Twain

CHAPTER I.

YOU don't know about me without you have read a book by the name of The Adventures of Tom Sawyer; but that ain't no matter. That book was made by Mr. Mark Twain, and he told the truth, mainly. There was things which he stretched, but mainly he told the truth. That is nothing. I never seen anybody but lied one time or another, without it was Aunt Polly, or the widow, or maybe Mary. Aunt Polly—Tom's Aunt Polly, she is—and Mary, and the Widow Douglas is all told about in that book, which is mostly a true book, with some stretchers, as I said before.

Now the way that the book winds up is this: Tom and me found the money that the robbers hid in the cave, and it made us rich. We got six thousand dollars apiece—all gold. It was an awful sight of money when it was piled up. Well, Judge Thatcher he took it and put it out at interest, and it fetched us a dollar a day apiece all the year round—more than a body could tell what to do with. The Widow Douglas she took me for her son, and allowed she would sivilize me; but it was rough living in the house all the time, considering how dismal regular and decent the widow was in all her ways; and so when I couldn't stand it no longer I lit out. I got into my old rags and my sugar-hogshead again, and was free and satisfied. But Tom Sawyer he hunted me up and said he was going to start a band of robbers, and I might join if I would go back to the widow and be respectable. So I went back.

The widow she cried over me, and called me a poor lost lamb, and she called me a lot of other names, too, but she never meant no harm by it. She put me in them new clothes again, and I couldn't do nothing but sweat and sweat, and feel all cramped up. Well, then, the old thing commenced again. The widow rung a bell for supper, and you had to come to time. When you got to the table you couldn't go right to eating, but you had to wait for the widow to tuck down her head and grumble a little over the victuals, though there warn't really anything the matter with them, — that is, nothing only everything was cooked by itself. In a barrel of odds and ends it is different; things get mixed up, and the juice kind of swaps around, and the things go better.

After supper she got out her book and learned me about Moses and the Bulrushers, and I was in a sweat to find out all about him; but by and by she let it out that Moses had been dead a considerable long time; so then I didn't care no more about him, because I don't take no stock in dead people.

Pretty soon I wanted to smoke, and asked the widow to let me. But she wouldn't. She said it was a mean practice and wasn't clean, and I must try to not do it any more. That is just the way with some people. They get down on a thing when they don't know nothing about it. Here she was a-bothering about Moses, which was no kin to her, and no use to anybody, being gone, you see, yet finding a power of fault with me for doing a thing that had some good in it. And she took snuff, too; of course that was all right, because she done it herself.

CONFLICT

---

noun \ˈkän-ˌflikt\
: a struggle for power, property, etc.: strong disagreement
between people, groups, etc., that results in often angry
argument : competitive or opposing action of
incompatibles : mental struggle resulting from
incompatible or opposing needs, drives, wishes, or external
or internal demands

point
noun \ˈpȯint\
: an idea that you try to make other people accept or
understand: a particular detail of an idea or argument
the point : the main or most important idea of something
that is said or written

The conflict is a discord that can have external aggressors
or can even arise from within the self. It can occur when
the subject is battling his inner discord, at odds with his
surroundings or it may be pitted against others in the story.
In literature, conflict is the result of competing desires or
the presence of obstacles that need to be overcome.
Conflict is necessary to propel a narrative forward; the
absence of conflict amounts to the absence of story.
Conflict is not about a fight, or verbal aggression. Conflict
is about the meeting of two opposing forces.

THE MOTHER
Gwendolyn Brooks

Abortions will not let you forget.
You remember the children you got that you did not get,
The damp small pulps with a little or with no hair,
The singers and workers that never handled the air.
You will never neglect or beat
Them, or silence or buy with a sweet.
You will never wind up the sucking-thumb
Or scuttle off ghosts that come.
You will never leave them, controlling your luscious sigh,
Return for a snack of them, with gobbling mother-eye.

I have heard in the voices of the wind the voices of my dim killed children.
I have contracted. I have eased
My dim dears at the breasts they could never suck.
I have said, Sweets, if I sinned, if I seized
Your luck
And your lives from your unfinished reach,
If I stole your births and your names,
Your straight baby tears and your games,
Your stilted or lovely loves, your tumults, your marriages, aches, and your deaths,
If I poisoned the beginnings of your breaths,
Believe that even in my deliberateness I was not deliberate.
Though why should I whine,
Whine that the crime was other than mine?--
Since anyhow you are dead.
Or rather, or instead,
You were never made.
But that too, I am afraid,
Is faulty: oh, what shall I say, how is the truth to be said?

48

You were born, you had body, you died.
It is just that you never giggled or planned or cried.
Believe me, I loved you all.
Believe me, I knew you, though faintly, and I loved, I loved you
All.

BOOKER T. AND W.E.B.
Dudley Randall

"It seems to me," said Booker T.,
"It shows a mighty lot of cheek
To study chemistry and Greek
When Mister Charlie needs a hand
To hoe the cotton on his land,
And when Miss Ann looks for a cook,
Why stick your nose inside a book?"
"I don't agree," said W.E.B.
"If I should have the drive to seek
Knowledge of chemistry or Greek,
I'll do it. Charles and Miss can look
Another place for hand or cook,
Some men rejoice in skill of hand,
And some in cultivating land,
But there are others who maintain
The right to cultivate the brain."
"It seems to me," said Booker T.,
"That all you folks have missed the boat
Who shout about the right to vote,
And spend vain days and sleepless nights
In uproar over civil rights.
Just keep your mouths shut, do not grouse,
But work, and save, and buy a house."
"I don't agree," said W.E.B.
"For what can property avail
If dignity and justice fail?
Unless you help to make the laws,
They'll steal your house with trumped-up clause.
A rope's as tight, a fire as hot,
No matter how much cash you've got.
Speak soft, and try your little plan,

But as for me, I'll be a man."
"It seems to me," said Booker T.--

"I don't agree,"
Said W.E.B.

WE BELLY BIG, BUT WE STILL HUNGRY
Eternal Mind

Hypertension
High fructose babies

Corn syrup still dripping from our breath
Predicting unpredictable behaviors
That once slept in secret labs now known as projects

Sold to prospects
Trying to feed
Empty bellies with government dollars and ghetto cents
Makes no sense

Unless you calculate the average rate
By the average weight
That the average weighs

Now the average sick
By the average diseased
Gives you an idea of the average death rate

Corporate business the USDA helps regulate

Swimming in Scrooge McDuck money
From the food pains we accumulate
The street pains we aggressively demonstrate

When we kill our self they can't be blamed

It's like we being fed to eat our fate
Now how much sense does it make
Not Bacon bits the whole pig
Big bank be at stake

Not time served the whole bid

They like yeah up your weight
Better yet increase your heart's rate
Chittlin your face
Enjoy the high blood pressure
Stroke upon your plate

Tired weight got the eye-diss
From carrying slaughter souls in the pits of our stomachs

We diabete our state

Dis-eased from disease

INI destruction never linked to food substances in we
Growing deep within we
Our stomachs serve as cemeteries

Flame broiled
Our talk Big Mac
Our walk IHOP stacked

Don't ever say animal worship is taboo
When most practice worshiping acts

Cannibalistic
Cannibal behaviors we internally script
Then act

When we consume animal acts
We consume
The acts of animals that determine our mood

Chemical reactions
React chemical acts

That internally cock back
Externally blast

What happens when foreign substances are made to attack
Unprepared Immune systems collapse
A taste of ignorance got us hungry for flesh

Hungry for vengeance
Hungry to test

Dehydrated souls
We thirst to put the heat to the flesh
Jungle concrete mentalities that rip through the vest

Open the chest

By any means
Addicted fiend's fiend to be fed
Street appetite beast for the bread

Unaware of the animal behavior we see
Unaware of the animal behavior we eat
Unaware of the animal behavior we be

So I was offered guidance in a glass of vegetable juice

Told to help the green pigmentation converse with light
like sun and melanin do

Photo this synthesis

Watch life give birth to truth

Similar to fresh wisdom fertilizing the youth
Instead of deadly similes dressed in yellow clothes and red
clown shoes

Spoken word explain
Stick to the root

Carefully plant poetic seeds
Receive nurture and bare the fruit

Detox

Remove the bowl that moves you
Free you from the bowel your mouth moves to
Colonic you
So you can stop being an ass

Yes

Simply cleanse you

Whispering in eardrums

Help me
Help you

Help you

THE UNIVERSITY OF SOUTH CENTRAL: My First White Friend, His First Black Friend, Freshman Year
Hiram Sims

They told me you're a criminal.
That all your people rob and steal
from folks who have the sort of mind
 to work for what they should conceal
from you. They said you're nothing but
a beast whose endless, violent rage
will hurt a thousand people's lives
before they lock you in a cage.
But you have never been to jail, so I'm confused.

They told me you're a colonist.
That all your people conquer soil
that God's given to other men,
then rape that continent of oil
or gold, or diamonds. Take your pick.
They said you've dug a million graves,
then filled them all with native men
and turned their children into slaves.
But your family owns no land, so I'm confused.

They told me you're a welfare case.
That all your people break their necks
to claim their government handouts,
and pray for reparation checks.
They said you waste our tax dollars
on aid that you don't really need,
then spend our country's charity
on menthol cigarettes and weed.
But both your parents work fulltime, so I'm confused

They told me you were filthy rich.
You own the towns and own the shops.
own the bridges, own the roads,
own the judges and the cops.
 Own the prisons and the jails
from east to west, from north to south,
and never worked for any of it.
Born with silver spoon in mouth.
But you don't even own your car, so I'm confused

They told me you're a Deadbeat Dad.
You spread your seed all over town,
then lie. Deny the fact that you
screw anything that's not nailed down.
Rather than raise your bastard children,
all your time is spent in court.
Begging judges not to take
your meager wage in child support.
But your pops raised you all your life, so I'm confused.

They told me you're a junkie.
That white folks got the cash to buy
the kinda drugs you snort and sniff
and shoot from needles to get high.
They said that all you trust-fund snobs
pop pills and smoke your crystal meth
to function. Just to study, while
you half near drink yourselves to death.
But you have never drank or smoked, so I'm confused.

They said to stay away from you
But I didn't, and now I know,
after knowing you,
that somebody lied to me.

THE DARKER BROTHER
Fud4thot

I am... The Darker Brother
and I too sing America
I be charcoal choco-latte
chanting
rise up, ye mighty people
rise up, ye mighty race

I am Negro
A dream variant of simplicity
Carved creative marble-breasted
Cracked leather etched into chalk lungs
Coughing a weary blues
I sneeze renaissance
then bless haiku

I be Ptah
fashioning the Universe
through harmonics and thought
Medu Neter chiseled in me chest plate
checkmate in three
me now know why the caged bird sings
so me drink suffering
and piss triumph

I am burnt cork
Greased paint
Spread like chocolate bar
Slice of melon rind
That wide

I be melanin
Nyuesi Infalm

pigmented to the third power
thee antithesis of pale

I am Harlem
"A Dream Deferred" and-
they send me to the kitchen
when company comes

I be Watts
Conceptions and Misconceptions
Blacks Arts Movement
Blues People
Negro Music in White America

I am *The Souls of Black Folk*
The sage of Anacostia
"Genius Child"
Busy with me oyster knife
Doctoring Toomers cut by Cane

I be *Black Magic*
Word sorcerer
360 Degrees of Blackness Coming at You
Black Feeling
Black thought
Black Talk
Re: Creation
My House
The Women and the Men
Cotton Candy on a Rainy Day
And *Those Who Ride the Night Winds*

I am sorrow
Sung thru lost vernacular
Spilled on Dixie's breast
Whipped with black belts
Bleeding solitary tears for glory

59

I am "A Negro Love Song"
A "Little Brown Baby"
"The Corn-Stalk Fiddle"
"The Haunted Oak"
"Ships That Pass in the Night"

I am an invisible
Shouting words felt but never heard
Muffled
Lips ostracized my nerves
Where in the kitchen
I eat
I laugh
And I grow
Stronger for the day, that I'm able to tell the world
How it feels to be colored me...

I am
Langston Hughes
Marcus Garvey
Amiri Baraka
Sonia Sanchez
Nikki Giovanni
Paul Laurence Dunbar
Zora Neale Hurston
John Blak
Lukuma Kwa Luja

translation -
Food4Thot! I am ...

The Darker Brother!

DRAMATIC MONOLOGUE

dramatic
adjective \drǝ-ˈma-tik\
: sudden and extreme: greatly affecting people's emotions
: attracting attention : causing people to carefully listen, look,

monologue
noun \ˈmä-nǝ-ˌlȯg, -ˌläg\
: a long speech given by a character in a story, movie, play, etc., or by a performer : a long speech made by one person that prevents anyone else from talking

A dramatic monologue is a long excerpt in a play, poem or story that reveals a character's thoughts and feelings. When we read a story, sometimes we can see what a character is thinking, but it isn't always so clear. When a writer allows a character to speak in a monologue, we get to see inside a character's head and then we better understand what motivates that character. Monologue comes from the Greek word *monos* meaning alone and *logos* means speech. It is a literary device, which is the speech or verbal presentation that a single character presents in order to express his/her collection of thoughts and ideas aloud. Often this character addresses an audience or another character. Monologues are found in dramatic mediums like films, plays and poetry. A great majority of the current spoken-word poets are actually trained actors.

SKINHEAD
Patricia Smith

They call me skinhead, and I got my own beauty.
It is knife-scrawled across my back in sore, jagged letters,
it's in the way my eyes snap away from the obvious.
I sit in my dim matchbox,
on the edge of a bed tousled with my ragged smell,
slide razors across my hair,
count how many ways
I can bring blood closer to the surface of my skin.
These are the duties of the righteous,
the ways of the anointed.
The face that moves in my mirror is huge and
pockmarked,
scraped pink and brilliant, apple-cheeked,
I am filled with my own spit.
Two years ago, a machine that slices leather
sucked in my hand and held it,
whacking off three fingers at the root.
I didn't feel nothing till I looked down
and saw one of them on the floor
next to my boot heel,
and I ain't worked since then.
I sit here and watch niggers take over my TV set,
walking like kings up and down the sidewalks in my head,
walking like their fat black mamas *named* them freedom.
My shoulders tell me that ain't right.
So I move out into the sun
where my beauty makes them lower their heads,
or into the night
with a lead pipe up my sleeve,

a razor tucked in my boot.
I was born to make things right.
It's easy now to move my big body into shadows,
to move from a place where there was nothing
into the stark circle of a streetlight,
the pipe raised up high over my head.
It's a kick to watch their eyes get big,
round and gleaming like cartoon jungle boys,
right in that second when they know
the pipe's gonna come down, and I got this thing
I like to say, listen to this, I like to say
"Hey, nigger, Abe Lincoln's been dead a long time."
I get hard listening to their skin burst.
I was born to make things right.
Then this newspaper guy comes around,
seems I was a little sloppy kicking some fag's ass
and he opened his hole and screamed about it.
This reporter finds me curled up in my bed,
those TV flashes licking my face clean.
Same ol' shit.
Ain't got no job, the coloreds and spics got 'em all.
Why ain't I working? Look at my hand, asshole.
No, I ain't part of no organized group,
I'm just a white boy who loves his race,
fighting for a pure country.
Sometimes it's just me. Sometimes three. Sometimes 30.
AIDS will take care of the faggots,
then it's gon' be white on black in the streets.
Then there'll be three million.
I tell him that.
So he writes it up
and I come off looking like some kind of freak,
like I'm Hitler himself. I ain't that lucky,
but I got my own beauty.
It is in my steel-toed boots,
in the hard corners of my shaved head.

I look in the mirror and hold up my mangled hand,
only the baby finger left, sticking straight up,
I know it's the wrong goddamned finger,
but fuck you all anyway.
I'm riding the top rung of the perfect race,
my face scraped pink and brilliant.
I'm your baby, America, your boy,
drunk on my own spit, I am goddamned fuckin' beautiful.
And I was born
and raised
right here.

DID I HAPPEN TO YOU OR YOU TO ME?
Mo Piquette

Dad always told me take responsibility
the world don't happen to you
you happen to the world
take responsibility he would say
ain't no point in blaming others
look just a little deeper, right in the mirror,
the same mirror, where my brother told me to find my best
friend,
right there under that skin, the same skin my mom told me
was a miracle.
See, my family gave me everything.
I am capable of anything.
So I take responsibility for my hand in this world
I don't even think about pointing that finger.

Take responsibility..
ringing through my ears
all my life.
The world don't happen to you
you happen to the world,

but what happens when
in this world of me happening to the world,
there happens a night with a man and a girl
fall asleep sweet heart in one bed
wake up in another
"you wanted it",
I remember that's what he said

in between my legs shattered

bits of him
bit of me
and his friend too
cowering over like the camera
just watching
or was he?
did he get a piece of me too?
did i happen to you
or you to me?

This couldn't be!

I happen to the world you see,
the world doesn't happen to me
so 3 cups of pills I take,
every 3 months make
my head a little more ill,
3 more pills for my sanity sake,
to kill off anything and everything you might have given
me
except the memory.
Barefoot I stood, looking in a mirror,
I search for the girl I called best friend,
but now layers of doubt disguise my skin.

So I curl into myself
take my dose of lessons learned
replay the memory
time loss, time blocked,
 blackout, blocked thoughts
thought, disguised as questions
thoughts of you, question me.

Replay the memory
each replay different with each "if only"
if only I wasn't

if only I did
if only I knew then,
if only i knew what?!

I'm unsure my memory is right recalling the night,
one whisper spirals me into a state of mistrust,
When I woke up, the whisper was...
"Don't worry, this stays between us."

Now, again, I'm given a responsibility.
How I react to that which happened to me
my reaction, my karma,
my karma, my fate.

I believe how people treat you is their karma
how you react is yours,
but I'm never quite sure how much taller I can can stand.
Feel like I always gotta be the bigger man
as I stand in ruins for another man's actions.

My life dreams replaced with fantasies of sought justice.

A desire I don't trust in the hands of others.
My whole world changed,
An absence of light took reign.

Yes, I'm lost
and I feel like my dignity was the cost.

CHILDREN OF A LESSER GOD
Deb Young

Ya know me na understand why my uncle John insist
fa hold up me hand while me asleep. And if me open up
me eye and look ina he face, he tell me to close ya eye don't
be shy, don't make no noise. Ca me nah wan ya motha ta
wake ina de place. Don't tell nobody what a go on. Me
have a special love fa you, ya motha na go understand, so
keep this between me and you. Last week him tkae his
time and him climb pon top a me, then he open up him
pants and he hol down me hands and ..And now it hurt
between me legs when me a walk.

Me have a spread me leg apart when
me a walk. Me have to sit down on the side when me at
school, because the benches feel to hard. De pickney dem
at school laff after me hehee. Dem point and jeer all day
long and me best friend Pam, tell me fa look pon me
skirt,when me turn it around me get a big alert. Me did a
bleed and bleed pon me uniform. Red blood, red blood
all day long. Blood is the colour of the rainbow when
brown girls consider suicide and love is not enough.
Uncle John me na like it when you touch me right there.
Mama said me shouldn't let nobody touch me right there.
Uncle John this is wrong, please let go of me hand. Uncle
John this is wrong please put on back ya pants. Tonight
she a go sleep with a knife.

Pam tell her uncle John that night should only touch his
wife. She tell him she na wan his special love, but him still
insist to take her from above. So tonight uncle John take
him time. Him climb pon top a her, she stick the knife inna
him spine.

Him never hol her hand, him never take off her pants and all him feel is pain, again, and again. All him feel is pain, again and again. All him feel is pain again, and again.

Excerpt from A Few Good Men

Kaffee: I want the truth!

Jessup: You can't handle the truth! Son, we live in a world that has walls, and those walls have to be guarded by men with guns. Who's gonna do it? You? You, Lieutenant Weinberg? I have a greater responsibility than you can possibly fathom. You weep for Santiago and you curse the Marines. You have that luxury. You have the luxury of not knowing what I know, that Santiago's death, while tragic, probably saved lives. And my existence, while grotesque and incomprehensible to you, saves lives! You don't want the truth, because deep down in places you don't talk about at parties, you want me on that wall. You need me on that wall. We use words like "honor", "code", "loyalty". We use these words as the backbone of a life spent defending something. You use them as a punchline. I have neither the time nor the inclination to explain myself to a man who rises and sleeps under the blanket of the very freedom that I provide, and then questions the manner in which I provide it! I would rather you just said "thank you", and went on your way. Otherwise, I suggest you pick up a weapon, and stand a post. Either way, I don't give a damn what you think you are entitled to!

Excerpt from JAWS, Quint

Japanese submarine slammed two torpedoes into our side, chief. It was comin' back, from the island of Tinian to Leyte, just delivered the bomb. The Hiroshima bomb. Eleven hundred men went into the water. Vessel went down in twelve minutes. Didn't see the first shark for about a half an hour. Tiger. Thirteen footer. You know, you know that when you're in the water, chief? You tell by lookin' from the dorsal to the tail. Well, we didn't know. `Cause our bomb mission had been so secret, no distress signal had been sent. They didn't even list us overdue for a week. Very first light, chief. The sharks come cruisin'. So we formed ourselves into tight groups. You know it's kinda like `ol squares in battle like a, you see on a calendar, like the battle of Waterloo. And the idea was, the shark nearest man and then he'd start poundin' and hollerin' and screamin' and sometimes the shark would go away. Sometimes he wouldn't go away. Sometimes that shark, he looks right into you. Right into your eyes. You know the thing about a shark, he's got lifeless eyes, black eyes, like a doll's eye. When he comes at ya, doesn't seem to be livin'. Until he bites ya and those black eyes roll over white. And then, ah then you hear that terrible high pitch screamin' and the ocean turns red and spite of all the poundin' and the hollerin' they all come in and rip you to pieces. Y'know by the end of that first dawn, lost a hundred men. I don't know how many sharks, maybe a thousand. I don't know how many men, they averaged six an hour. On Thursday mornin' chief, I bumped into a friend of mine, Herbie Robinson from Cleveland. Baseball player, bosom's mate. I thought he was asleep, reached over to wake him up. Bobbed up and down in the water, just like a kinda top. Up ended. Well, he'd been bitten in half below the waist. Noon the fifth day, Mr. Hooper, a Lockheed Ventura saw us, he swung in low and he saw us.

He'd a young pilot, a lot younger than Mr. Hooper, anyway he saw us and come in low. And three hours later a big fat PBY comes down and start to pick us up. You know that was the time I was most frightened? Waitin' for my turn. I'll never put on a lifejacket again. So, eleven hundred men went in the water, three hundred and sixteen men come out, the sharks took the rest, June the 29, 1945. Anyway, we delivered the bomb.

INSPIRATION

noun \ ˌin(t)-spə-ˈrā-shən, -(ˌ)spi-\

: something that makes someone want to do something or that gives someone an idea about what to do or create : a force or influence that inspires someone: a person, place, experience, etc., that makes someone want to do or create something: a good idea: a divine influence or action on a person believed to qualify him or her to receive and communicate sacred revelation

Muse: a source of inspiration; *especially* : a guiding genius

Inspiration is the act or power of exercising an elevating or stimulating influence upon the intellect or emotions; the result of such influence which quickens or stimulates; as, the inspiration of occasion, of art, etc.The Muses in Greek mythology are the goddesses of the inspiration of literature, science, and the arts. They were considered the source of the knowledge embodied in the poetry, song-lyrics, and myths that were related orally for centuries in these ancient cultures. In current English usage, "*muse*" can refer in general to a person who inspires an artist, writer, or musician. Inspiration is the fuel that guides creative writers. If we understand what inspires us, we can manipulate the source to create more work.

WE ARE VIRGINIA TECH
Nikki Giovanni

We are sad today, and we will be sad for quite a while. We are not moving on, we are embracing our mourning.

We are Virginia Tech.

We are strong enough to stand tall tearlessly, we are brave enough to bend to cry, and we are sad enough to know that we must laugh again.

We are Virginia Tech.

We do not understand this tragedy. We know we did nothing to deserve it, but neither does a child in Africa dying of AIDS, neither do the invisible children walking the night away to avoid being captured by the rogue army, neither does the baby elephant watching his community being devastated for ivory, neither does the Mexican child looking for fresh water, neither does the Appalachian infant killed in the middle of the night in his crib in the home his father built with his own hands being run over by a boulder because the land was destabilized. No one deserves a tragedy.

We are Virginia Tech.

The Hokie Nation embraces our own and reaches out with open heart and hands to those who offer their hearts and minds. We are strong, and brave, and innocent, and unafraid. We are better than we think and not quite what we want to be. We are alive to the imaginations and the possibilities. We will continue to invent the future through our blood and tears and through all our sadness.

We are the Hokies.

We will prevail.

We will prevail.

We will prevail.

We are Virginia Tech.

INVICTUS
William Ernest Hensley

Out of the night that covers me,
Black as the Pit from pole to pole,
I thank whatever gods may be
For my unconquerable soul.

In the fell clutch of circumstance
I have not winced nor cried aloud.
Under the bludgeonings of chance
My head is bloody, but unbowed.

Beyond this place of wrath and tears
Looms but the Horror of the shade,
And yet the menace of the years
Finds, and shall find, me unafraid.

It matters not how strait the gate,
How charged with punishments the scroll.
I am the master of my fate:
I am the captain of my soul.

THE CRAFTSMAN
Marcus B. Christian

I ply with all the cunning of my art
This little thing, and with consummate care
I fashion it—so that when I depart,
Those who come after me shall find it fair
And beautiful. It must be free of flaws—
Pointing no laborings of weary hands;
And there must be no flouting of the laws
Of beauty—as the artist understands.

Through passion, yearnings infinite—yet dumb—
I lift you from the depths of my own mind
And gild you with my soul's white heat to plumb
The souls of future men. I leave behind
This thing that in return this solace gives:
"He who creates true beauty ever lives."

HAVE YOU FORGOTTEN
Darryl Worley

I hear people saying we don't need this war
But, I say there's some things worth fighting for
What about our freedom and this piece of ground
We didn't get to keep 'em by backing down
They say we don't realize the mess we're getting in
Before you start your preaching let me ask you this my friend

Have you forgotten how it felt that day?
To see your homeland under fire
And her people blown away
Have you forgotten when those towers fell?
We had neighbors still inside going thru a living hell
And you say we shouldn't worry 'bout bin Laden
Have you forgotten?

They took all the footage off my T.V.
Said it's too disturbing for you and me
It'll just breed anger that's what the experts say
If it was up to me I'd show it everyday
Some say this country's just out looking for a fight
Well, after 9/11 man I'd have to say that's right

Have you forgotten how it felt that day?
To see your homeland under fire
And her people blown away
Have you forgotten when those towers fell?
We had neighbors still inside going thru a living hell
And we vowed to get the one's behind bin Laden
Have you forgotten?

I've been there with the soldiers
Who've gone away to war
And you can bet that they remember
Just what they're fighting for

Have you forgotten all the people killed?
Yeah, some went down like heroes in that Pennsylvania
field
Have you forgotten about our Pentagon?
All the loved ones that we lost and those left to carry on
Don't you tell me not to worry about bin Laden
Have you forgotten?

Have you forgotten?
Have you forgotten?

PLACE

• *a* : physical environment : <u>space</u> *b* : a way for admission or transit *c* : physical surroundings : <u>atmosphere</u> *2 a* : an indefinite region or expanse *<all over the place> b* : a building or locality used for a special purpose *<a place of learning> <a fine eating place> c archaic* : the three-dimensional compass of a material object *3 a* : a particular region, center of population, or location *<a nice place to visit> b* : a building, part of a building, or area occupied as a home *<our summer place>*

In literature, the word "setting" or "place" is used to identify and establish the time, place and mood of the events of the story or poem. It helps in establishing where and when and under what circumstances the story is taking place. Circumstance is the most important element, because when the environment creates both the context and the conflict that arises in the writing. For example, a narrative that takes place in prison brings with it certain implied problems with authority, race relations and confinement conflicts. As writers, place also serves as an inspiration, which often results in homages to our home, or warnings about the dangers therin. Our endeavor as writers should be to understand how a given country, state, city or street creates the context of conflict/resolution, and use it to move our sotry forward.

PROBLEMS WITH HURRICANES

Victor Hernandez Cruz

A campesino looked at the air
And told me:
With hurricanes it's not the wind
or the noise or the water.
I'll tell you he said:
it's the mangoes, avocados
Green plantains and bananas
flying into town like projectiles.
How would your family
feel if they had to tell
The generations that you
got killed by a flying
Banana.
Death by drowning has honor
If the wind picked you up
and slammed you
Against a mountain boulder
This would not carry shame
But
to suffer a mango smashing
Your skull
or a plantain hitting your
Temple at 70 miles per hour
is the ultimate disgrace.
The campesino takes off his hat—
As a sign of respect

toward the fury of the wind
And says:
Don't worry about the noise
Don't worry about the water
Don't worry about the wind —
If you are going out
beware of mangoes
And all such beautiful
sweet things.

I KNOW THESE PARTS...
Food4Thot

get'cho butt up
get ready for school
was the alarm I heard every morning
removing roaches from Sugar Smacks
to help quiet stomach rumblings
crack pipes
used needles
condoms
littered path to education

daylight breaks
piercing gunshot hole in wooden fence
flowers beneath
represent victim

dogs bark
as tho they see evil spirits
causing mischief
buckets crank
but never start
leaving room for shade-tree mechanics to worsen
problems!
businessman gets blow job in brand-new Mercedes
hours later
carcass of Mercedes sits on four crates

 I know these parts... well!

where I dreamed in high definition
awake and TiVo fairy tales
aligning parallels with reality
birthing clarity

through divine assignments
I've been battle tested
on these streets
told, "better policeman catch you with pistol"
than them jackers to catch you without heat
so youngins packed heat like oven
grinding on block like bad brakes
metal to metal
headed for collision
lil man's 3rd eye vision's impaired while smoking dust
everything's in slow motion now
he can't feel his face now
car flipped over
dead at thirteen
mother's only child
daddy's cracked out
his whereabouts?
go figure!!!

pastor see youngsters hustling on corners and yell…
"REPENT NOW OR BURN IN HELL!!!"
not realizing he's burning now
'cause he's preaching
with mistress's vagina stench on tongue
very life contradicts what he's supposed to be standing on
…and we should take the pastor serious?
Father, please help us…

revolutionary man yells, "BLACK POWER!"
power yells back, "NOT WITHOUT CAPITAL!"
movement paralyzed in its tracks…
tracking history through needle tracks
up panther's arms
only reveals dependency!
no clemency for the poor
with liquor stores on every corner

coroners stay busy 'round here
bodies get dumped and found 'round here...
on a daily...
another homicide
retaliation makes it genocide
less work for police force
medi-Cal / minus healthcare / plus HMO / equals fast
death—
of course...

I know these parts
I know these parts...

Well!

SHEEV'S GLORY
Kendall Hanner

"Inhale air, exhale flame and behold the inferno of justice.
The code by which I live, words to guide my spear."

This phrase spirals through Sheev's mind as he spurts
through the fair paved routes of his origins. Toor Shul, the
pillar of hearth. A grand kingdom that yields an ivory-
gold aura of purity. The streets envelope its residents in a
cloth of freedom, and the sentinels like Sheev enforce this
sanctuary with sword and shield. Sheev's hasty trek to the
frontlines blurs the alabaster structures around him.
"Clinck-clack," "thump-thump," the rhythmic whisper of
his dancing scarlet armor mixed with the rise and fall of
his feet, lulls Sheev's vision into central acuity. "I mustn't
linger, faster, faster" he cries out in his head, expediting
his pace swinging his polearm at a low. To and fro it sways
in his right hand with the edge facing the searing horizon
ahead.

"Yo" a familiar voice of tenderness screeched out to him.

Sheev slows himself to a halt and turns around. "Tamul
show ye self I know it be you," He exclaimed.

A woman plated in red steps out from an ally to the left
and into a beam of early morning light. Her Hazel skin
shined through the open joints of her gear. Curly black
threads fall past her shoulders and down her back. She
wields two sabers, one sheathed on both her hips angled
backwards.

"What's a fairhead like you prowling for" Sheev asks.

"I'm to gather you. Ye lallygagging halts the advance," she answers.

She then propels herself into a jog past Sheev. He sees the medallion of adulation he gifted her bouncing above her plated breast. In Toor Shul, males would present a medallion forged from Theolium and branded with their family's crest as a gesture for marriage. Tamul recently accepted his proposal but gave no answer at the time. Seeing it strapped around her neck with string and close to her heart overwhelmed him with hope, hope for the Shulian dream, a two story cottage, three fair children, and four golden reins.

***

By Midday the two sentinels reached the rendezvous.,Yol, a small town in the outer ring of the kingdom. Here the buildings have been coated in smog and ash as the city burns just five hundred meters ahead. A carbon filtered scent of scorched flesh wafts through the air. Tamul and Sheev stopped in front of the encampment which was a four story housing area surrounded by smaller buildings. Thirty or so soldiers patrol and guard the area . Sheev turned to speak to Tamul.

"What holds ye tongue" he asks Tamul, "you've not spoke a word since our voyage began".

Tamul's lips formed a thin smile as she stares at the burning town ahead "Man's red flower. Isn't it a beaut, a rose of power," she asked.

"Mayhap if it choose to bloom any place but hither,"Sheev commented quickly.

"We always speak of burning passion, simple truths, and absolute power. Why is it we don't use tactics like that. Burn and raid those who oppose us" she asks.
"Such tactics are used only by the weak" Sheev counseled.

Tamul walks past the four watch guards ending the conversation. Sheev followed her through the doorless entrance. Once inside they see where three walls that separated the homes were completely shattered, expanding the room enough for an entire platoon to sit bundled up together. A mesh of worn red iron covered the walls leaving a gaping trail from the entrance, to the center, and across to the stairs on the other side. In the center of the room were four cubed tables joined together, half eaten loaves of bread and many wooden jugs and cups were scattered across them. A large pale man with a red beard and small beady blue eyes leaned against the table watching the entrance.

"Bout time" Exclaimed the bear like figure to Sheev.

A Timber buckler was strapped to the man's right forearm and a broad short sword hung at his hip. The large man grabs a jug and holds it out In front of him in an offering gesture.

"A swig of Adam's Ale" the man barked.

Sheev places his hand on the handle of the jug "garmmarcy Ramun but is this all we have" he asks.

"Ye misunderstood me. It is not a lack of variety that I present, tis but a swig is all we have to offer." Ramun lead the room into a burst of laughter.

"Ye quite the jester eh. perchance you look the part as well," Sheev snarled back with a grin on his face.

He snatched the jug from Ramuns paw and leaped onto the table kicking cups and bread in every which way. A jug in his left, a halberd in his right, Sheev downed the last drops of liquid for the camp.

Throwing the empty jug down he shouts, "bare ye pride and ready your arms for Sheev be a hither now. After I report to Lord Stefanus we shall strike back and end this raid. The fools of Ru Maar will know the extent of a Shulians wraith." Each soldier stood to their feet and shouted at the top of their lungs. "Recite with me," Sheev bellowed over his men continuing his speech, "Inhale air, exhale flame and behold the inferno of justice." The crowd of over four hundred shouted the code with enthusiastic patriotism. With his men rallied up Sheev took off to see Lord Stefanus, with Ramun and Tamul in his wake.

The squad of three sentinels take a knee upstairs before Stefanus. A bald man in ruby steel. High lord of the western region of Toor Shul.

"My Lord the escort was successful, the samaritans of the west were pushed back to safety along with ye son," pledged Sheev.

"Garmmarcy to you my friend garmmarcy," said Stefanus. "Tho I am glad to hear ye escort was a success it took much longer than expected. Our enemy has taken the majority of Yol and set fire to its routes. Stand and let's not waste daylight's soothing touch".

The sentinels rise in one synchronized movement following their commander downstairs and into the battle field. Stefanus marched into the burning pits of Yol.

***

His bodyguards, three hand picked sentinels, stride behind him in a triangular formation; over four hundred disciplined soldiers follow as well. Their steps create a roar of stampeding justice down the routes laced with burning buildings here and there. Suddenly a thunderous crack followed by a deafening yelp came from Sheev's right. He turns to see Ramun's buckler raised up covering his face. A single arrow lay drilled in the center of the raised shield. Sheev's eyes follow the length of the arrow through the shield, Ramun's forearm, and into his left eye. The mighty sentinel was now nailed to his buckler unable to lower his arm or else rip out his eyeball. Ramun yelped with agony dropping the sword from his free hand. Before his blade hit the pavement a second arrow came flying from ahead. Once again targeting Ramun, the edged tip crashed through the buckler but this time ending it's flight in Ramun's neck. He turned slightly left and locked eyes with Sheev as his two and a half meter figure fell back gurgling on his own blood. The platoon fell silent as one of the four leaders was defeated in mere seconds upon entering the battle.

A roar of morale came from the enemy signaling that this was no coincidence, but a well planned ambush that they walked into. Placed in a cross road men and women in violet chainmail sprinted from their hiding spots and through flames. They flanked the crimson soldiers of Toor Shul from three sides. Anxiety ascended through Sheev as he turned his attention to the enemy before him. A formation of many soldiers in every direction challenging his life, but he saw only one target. A tall man equipped with velvet leather armor, slowly lowered a well made bow throwing it to the side. The ominous figure then drew his longsword from its sheath and began to walk forward, aware of Sheev's gaze. The assailant smiled revealing sharp blackened teeth. Many scars ran horizontally across the hooded man's face.

Before Stefanus could command his people to attack, Sheev had already dived into the fray wielding his polearm. Sheev did not carry a normal spear. He used a glaive which is a type of halberd. Where a spear is made for poking and stabbing an opponent, the glaive was forged to hack and slash through armor and limbs, but is still capable of a deadly thrust. Sheev wasted no movements; every time he swung his weapon he downed a new foe.

He danced in half circles slashing his weapon back and forth. stopping his blade in mid swing to his right he reversed the blade with a swift flick of the wrist. The glaive twists and sings through the air dashing through rusted mail releasing the contents of someone's stomach on the pave. "Six" he counts in his head, he then thrusts the butt end of his weapon behind him, a crunching resistance, and a scream lets him know that his attack landed into someone's nose. Sheev thrusts his weapon forward into the neck of a young woman armed with an axe. He turns into a full one-eighty pivot as he pulls the blade out of the victim, and
hacks off the head of a man holding his nose. "Eight" he whispers to himself.

He crouches into his battle stance readying his weapon at a low. He has been lead away from his people and surrounded by a weary sea of purple. His eyes focus in on the archer fighting a wave of red iron with ease. The tall assailant begins to fight his way to Sheev. After ten seconds and four more kills, Sheev stood before Ramun's killer. The sounds of combat surrounded the two while their weapons clashed. Fire danced across the pave swallowing the dead. As Sheev began his assault he spotted Tamul. She was locked in on a target; she weaved through the blades like a leaf in the wind. There was nothing he could do but shout when he finally noticed who she was stalking. He worked himself into a defensive stance to keep the assailant at bay. "My lord" Sheev bellowed, but it was too late Tamul was already within range. She plunged both of her blades into Stefanus's back. The commander coughed up a spout of blood as Tamul finished him off. She thrusts her sabers forward until the tips breached from his chest plate.

Sheev catching wind of the situation shouts "stand fast", every soldier in red fades into a defensive style. With a quick glance he could count more red than purple in any direction. This puts Sheev at ease.

Still locked in combat with the assailant, Sheev begins to push him backwards no longer allowing his enemy to counter or strike back. "I must end this" Sheev cries out in his head, "I'm next no doubt". His glaive sings through the air missing its intended target, but slashing and ripping through the velvet minions in chainmail near by. After seeing four of his men fall to this wild array of attacks, the assailant lunges out in anger just as Sheev wanted. The assailant's blade slides into range as Sheev raised his weapon up for a downward vertical attack. With a high pitch cringing sound of metal sliding against metal the enemy's blade cuts through Sheev's armor. The remaining sentinel predicted this move and slid to the right controlling where this jab would land, it only scratched the side to Sheev's gear ripping no flesh, spilling no blood. With an absolute strike, he pulls his glaive in a downward sweep and into the vile murderer's shoulder.
The cut was so precise and fast it made no sound and left no blood on the blade. A agonizing screech came from

behind mottled black teeth. The man's sword arm slide off from his body and hit the ground. Sheev swings his weapon around like a twister in a storm. This last attack cuts the enemy's commander throat open. "Now you shall know fury" Sheev chants out loud in victory and kicks his body into a pit of nearby flames. "Behold justice".

Sheev looks around the still burning battlefield to see that Tamul had been encircled by a his platoon. He walked over to the angry mob. Passing scorched corpses that decorate the route. He sees his charge, lord Stefanus who now lays in cold blood. "At ease men," Sheev commanded and they parted a path for him.

He then saw a soldier behind Tamul reading a spear. Sheev's body reacted on instinct; he had no ruling over his limbs or the actions they would make next. Sheev dropped his weapon and closed the gap between him and Tamul with godly speed. He grabbed Tamul by the waist and spun her around taking the spear in the back. It slid through him leaving a length of two feet protruding from his stomach.

"Why" Tamul asked in confusion.

Sheev said nothing, he just reached around her waist with his right arm tightening his grip and snagged the medallion of adulation with his left hand. He then pulled Tamul closer to him, impaling her with the same spear. She let out a short muffled scream as Sheev pulled her body towards his, forcing the spear to rip through her back.

The soldier holding the spear did not let go he was too shocked to move. All was still even the wind and fire stood in silence to watch the moments of faith reveal itself.

Sheev intimately wrapped his right arm around her and embraced her fully. Slowly he removes the Medallion from around her neck and let his left arm dangle without dropping the contents of his hand.

"It was not always so" Tamul whispered to him, "I.." she hesitates for a moment choking on her words. "I do still". Sheev interrupted her confession by kissing her with bloody lips.

He untangles his mouth from hers and whispers "and the weak shall fear and flee in terror from the name of justice, I sentence you to death, you treacherous wench".

LEXICON

noun \ˈlek-sə-ˌkän *also* -kən\
: the words used in a language or by a person or group of people*a* : the vocabulary of a language, an individual speaker or group of speakers, or a subject

Jar·gon
noun \ˈjär-gən, -ˌgän\
: the language used for a particular activity or by a particular group of people: the technical terminology or characteristic idiom of a special activity or group

A lexicon is the vocabulary of a person, language, or branch of knowledge (such as nautical or medical). In linguistics, a lexicon is a language's inventory of lexemes. The word "lexicon" derives from the Greek λεξικόν (*lexicon*), neuter of λεξικός (*lexikos*) meaning "of or for words".Linguistic theories generally regard human languages as consisting of two parts: a lexicon, essentially a catalogue of a language's words (its wordstock); and a grammar, a system of rules which allow for the combination of those words into meaningful sentences. Jargon is a literary term that is defined as a use of specific phrases and words by writers in a particular situation, profession or trade. These specialized terms are used to convey hidden meanings accepted and understood in that field. Jargon examples are found in literary and non-literary pieces of writing.

Home Synonyms abode, diggings, domicile, dwelling, fireside, habitation, hearth, hearthstone, house, lodging, pad, place, quarters, residence, roof

Related Words accommodations, housing, nest, residency, shelter; bungalow, cabin, casita, chalet, cottage; duplex, ranch, ranch house, saltbox, semi [*chiefly British*], split level, townhome, town house, tract house, triplex; apartment, apartment house, condominium, flat, tenement, tenement house, walk-up; penthouse, salon, suite; barracks, billet, boardinghouse, dorm, dormitory, lodging house, lodgment , room(s), rooming house; castle, château, countryseat, estate, hall, manor, manor house, mansion, palace, villa; farmhouse, grange, hacienda, homestead; double-wide, houseboat, house trailer, mobile home, motor home, recreational vehicle, trailer; hermitage, manse, parsonage, rectory, vicarage; hooch [] hovel, hut, hutch, shack, shanty

THE CONTRACTOR'S INHERITANCE
Hiram Sims

I lay these words on the paper
like 2 by 4's 16 inches on center
Cut these diagonal phrases in half and
drop them down with this sawzall pen
I chisel away at these stanzas one lonely
shingle at a time till
The words are level and that bubble
is In between the two black lines.

I measure these syllables twice,
 then cut once with this table saw
Pushing the three quarter-inch plywood
with both thumbs through the blade
 Dig out this retrofitted trench of stanzas,
then set the forms,
rebar first, then cold gray concrete.

I lay the floor joyces of this sonnet,
then build the bearing walls of pentameter verse.
I run the copper pipes from the street
to this lyrical structure
Run the #12 romex wire through each syntaxed stud
until I got juice runnin' through this joint.

I make, with my own two hands
this Gabriel pitch roof of rhythm and rhyme
Roll the black paper over the sheathing
of this muse and melt these lines together
with that hot bubbling black tar
that'll burn your ass up if it touches your skin.

I hang that awkward drywall last,
cut the molding that the owner will like
 at a 45% angle, then walk out the door
and leave the rest for the painters while I sit back,
look at what I've done
And thank God I had a pops
who showed me everything he knows

WETBACK
Carlo Ornelas

I'm the wetback, my water soaked shoes left a wet track
I got deported twice, but that was just a minor setback
Cause I'm strong like the current of the Colorado River
The tone of my courage made the border patrol shiver
I been through all the borders: El Paso, Tijuana,
Agua Prieta, Palomas, I move like smoke of marihuana
I'm smooth and unnoticed,
Some label me as Illegal
But if they would really notice,
I'm a reflection of their ego
I'm the reason why the Government created Border Patrol
They already took our land but they'll never take my soul
I was blind to the fact that this land belonged to me
Now I'm a slave in the place where my ancestors were royalty
They stole my history, my beliefs, even my pride
The Jews were not the only ones to suffer genocide
Now I have to sneak in to the land that I once ruled…
They told us were Illegal, now I know that we were fooled
What's my name? Where am I from?
I know that you don't know
That's why you label me simply as a U.F.O…
An alien, an Unidentified Foreign Object,
But you should think twice
About the words that you select
I'm the wetback, son of the rain and the pain
My brain remains trapped by an invisible chain
Society is my prison, from the water I have risen
I'm not being treated fair, why won't anybody listen?
Borders are just stupid reasons made by Man
To have land to their name and to have the upper hand
The government's a backstabbing, land thieving crook,

Why don't they write about that in the history book?
But the words I say are senseless,
You can never believe me
Because I'm trapped and defenseless
In the "Land of the Free"…
I'm the Wetback,
My water soaked shoes left a wet track,
I got deported twice, but that was just
A minor setback.

COMPUTER WORDPLAY
Tommy Chun

I met this single black white female
She was a valley-gangsta chick
A little confused, she said she was selling a bit.
I said, well if you're selling a bit? then I'm buying a bit.
She said she wanted to have cyber sex with me
So I sent her an email saying
Once you are on my web page
I'll know if we are IBM compatible.
My extension is longing for a power source
And your DSL is like an open bank.
I said I'm tired of playing with my palm pilot
Jump on your Netscape Navigator and get in my Internet Explorer.
And we can take a short cut through my neighborhood
And meet at my Interactive Playstation.
You know once she arrived at my site I served-her.
I interfaced with her floppy disk
I downloaded my hard drive into her software
As I was searching for viruses in the system
As I was about to set my margins
She jumped on my laptop
As she started scanning me for Megabytes
It wasn't Micro..soft
So she grabbed my mouse and double-clicked
I started to curs-or!
I said Mrs. Macintosh what the font are you doing!
Things were starting to get terminal
So that's when I opened my zip drive
Put on my surge protecter and polished my apple
Logged on? and hit the backspace
And jumped out the mutha-fuckin window .DOT. COM
And she said
YAHOOOOOOOOOOOOOOOOOOOOOOOOOOOOOOOO!!!!

THE USE OF FORCE
William Carlos Williams

They were new patients to me, all I had was the name, Olson. Please come down as soon as you can, my daughter is very sick.

When I arrived I was met by the mother, a big startled looking woman, very clean and apologetic who merely said, Is this the doctor? and let me in. In the back, she added. You must excuse us, doctor, we have her in the kitchen where it is warm. It is very damp here sometimes.

The child was fully dressed and sitting on her father's lap near the kitchen table. He tried to get up, but I motioned for him not to bother, took off my overcoat and started to look things over. I could see that they were all very nervous, eyeing me up and down distrustfully. As often, in such cases, they weren't telling me more than they had to, it was up to me to tell them; that's why they were spending three dollars on me.

The child was fairly eating me up with her cold, steady eyes, and no expression to her face whatever. She did not move and seemed, inwardly, quiet; an unusually attractive little thing, and as strong as a heifer in appearance. But her face was flushed, she was breathing rapidly, and I realized that she had a high fever. She had magnificent blonde hair, in profusion. One of those picture children often reproduced in advertising leaflets and the photogravure sections of the Sunday papers.

She's had a fever for three days, began the father and we don't know what it comes from. My wife has given her things, you know, like people do, but it don't do no good. And there's been a lot of sickness around. So we tho't you'd better look her over and tell us what is the matter.

As doctors often do I took a trial shot at it as a point of departure. Has she had a sore throat?

Both parents answered me together, No . . . No, she says her throat don't hurt her.

Does your throat hurt you? added the mother to the child. But the little girl's expression didn't change nor did she move her eyes from my face.

Have you looked?

I tried to, said the mother, but I couldn't see.

As it happens we had been having a number of cases of diphtheria in the school to which this child went during that month and we were all, quite apparently, thinking of that, though no one had as yet spoken of the thing.

Well, I said, suppose we take a look at the throat first. I smiled in my best professional manner and asking for the child's first name I said, come on, Mathilda, open your mouth and let's take a look at your throat.

Nothing doing.

Aw, come on, I coaxed, just open your mouth wide and let me take a look. Look, I said opening both hands wide, I haven't anything in my hands. Just open up and let me see.

Such a nice man, put in the mother. Look how kind he is to you. Come on, do what he tells you to. He won't hurt you.

At that I ground my teeth in disgust. If only they wouldn't use the word "hurt" I might be able to get somewhere. But I did not allow myself to be hurried or disturbed but speaking quietly and slowly I approached the child again.

As I moved my chair a little nearer suddenly with one catlike movement both her hands clawed instinctively for my eyes and she almost reached them too. In fact she knocked my glasses flying and they fell, though unbroken, several feet away from me on the kitchen floor.

Both the mother and father almost turned themselves inside out in embarrassment and apology. You bad girl, said the mother, taking her and shaking her by one arm. Look what you've done. The nice man . . .

For heaven's sake, I broke in. Don't call me a nice man to her. I'm here to look at her throat on the chance that she might have diphtheria and possibly die of it. But that's nothing to her. Look here, I said to the child, we're going to look at your throat. You're old enough to understand what I'm saying. Will you open it now by yourself or shall we have to open it for you?

Not a move. Even her expression hadn't changed. Her breaths however were coming faster and faster. Then the battle began. I had to do it. I had to have a throat culture for her own protection. But first I told the parents that it was entirely up to them. I explained the danger but said that I would not insist on a throat examination so long as they would take the responsibility.

If you don't do what the doctor says you'll have to go to the hospital, the mother admonished her severely.

Oh yeah? I had to smile to myself. After all, I had already fallen in love with the savage brat, the parents were contemptible to me. In the ensuing struggle they grew more and more abject, crushed, exhausted while she surely rose to magnificent heights of insane fury of effort bred of her terror of me.

The father tried his best, and he was a big man but the fact that she was his daughter, his shame at her behavior and his dread of hurting her made him release her just at the critical times when I had almost achieved success, till I wanted to kill him. But his dread also that she might have diphtheria made him tell me to go on, go on though he himself was almost fainting, while the mother moved back and forth behind us raising and lowering her hands in an agony of apprehension.

Put her in front of you on your lap, I ordered, and hold both her wrists.

But as soon as he did the child let out a scream. Don't, you're hurting me. Let go of my hands. Let them go I tell you. Then she shrieked terrifyingly, hysterically. Stop it! Stop it! You're killing me!

Do you think she can stand it, doctor! said the mother.

You get out, said the husband to his wife. Do you want her to die of diphtheria?

Come on now, hold her, I said.

Then I grasped the child's head with my left hand and tried to get the wooden tongue depressor between her teeth. She fought, with clenched teeth, desperately! But now I also had grown furious--at a child. I tried to hold myself down but I couldn't. I know how to expose a throat for inspection. And I did my best. When finally I got the wooden spatula behind the last teeth and just the point of it into the mouth cavity, she opened up for an instant but before I could see anything she came down again and gripping the wooden blade between her molars she reduced it to splinters before I could get it out again.

Aren't you ashamed, the mother yelled at her. Aren't you ashamed to act like that in front of the doctor?

Get me a smooth-handled spoon of some sort, I told the mother. We're going through with this. The child's mouth was already bleeding. Her tongue was cut and she was screaming in wild hysterical shrieks. Perhaps I should have desisted and come back in an hour or more. No doubt it would have been better. But I have seen at least two children lying dead in bed of neglect in such cases, and feeling that I must get a diagnosis now or never I went at it again. But the worst of it was that I too had got beyond reason. I could have torn the child apart in my own fury and enjoyed it. It was a pleasure to attack her. My face was burning with it.

The damned little brat must be protected against her own idiocy, one says to one's self at such times. Others must be protected against her. It is a social necessity. And all these things are true. But a blind fury, a feeling of adult shame, bred of a longing for muscular release are the operatives. One goes on to the end.

In a final unreasoning assault I overpowered the child's neck and jaws. I forced the heavy silver spoon back of her teeth and down her throat till she gagged. And there it was--both tonsils covered with membrane. She had fought valiantly to keep me from knowing her secret. She had been hiding that sore throat for three days at least and lying to her parents in order to escape just such an outcome as this.

Now truly she was furious. She had been on the defensive before but now she attacked. Tried to get off her father's lap and fly at me while tears of defeat blinded her eyes.

The Syndicate Wars: Origin
Jesse James Felice

A War Is Coming.

Too long has my home, the city of Midnight, been engulfed by rampant violence. "We did not seek nor did we provoke an assault on our freedoms and our way of life. We did not expect nor did we invite a confrontation with evil. Yet the true measure of a people's strength is how they rise to master that moment when it does arrive." 2977 people have been killed, and more than 6000 have been injured since the night of the fires, the night the Shadaloo Syndicate laid waste to our city. "72 law enforcement officers were killed; when after having heard the initial explosion from their precinct they ran into the fires to get people out... ran "into" the fires. The streets of heaven are too crowded with angels tonight. They're our students and our teachers and our parents and our friends. The streets of heaven are too crowded with angels, but every time we think we have measured our capacity to meet a challenge, we look up and we're reminded that that capacity may well be limitless. This is a time for heroes. We will do what is hard. We will do what is necessary. This is a time for heroes, and we reach for the stars."

Shadaloo & Zanzibar Land.

I was in full MOP gear on a mission with my JSOC unit when it happened, things went bad quick and the city of Midnight went dark; it was a massacre. The guys I was training with were from all over, Seal Team 2 out of Little Creek, Virginia, Team 5 out of Coronado, California, the Blue Devils Assault squad, the Black Knights Recon, and

Vehicle Team 1 from Pearl Harbor. We even had a few guys from the original Team 6 out of Damn Neck which had been disbanded in the late 80's; they were smart, experienced, seasoned, they had seen a lot of action, and lost too many brothers. Black Knights Recon had been gathering data since Shadaloo had arrived in Midnight, this wasn't just another mob. Shadaloo was known as one the most dangerous crime organizations in the world.

They were para-military, and specialized in biochemical drugs and arms. They're well funded and highly organized skilled and covert criminals, fighters, and mercenaries. Reports indicated they had enough technology and weapons sufficiently advanced to rival a medium-sized nation. Shadaloo originated in Zanzibar Land, a heavily fortified state in Central Asia, located between the former Soviet Union, China, Pakistan, and Afghanistan, all the romantic weekend get-away spots. It was founded by one of the legendary mercenaries, a Russian, fringe, wet-work operative known as Solidus, a man hell bent on achieving world domination through chemically manipulating and genetically enhancing super soldiers.

The area, formerly "Zanzibar province, is an autonomous zone of the USSR. Despite military intervention, Zanzibar was able to win its sovereignty. Primary credit for the success was generally given to the mercenaries from around the world that participated in the war. Because of this, Zanzibar Land's war of independence was also known as the "Mercenary War," bringing back to global attention the profession of the gun for hire." "Add all that up, I don't know what the fuck it means but you got some bad ass perpetrators and they're here to stay."

Like A Thief In The Night.

We stared at each other over beers after the successful completion of our mission; the mood was bittersweet, things had gotten worse in Midnight…Master Chief put his beer down, subtly surveyed the entrances and the patrons present at the bar, and then turned back to us with determined eyes. "We have to do something" he said. We all knew it, we knew the cost too. It was time. We had finished our mission a week early and were ordered to lay low for a few weeks until the geo-political dust from our mission had settled. We went dark, off the grid, quite into the night. We had to be good, we had to be the best. We had to take back our city like a thief in the night: no prints, no paper trail, no leading evidence. We wanted to make it easy for Midnight's local LEO's to look the other way. The stomach churning part was that we didn't NEED to; even if they had found evidence linking to us they wouldn't have cared. They had all lost so much and just wanted it to stop.

We also had to be careful, we were the good guys, we had to minimize collateral damage and avoid getting the community involved as much as was possible. Retribution from the Shadaloo would be a body blow to the city; we had to be swift, proficient, and stay hidden in the cover of darkness. No one could know, just us. Thus we fashioned ourselves a new unit name and new identities for the mission. We spent three days doing reconnaissance with the Black Knights, another three days on mission strategy, op tech, and weapons training. We needed to know everything we could about our enemy. We needed to know the city, its infrastructure, anything that would give us an edge. On the seventhth day we rested, we had to be focused and alert, no sense in a sloppy soldier getting everyone killed.

N-7, 2300 hours, we departed for one of the neighboring

islands off the city's coast; we secured transport from our informant Keyser Soze who ran a smuggling operation from a landing strip in Cuba. In addition to the weapons package he had also been able to secure three six person modified go-fast boats used during a SEAL training exercise in Mississippi; those babies can do over 80 knots. He'd said he'd won them in card game; we didn't ask. We were locked and loaded, coms were up, boats were fueled, safeties were off. We were good to go; Section 8 was ready!

The City Of Midnight

Day 8. Hope flickers, it waxes and wanes with each passing day. The misery that has engulfed my once fair city is heavy like a thick fog, but there are those of us that are trained and willing to put everything on the line. We are Section 8, a specialized, off the books, unsanctioned, black op that has but one purpose, annihilate the Shadaloo Syndicate. We made camp on one of the uninhabited islands 100 miles east of Midnight, a little over an hour by boat. We arrived early on day 8 of our 14-day op, the first seven of which were used for recon and weapons prep.

We reviewed our mission objectives, synchronized our watches, readied our weapons, checked our gear, and swapped good bye letters to give to each others families. At 2100 hours we proceeded to the boats. There were 18 of us, 6 men to a boat, 3 targets, each with different coordinates and mission parameters. Once at the target six men would split into 3 groups, 2 men on the front, 2 men in back, and 2 coming in from the roof. We would take Shadaloo down in stages, night 1 of the assault, designated N-8, was a coordinated simultaneous attack on Shadaloo's infrastructure, aimed at destabilizing their three main bases of operation, HQ, a weapons Depot, and Shadaloo's control over the city's port, platform 9 and ¾. We'd hit'em hard, cut off their legs, and beat them to a calculated pulp. We had the element of surprise, a formidable advantage in battle.

The Hairy Edge

We approached the HQ perimeter fence from the river bank, team B and team C respectively surrounded the Weapons depot and the port's control room and causeway. The fence consisted of motion detectors, bio-metric pressure plates, and motion activated sentries, fortunately we had better toys than they did, which was really saying something considering these guys must have paid a fortune for their op tech; you can get next gen stuff on the black market but you'll have to pay for it. We navigated the perimeter's security defenses without being detected, 6 of us split into three groups and spread out, it was knives and tranq guns only from here on out. Collectively we encountered 15 guys patrolling the outer yard; the great thing about tranquilizer guns is that they don't make noise when you fire them. We dispatched non lethal but effective force to 12 of the 15 guards, 3 had to be taken out with a knife, quickly, quietly, yep, through the neck tends to do the trick. The bombs would take care of the rest, these fuckers are lucky, they get to die in their sleep.

We set charges at key structure points, just enough explosives to collapse each section in on itself. The exterior charges were set, now for the interior. The PAN card we acquired from one of the guards proved to be most useful, enabling us to access the generator room. The few schematics of the facility we were able to drudge up showed panic sensors in the walls and ground which would lock down in the event of an explosion, C-4 was out, and besides, that would draw way to much attention. Exterior charges were set, we got into position, set our night vision to interior mode, and blew the lights and the front and back doors of the main building, which was fashioned into the side of a mountain. I crashed the party through the roof with my fellow brother. At that moment, as I dropped down into the break room, it was as if everything froze for a split second. Time stopped.

There were two Russian mercs sitting on a couch in the corner playing call of duty, the irony wasn't lost on me. Off to the side were four guys shooting a game of billiards, they had taken their Kalashnikovs out of their jackets to play and rested them on the edge of the table next to the blue chalk. There were a couple of assholes in the back playing with their guns; there's nothing I hate more than a pussy with a gun in his hand, what ever happened to the good bad guys, tough guys with a pussy in their hand, kids these days. They didn't know what hit them. The two playing Call of Duty each got two in the chest and one in the head, the four playing pool got the Swiss cheese treatment from my partner's rifle, And the two playing with themselves in the back, I mean with their guns got their fingers and dicks blown off by Master Chief's glorious entrance from the front door. 5 seconds to clear the room, not bad, but we didn't have time to celebrate.

You could hear the droves of pissed off Russians stampeding hurriedly towards us, their emotions were running high, we were counting on that. In their rush to confront the team that just devoured their comrades in a barrage of bullets they forgot to check for trip wires...oops, you didn't need that leg did you? Gun fire erupted from every direction, chaos ensued, but it was our kind of chaos, controlled; we train for this. The break room battle for the last bag of M&Ms was over, victory was ours, or in this case the vending machine. We made our way towards central operations, taking out guards every 30 feet or so.

Things got progressively harder as we moved deeper into the enemy's lair, I took one in the shoulder, my buddy took one in the arm, but nothing was going to stop us from completing our mission.

After peeling back Shadaloo's defenses in what seemed like hours we were getting closer, we had been smart about our ammunition consumption and only used firearms when necessary, our trip wires had been well placed to maximize efficiency, in other words we were being smart about kickin' ass. We made it through the break room, the armory, and the brig, down the shaft, through the halls, past security level 5, and finally, there it was, the central command center. Charges had been set all over the base, inside and out, we were ready to end this campaign on a high note. We placed one final charge on the giant bay doors leading to central operations, this time with specialized explosives used for penetrating armored doors. We set the remote and detonated a person sized hole in the wall. As we entered the brains of the Shadaloo's operation a giant black stealth fighter took off from a cavernous missile silo which opened up from the ceiling, son of a bitch. We regrouped and made for the exit, leaving a trail of carnage and chaos behind us. We made it to the entrance, picking off a few more guards that had felt it wise to challenge us. From the entrance we made our way to the boats, once beyond the perimeter we detonated the charges and burned Shadaloo's operations to the ground.

The Aftermath

We looked up at the night sky with satisfaction. We had accomplished what we had set out to, drive Shadaloo out, even if only temporarily. You win some and you lose some. We didn't get everything we wanted that night, we knew

Solidus would be back, but by all accounts we had won the night. Reports were coming in from the port and the weapons depot, we had successfully taken both. 2 of my brothers were killed in action.

That night, we few, we happy few, we band of brothers stood together, in one voice, and said we will not quietly go into the night; we will fight on and make a better tomorrow for our brothers and mothers, and fathers and daughters.

BOREDOM

noun \\'bȯr-dəm\\
: the state of being bored: the state of being weary and restless through lack of interest

Dull

adjective \\'dəl\\
: not exciting or interesting: having an edge or point that is not sharp: mentally slow : STUPID**b** : lacking zest or vivacity : LISTLESS <a *dull* performance>: slow in action : SLUGGISH**a** : lacking in force, intensity, or sharpness <a *dull* ache>**b** : not resonant or ringing <a *dull* booming sound>: lacking sharpness of edge or point <a *dull* knife>: lacking brilliance or luster <a *dull* finish>

Opening lines are the initial portions of dialogue or text in a written book often constituted by at least the first sentence or a fragment thereof. A good opening line, or incipit, is usually considered desirable. A number of them are so well-known that they are remembered long after the book, while others are so famous that they can end up parodied. When we perform our work, we usually have four seconds before the listener decides whether they are going to continue listening, or tune out. The more powerful our opening lines are, the greater chance we have of holding the reader's attention

HOMAGE TO MY HIPS
Lucille Clifton

these hips are big hips.
they need space to
move around in.
they don't fit into little
petty places. these hips
are free hips.
they don't like to be held back.
these hips have never been enslaved,
they go where they want to go
they do what they want to do.
these hips are mighty hips.
these hips are magic hips.
i have known them
to put a spell on a man and
spin him like a top

THE IDEA OF ANCESTRY
Etheridge Knight

Taped to the wall of my cell are 47 pictures: 47 black
faces: my father, mother, grandmothers (1 dead), grandfathers (both dead), brothers, sisters, uncles, aunts,
cousins (lst and 2nd), nieces, and nephews. They stare
across the space at me sprawling on my bunk. I know
their dark eyes, they know mine. I know their style,
they know mine. I am all of them, they are all of me;
they are farmers, I am a thief, I am me, they are thee.

I have at one time or another been in love with my
mother, 1 grandmother, 2 sisters, 2 aunts (1 went to the
asylum), and 5 cousins, I am now in love with a 7-year-old
niece (she sends me letters written in large block print,
and her picture is the only one that smiles at me).

I have the same name as 1 grandfather, 3 cousins, 3
nephews, and 1 uncle, The uncle disappeared when he
was 15, just took off and caught a freight (they say). He's
discussed each year
when the family has a reunion, he causes uneasiness in
the clan, he is an empty space, My father's mother, who is
93 and who keeps the Family Bible with everybody's birth
dates (and death dates) in it, always mentions him, There
is no place in her Bible for "whereabouts unknown."

Each fall the graves of my grandfathers call me, the brown
hills and red gullies of Mississippi send out their electric
messages, galvanizing my genes. Last yr

like a salmon quitting the cold ocean—leaping and
bucking up his birthstream

Ihitchhiked my way from LA with 16 caps in my pocket and a monkey on my back. And I almost kicked it with the kinfolks. I walked barefooted in my grandmother's backyard

I smelled the old land and the woods

I sipped cornwhiskey from fruit jars with the men

I flirted with the women

I had a ball till the caps ran out and my habit came down. That night I looked at my grandmother and split

my guts were screaming for junk

but I was almost contented

I had almost caught up with me.

 (The next day in Memphis I cracked a croaker's crib for a fix.)

This yr there is a gray stone wall damming my stream, and when the falling leaves stir my genes, I pace my cell or flop on my bunk and stare at 47 black faces across the space, I am all of them, they are all of me, I am me, they are thee, and I have no children to float in the space between.

A MOTHERS REASONS
Ereene Allen

Someone said I treat my son like a baby.
I said I treat him like I'll never see him again.
If I did it'd only be to identify his 5'9, butter toned
body now masked with the blood that once pumped upward
through veins towards his compassionate heart
laying dead in a street he rode bikes and skateboards
up and down as a child.

A street he played touch football on with friends
who knew him far beyond his name.
It is without validation that cops see boys with coarse hair,
tan, brown, nude, mauve, black, blue black, midnight
skin full of melanin. Husky frames, wearing basketball shorts,
hoodies, pants saggin, comin' from the store, playin in the park
with a toy gun, alone, actin a fool in their grandmama's living
room.

It is not fair they see boys as young as twelve up to and beyond
my own sons' ambitious ready for college age of seventeen as a
threat,
a weak excuse to kill on sight.
I refuse to accept that as a reason for them to target him,
dislodge his livelihood into areas of existence I am only left to
imagine. Tasting fear from the tip of my tongue to the back of
my throat hoping one day I won't have to choke on the reality
that my son is gone…

The reality that I won't get another chance to massage my
fingers through his thick coiled hair as he sits me down and lays
his head on my shoulder and says "mom, can we talk," then
melts into my lap with concerns about me, him, his father, this
society.
 Trayvon Martin, who lost his life by way of a rejected cop, his
crime no crime at all, a junk food stop.

Cameron Tillman, Tamir Rice, Laquan Mcdonald, all murdered at the hands of a force once respected,
 now considered a tax payers agony, a black mothers insanity, but I treat him like a baby.
 I treat him as if any moment as soon as the next a cop is waiting to snatch him from the future that he'll never meet, the tax bracket he always seeked.
Seven figures, he said "and the first thing I'm buying is a yellow Lamborghini for me, a red one for you."

Say I treat my son like a baby I will say I treat my son like I'll never be able to cook for him again, laugh, debate, and educate him…again.

See him walk across the stage to receive his diploma from high school, bachelors degree from Tuskegee, masters from wherever his heart steers him.

Until those hired to protect and serve does just that, I will continue to treat my son like the baby I birthed, protected from bullies on playgrounds turf and the corrupt cops that flood the streets of our communities, day to day.

38 BEST FIRST LINES FROM NOVELS

1. Call me Ishmael. —Herman Melville, *Moby-Dick* (1851)
2. It is a truth universally acknowledged, that a single man in possession of a good fortune, must be in want of a wife. —Jane Austen, *Pride and Prejudice*(1813)
3. A screaming comes across the sky. —Thomas Pynchon, *Gravity's Rainbow* (1973)
4. Many years later, as he faced the firing squad, Colonel Aureliano Buendía was to remember that distant afternoon when his father took him to discover ice. —Gabriel García Márquez, *One Hundred Years of Solitude* (1967; trans. Gregory Rabassa)
5. Lolita, light of my life, fire of my loins. —Vladimir Nabokov, *Lolita* (1955)
6. Happy families are all alike; every unhappy family is unhappy in its own way. —Leo Tolstoy, *Anna Karenina* (1877; trans. Constance Garnett)
7. riverrun, past Eve and Adam's, from swerve of shore to bend of bay, brings us by a commodius vicus of recirculation back to Howth Castle and Environs. —James Joyce, *Finnegans Wake* (1939)
8. It was a bright cold day in April, and the clocks were striking thirteen. —George Orwell, *1984* (1949)
9. It was the best of times, it was the worst of times, it was the age of wisdom, it was the age of foolishness, it was the epoch of belief, it was the epoch of incredulity, it was the season of Light, it was the season of Darkness, it was the spring of hope, it was the winter of despair. —Charles Dickens, *A Tale of Two Cities* (1859)
10. I am an invisible man. —Ralph Ellison, *Invisible Man* (1952)
11. The Miss Lonelyhearts of the New York Post-Dispatch (Are you in trouble?—Do-you-need-advice?—Write-to-

Miss-Lonelyhearts-and-she-will-help-you) sat at his desk and stared at a piece of white cardboard. —Nathanael West, *Miss Lonelyhearts* (1933)

12. You don't know about me without you have read a book by the name of *The Adventures of Tom Sawyer*; but that ain't no matter. —Mark Twain, *Adventures of Huckleberry Finn* (1885)

13. Someone must have slandered Josef K., for one morning, without having done anything truly wrong, he was arrested. —Franz Kafka, *The Trial* (1925; trans. Breon Mitchell)

14. You are about to begin reading Italo Calvino's new novel, *If on a winter's night a traveler*. —Italo Calvino, *If on a winter's night a traveler* (1979; trans. William Weaver)

15. The sun shone, having no alternative, on the nothing new. —Samuel Beckett, *Murphy* (1938)

16. If you really want to hear about it, the first thing you'll probably want to know is where I was born, and what my lousy childhood was like, and how my parents were occupied and all before they had me, and all that David Copperfield kind of crap, but I don't feel like going into it, if you want to know the truth. —J. D. Salinger, *The Catcher in the Rye* (1951)

17. Once upon a time and a very good time it was there was a moocow coming down along the road and this moocow that was coming down along the road met a nicens little boy named baby tuckoo. —James Joyce, *A Portrait of the Artist as a Young Man* (1916)

18. This is the saddest story I have ever heard. —Ford Madox Ford, *The Good Soldier* (1915)

19. I wish either my father or my mother, or indeed both of them, as they were in duty both equally bound to it, had minded what they were about when they begot me; had they duly considered how much depended upon what they were then doing;—that not only the production of a rational Being was concerned in it, but that possibly the happy

formation and temperature of his body, perhaps his genius and the very cast of his mind;—and, for aught they knew to the contrary, even the fortunes of his whole house might take their turn from the humours and dispositions which were then uppermost:—Had they duly weighed and considered all this, and proceeded accordingly,—I am verily persuaded I should have made a quite different figure in the world, from that, in which the reader is likely to see me. —Laurence Sterne, *Tristram Shandy* (1759–1767)

20. Whether I shall turn out to be the hero of my own life, or whether that station will be held by anybody else, these pages must show. —Charles Dickens, *David Copperfield* (1850)

21. Stately, plump Buck Mulligan came from the stairhead, bearing a bowl of lather on which a mirror and a razor lay crossed. —James Joyce, *Ulysses* (1922)

22. It was a dark and stormy night; the rain fell in torrents, except at occasional intervals, when it was checked by a violent gust of wind which swept up the streets (for it is in London that our scene lies), rattling along the house-tops, and fiercely agitating the scanty flame of the lamps that struggled against the darkness. —Edward George Bulwer-Lytton, *Paul Clifford* (1830)

23. One summer afternoon Mrs. Oedipa Maas came home from a Tupperware party whose hostess had put perhaps too much kirsch in the fondue to find that she, Oedipa, had been named executor, or she supposed executrix, of the estate of one Pierce Inverarity, a California real estate mogul who had once lost two million dollars in his spare time but still had assets numerous and tangled enough to make the job of sorting it all out more than honorary. —Thomas Pynchon, *The Crying of Lot 49* (1966)

24. It was a wrong number that started it, the telephone ringing three times in the dead of night, and the voice on the other end asking for someone he was not. —Paul Auster, *City of Glass* (1985)

25. Through the fence, between the curling flower spaces, I could see them hitting. —William Faulkner, *The Sound and the Fury* (1929)

26. 124 was spiteful. —Toni Morrison, *Beloved* (1987)

27. Somewhere in la Mancha, in a place whose name I do not care to remember, a gentleman lived not long ago, one of those who has a lance and ancient shield on a shelf and keeps a skinny nag and a greyhound for racing. —Miguel de Cervantes, *Don Quixote* (1605; trans. Edith Grossman)

28. Mother died today. —Albert Camus, *The Stranger* (1942; trans. Stuart Gilbert)

29. Every summer Lin Kong returned to Goose Village to divorce his wife, Shuyu. —Ha Jin, *Waiting* (1999)

30. The sky above the port was the color of television, tuned to a dead channel. —William Gibson, *Neuromancer* (1984)

31. I am a sick man . . . I am a spiteful man. —Fyodor Dostoyevsky, *Notes from Underground* (1864; trans. Michael R. Katz)

32. Where now? Who now? When now? —Samuel Beckett, *The Unnamable* (1953; trans. Patrick Bowles)

33. Once an angry man dragged his father along the ground through his own orchard. "Stop!" cried the groaning old man at last, "Stop! I did not drag my father beyond this tree." —Gertrude Stein, *The Making of Americans* (1925)

34. In a sense, I am Jacob Horner. —John Barth, *The End of the Road* (1958)

35. It was like so, but wasn't. —Richard Powers, *Galatea 2.2* (1995)

36. —Money . . . in a voice that rustled. —William Gaddis, *J R* (1975)

37. Mrs. Dalloway said she would buy the flowers herself. —*Virginia Woolf*, Mrs. Dalloway (1925)

38. All this happened, more or less. —Kurt Vonnegut, *Slaughterhouse-Five* (1969)

NARRATIVE ARC

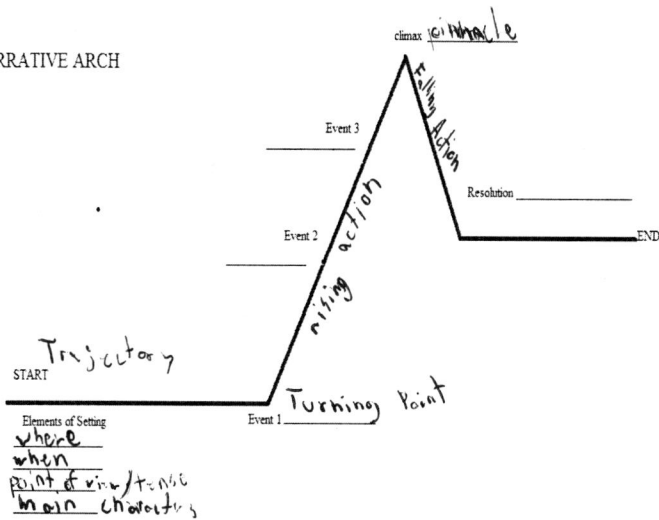

Fight
1 V 1
group V group
man V fear

NARRATIVE ARCH

climax Climax le

Event 3

Event 2

Falling Action

Resolution

END

action

rising

Trajectory

START

Turning Point

Elements of Setting
where
when
point of view / tense
main characters

Event 1

Sometime simply called "arc" or "story arc," narrative arc refers to the chronological construction of plot in a novel or story. Typically, a narrative arc looks something like a pyramid, made up of the following components: exposition, setting, main characters, trajectory, turning point, rising action, climax, falling action, and resolution. Narrative is a report of related events presented to the listeners or readers in words arranged in a logical sequence. A story is taken as a synonym of narrative. A narrative or story is told by a narrator who may be a direct part of that experience and he or she often shares the experience as a first-person narrator. Sometimes he or she may only observe the events as a third-person narrator and gives his or her verdict.

THE BALLAD OF RUDOLPH REED
Gwendolyn Brooks

Rudolph Reed was oaken.
His wife was oaken too.
And his two good girls and his good little man
Oakened as they grew.

"I am not hungry for berries.
I am not hungry for bread.
But hungry hungry for a house
Where at night a man in bed

"May never hear the plaster
Stir as if in pain.
May never hear the roaches
Falling like <u>fat</u> rain.

"Where never wife and children need
Go blinking through the gloom.
Where every room of many rooms
Will be full of room.

"Oh my home may have its east or west
Or north or south behind it.
All I know is I shall know it,
And fight for it when I find it."

The agent's steep and steady stare
Corroded to a grin.
Why you black old, tough old hell of a man,
Move your family in!

Nary a grin grinned Rudolph Reed,
Nary a curse cursed he,
But moved in his House. With his dark little wife,
And his dark little children three.

A neighbor would look, with a yawning eye
That squeezed into a slit.
But the Rudolph Reeds and children three
Were too joyous to notice it.

For were they not firm in a home of their own
With windows everywhere
And a beautiful banistered stair
And a front yard for flowers and a back for grass?

The first night, a rock, big as two fists.
The second, a rock big as three.
But nary a curse cursed Rudolph Reed.
(Though oaken as man could be.)

The third night, a silvery ring of glass.
Patience arched to endure,
But he looked, and lo! small Mabel's blood
Was staining her gaze so pure.

Then up did rise our Roodoplh Reed
And pressed the hand of his wife,
And went to the door with a thirty-four
And a beastly butcher knife.

He ran like a mad thing into the night
And the words in his mouth were stinking.
By the time he had hurt his first white man
He was no longer thinking.

By the time he had hurt his fourth white man

Rudolph Reed was dead.
His neighbors gathered and kicked his corpse.
"Nigger--" his neighbors said.

Small Mabel whimpered all night long,
For calling herself the cause.
Her oak-eyed mother did no thing
But change the bloody gauze.

COMPTONIAN FOLKTALE
Hiram Sims

Once upon a time there lived a whore
of meager wages and of meager hope,
who walked the streets of Compton every night
in search of tricks to fill her veins with dope.

And every night those men did surely come
to feast upon her flesh and weary bones,
that every morning woke to alley streets
laden with trash, and everything she owns.

She, like the rest of us, hated her job
and took no joy in work, derived no thrill,
from letting men deposit wasted seeds
into a womb no child would ever fill.

One morning after her crack-induced sleep,
she lifted herself from that alley floor,
and screamed with every fiber of her frame
"It's over, I can't live this life no more!"

She took her earnings from the night before
and walked into the Goodwill right off Brutes,
where she bought three nice dresses and two pair
of stockings to go with her hooker boots.

She got dressed, combed her hair and greased her scalp,
then walked right into Mom's Cleaners on Hyde
and said, " The sign outside says you need help.
My Daddy owned a Cleaners fo' he died…

I worked there thirteen years cleanin' them clothes
and if you let me work here, you gon' see,
I'll be da best employee thatchu got,
Please Ma'm, gimme this job, just trust me."

She looked her up and down, then crossed her arms
and said, "Who the hell do you think you are?
You think just cuz you bought a dress, these folks
don't know you sell your ass behind that bar?

Every night my husband leaves my house
and spends My Money in your alley streets,
then brings your stink into our marriage bed
and marinates your sweat in my white sheets!

Listen to me good, unlike my Man
I'd never give my money to a whore.
I'd slit my throat before I'd ever let
a tramp like you work in my Goddam store!!"

She walked out of that place with head hung low,
then marched to Jerry's Liquor up the street,
and bought a pint of Vodka, which she took
back to her alley home to claim her seat.

And there she sits today, her dress still on.
A mound of broken flesh and broken hope,
who waits in Compton alleys every night
for tricks, that she might numb her pain with dope.

CHILDREN'S BEDTIME STORY
Slick Rick

Here we go,
Once upon a time not long ago,
When people wore pajamas and lived life slow,
When laws were stern and justice stood,
And people were behavin' like they ought ta good,
There lived a lil' boy who was misled,
By anotha lil' boy and this is what he said:
"Me, Ya, Ty, we gonna make sum cash,
Robbin' old folks and makin' tha dash",
They did the job, money came with ease,
But one couldn't stop, it's like he had a disease,
He robbed another and another and a sista and her brotha,
Tried to rob a man who was a D.T. undercover,
The cop grabbed his arm, he started acting erratic,
He said "Keep still, boy, no need for static",
Punched him in his belly and he gave him a slap,
But little did he know the lil' boy was strapped,
The kid pulled out a gun, he said "Why did ya hit me ?",
The barrel was set straight for the cop's kidney,
The cop got scared, the kid, he starts to figure,
"I'll do years if I pull this trigga",
So he cold dashed and ran around the block,
Cop radioes it to another lady cop,
He ran by a tree, there he saw this sista,
A shot for the head, he shot back but he missed her,
Looked around good and from expectations,
So he decided he'd head for the subway stations,
But she was coming and he made a left,
He was runnin' top speed till he was outta breath,
Knocked an old man down and swore he killed him,
Then he made his move to an abandoned building,

Ran up the stairs up to the top floor,
Opened up the door there, guess who he saw?,
Dave the dope fiend shootin' dope,
Who don't know the meaning of water nor soap,
He said "I need bullets, hurry up, run!"
The dope fiend brought back a spanking shotgun,
He went outside but there was cops all over,
Then he dipped into a car, a stolen Nova (?),
Raced up the block doing 83,
Crashed into a tree near university,
Escaped alive though the car was battered,
Rat-a-tat-tatted and all the cops scattered,
Ran out of bullets and still had static,
Grabbed a pregnant lady and out the automatic,
Pointed at her head and he said the gun was full o' lead,
He told the cops "Back off or honey here's dead",
Deep in his heart he knew he was wrong,
So he let the lady go and he starts to run on,
Sirens sounded, he seemed astounded,
Before long the lil' boy got surrounded,
He dropped the gun, so went the glory,
And this is the way I have end this story,
He was only seventeen, in a madman's dream,
The cops shot the kid, I still hear him scream,
This ain't funny so don't ya dare laugh,
Just another case 'bout the wrong path,
Straight 'n narrow or yo' soul gets cast(?). kid gets shot

Good night.   They chase him

kid is dead. The End

gets caught

wants to steal

steals

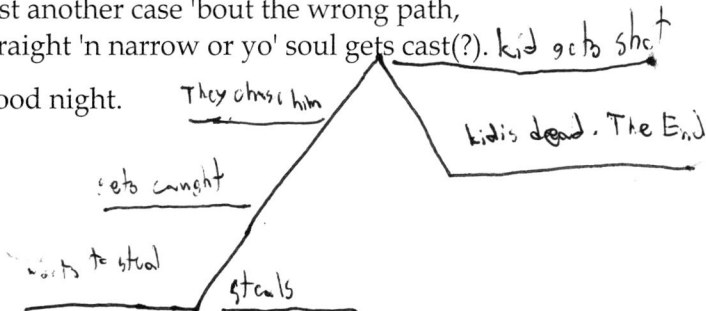

Probably LA or NY or London
A time not long ago
maybe the 80's

133

ETHEL
Jam Javier

Princess Ethel watched her younger sister silently from the high windows of her tower. She had done this every day, making sure her heart was always filled with hatred and bitterness. She woke up morning after morning and made a point to find characteristics about her sister that were unfair, irritating or resentful.

On that specific morning, it was young Princess Lily's hair. She had long and wavy hair, down to her lower back, and it was a beautiful shade of the colors brown and red. On some occasions, with the perfect hit of sunlight, it looked almost pink. It appeared as though a cherry blossom tree in autumn grew on top of Lily's head.

"It's because she's got servants brushing it all night long. Yes, that must be it. She waits for me to fall asleep, then calls all the castle's helpers to her room. And they brush... and brush... and brush," Ethel muttered under her breath. She pulled on her own long hair, the color of tree bark, and sniffed it. "Mine has a stench. And it's dull."
Ethel's reverie was interrupted by her maid.

"Princess Ethel, your breakfast is ready."
"What is it?" She asked suspiciously.
"Your favorite, young miss, pumpkin soup." The maid attempted a smile.
"Did Lily have some of it?"
"Why, yes, Princess."
"Then I don't want it," Ethel whispered.
"But, miss, you must eat. You haven't been looking healthy these past weeks. You'll starve, Princess!" The maid exclaimed, in a worried tone.

"Make me something she doesn't like," Ethel ordered.

"The only thing she doesn't like is…" The maid had to think first. "Well, meat. And you never liked meat either."

"Then… I'm having meat for breakfast," Ethel stated, continuing to look out the window.

***

"Today, it stops, Ethel!" Derek shook his head. "Pardon me, Ethel. We are friends, yes, we are. I have always been there for you, and you have always been there for me. We grew up together and I care about you, but we need to put an end to this!"

"What?" Ethel asked incredulously. "End to what?"

Derek sighed heavily. "You disparage your sister all the time, and it drives me mad! She is a good person, she loves you, she minds her own business, she doesn't harm anything or anybody. She's always so happy and most of all she does not deserve her older sister saying so many offensive and may I say, incorrect things about her!"

Ethel was pacing back and forth in the garden where she and Derek, her only friend (the son of the baker down the dirt path), always got together to play or talk.

Ethel scoffed. "How can you possibly say 'incorrect'? Don't you agree that everyone favors her over me? Don't you see that she takes advantage of everybody and manipulates them when she smiles phonily? She is a fraud, that's what she is! She wants my castle playing at the palm of her hands and she wants to take my kingdom from me!"

"She is not, Ethel. You are making these things up in your head." Derek calmly answered. "She worries about you. She's saddened by the fact you hardly speak to her, that you are always sneering, that you don't frolic in the sun-- that you are pale. And the dark circles under your eyes… she thinks you don't sleep. You're her older sister. She cares about you, deeply."

135

"She... what?" Ethel gave Derek a piercing look. She started advancing eerily towards him, contempt evident in her eyes. "How do you know all this? How she feels? What she thinks?"

"Well I..." Derek stammered. "I... do speak with her at times."

Ethel stared at him scornfully. "You know how I feel about her."

Derek sighed. "I do know. I listened to you for eight years talk about your younger sister as if she were this awful creature. But I realized, you're wrong..."

Derek's voice lightened and he even chuckled a bit, and this small but significant change made the hair on Ethel's arms rise with fury. She swallowed back the building rumble in her throat and curled her bony hands into hard, white-knuckled fists.

"She's wonderful. I never could tell you, but she is! She's clever and funny... genuine, kind. She rescued a weak dove four days ago, you know, treated her broken wing so it could fly. Her perspective is fresh and optimistic. She breathes life into stillness. She makes the best wreaths out of flowers, too! She's got these gorgeous green eyes and porcelain skin. A face that beautiful is just a miracle of nature. Give her a chance, will you? You'd like her..."

Something inside Ethel snapped. She couldn't believe what she was hearing. This was Derek, the only thing that was hers. And he was praising Lily like a lovesick fool.

"Ethel, I think I'm in love with your sister." He concluded. "I'm sorry."

Ethel merely nodded, and cast her eyes upon ground.

***

That same night, just like many nights prior, dinner was served.

"I had a lovely day, Martha! It was quite fascinating, feeding those chickens. I'd love to do it again tomorrow. Will you tell Mr. Dino I enjoyed it very much?" Lily giggled with one of the servants as she ate her vegetables.

Ethel gazed at Lily distrustfully. She couldn't understand how everyone was deceived by her bogus charm.

"And by the way, I appreciate the basin of water you put in my quarters, Martha. It is the first thing I look forward to when I wake up in the morning. I certainly love the cool temperature on my face."

"You're always very welcome, Miss Lily. I've been filling up that basin every night for about fifteen years now. And you thank me for every little thing, Princess," Martha replied lovingly.

Ethel glared and lost her appetite. She didn't finish her meal. She picked up her plate, stomped over to the maid named Martha, and threw the contents of it to her face. Martha, Lily and the rest of the servants in the dining room gasped in shock.

Then Ethel scowled at Lily, smiled sarcastically at Martha and retorted, "That, is for never putting a 'basin of water'"-she copied Lily's higher pitched tone- "in my quarters."

Then Ethel ran up three flights of stairs. The entire castle shook when she banged her large, oak doors shut.

Under her covers, Ethel couldn't sleep. She stared up to her ceiling and counted the spider webs. No one was allowed to clean her quarters. She made a mental note to herself to try and collect some flies for the spiders living in her space. She thought that some company would be nice, since Derek was about to leave her for her sister.

Derek's voice then echoed in her ears. She's got these gorgeous green eyes and porcelain skin. A face that beautiful is just a miracle of nature. Give her a chance, will you? You'd like her…

Ethel dreamed of screaming that night, and woke up in the morning leering.

***

The next day, Ethel peered out once again from the high windows of her tall towers and looked down to find Lily. Ethel saw her, having what seemed like a pleasant conversation with Derek. Ethel paid closer attention to Derek, his eyes squinting from smiling too broadly. Then Derek all of a sudden touched Lily's face, pulled it closer to his, and kissed her.

Ethel's heart broke, and her mind reeled. She ran to the back of the castle, mounted her horse and rode several miles to meet with Willa.

"What in the world will you need this much acid for, Princess?" she wondered.

"Just for my room, Willa… it's about time I clean it, rid it of its dirty… spots." Ethel responded absent-mindedly, as she examined the clear liquid in the tall flask.

"This is very strong. Use it well." Willa's voice was raspy.

"Believe me…" Ethel droned, "I will."

***

Before dawn, Ethel cautiously and carefully made her way to her younger sister's room. It was a challenge to open the doors without making a sound, but since the maids all had a separate sleeping area, Ethel got away with the soft thud the doors made.

Ethel stood beside the bed and watched Lily breathe and sleep. She stood there and cursed at Lily's beautiful features, cursed her parents for dying without making her feel just as important as Lily, and cursed Derek for choosing Lily, just like everybody else did.

Lily, Lily, Lily. It was all about Lily, Ethel thought.

She quietly walked to Lily's vanity area and spotted the wooden basin that Lily was very fond of. True to Martha's words, it was filled, perhaps two inches from the brim. The

138

water felt cool, perfect, like the temperature Lily had spoken of.

Then Ethel took out the tall flask from her pocket and emptied out its strong and foul-smelling contents to the basin. Then she walked to the balcony, threw the flask as far as she could into the woods that was their backyard, and skipped all the way back to her room.

She happily jumped into her bed and snuggled with her raggedy pillow. Let's see if she'll still be beautiful in the morning.

Later that morning, Ethel was awoken untimely by tiny legs.

Groggy and upset, she forced her eyes open. Then she saw a spider, the size of a golf ball crawling on her face. Out of morning disorientation, instinct and shock (even though she did welcome the idea), she screamed and hit the spider dead, flat on her face. Some of the juice of the dead spider splattered on her forehead, nose and left eye. Ethel jumped up to her feet and ran to anything that could alleviate the situation.

She saw a basin full of water a few feet away; and without thinking, Ethel immersed her face into it.

Then there was an ear-splitting scream of excruciating pain from the highest room up in the tallest tower.

***

"Did you hear that?" Derek looked around the woods as Lily bent over to pick up some wild flowers from the bush. "I thought I heard someone screaming… thought I heard Ethel."

"I didn't hear anything." She answered innocently.

"Perhaps, not." Derek mused. "Besides, Ethel doesn't wake up this early."

"No," Lily agreed. "And I think she'll have a better morning today."

"Why is that?" Derek inquired.

"Well, I figured Ethel would want to wash her face in the morning to start off her day. So before the sun rose, I snuck into her quarters to let her have my basin. She was complaining about it the other night at dinner, so I decided to surprise her."

Short story —Film

COLLABORATE

90 sec ~6min
I ant created the othe ort

verb \kə-'la-bə-ˌrāt\
: to work with another person or group in order to achieve
or do something: : to work jointly with others or together
especially in an intellectual endeavor: to cooperate with an
agency or instrumentality with which one is not
immediately connected

CALIBRATE

to adjust or mark (something, such as a
measuring device) so that it can be used in an
accurate and exact way: determining the
deviation from a standard so as to ascertain the
proper correction factors: to adjust precisely for
a particular function

Collaboration is working with others to do a task and to
achieve shared goals. It is a recursive[1] process where two
or more people or organizations work together to realize
shared goals, (this is more than the intersection of common
goals seen in co-operative ventures, but a deep, collective
determination to reach an identical objective. Some of the
greatest poems and stories are collaborations between
literature and other artforms. Here are some examples.

NIGGAS ARE SCARED OF REVOLUTION!
The Last Poets

Niggas are scared of revolution

but niggas shouldn't be scared of revolution
because revolution is nothing but change
and all niggas do is change

niggas come home from work and change into pimping
clothes and hit the streets to make some quick change
nigger change thier hair from black to red to blonde and
hope like hell thier looks will change
niggas kill other niggers
just because one didnt receive the correct change
niggas change from men to women
from women to men
niggas change/ change/ change
you hear niggas say thing are changing/ things are
changing yeah things are changing, niggas change into
black nigga things black nigga things that go thru all kinds
of changes the change in the day that makes them rant and
rave black power/ black power
and the change that comes over them at night
as thy sigh and moan
white thighs /oooh white thighs
niggas are always going through bullshit change
but when it comes to a real change
niggas are scared of revolution

niggas are actor/niggas are actors
niggas act like they are in such a hurry
to catch the first act of the great white hope
niggas tyr to act like malcolm and when the white man
doesnt react toward them like he did malcolm

142

niggas want to act violently
niggas act so kooool and slick
causing white people to say:
"what makes them niggas act like that?"
niggas act like you aint never seen nobody act before
but when it comes to acting out revolution
niggas say- i can't dig them actions!
niggas are scared of revolution

niggas are very untogether people
niggas talk about getting high
and ridin around in els
niggas should get high and ride to hell
niggas talk about pimping

pimping that /pimping what
pimping your pimping mine
just to be pimping /is a hell of a line
niggas ar very untogether people

niggas talk about the mind
talk about- my miind is stronger than yours
i got that *****es mind up tight
niggas dont know a damn thing about the mind
or they'd be right
niggas are scared of revolution

niggas fuck /niggas fuck/ fuck/ fuck
niggas loove the word fuck they think they so fuckin cute
they fuck you around
the first thing they say when they get mad is fuck it
you play a little too much with them
and they say fuck you
when it's time to tcb

niggers be somewhere fucking and if you
try to be nice to them
they fuck over you
niggas dont realize that while they are doing all this
fucking that they are getting fucked around
but when they do realize it's too late so niggas just get
fucked up niggas just get fucked up
niggas talk about fucking
fucking that /fucking this/fucking yours /fucking my sis
not knowing what they are fucking for
aint fucking for love and appreciation
just fuckin to be fucking
niggas fuck
white thighs/ black thighs/ yellow thighs/ brown thighs
niggas fuck ankles when they run out of thighs
niggas fuck sally , linda and sue
and you don't watch out
niggas will fuck you
niggas would fuck fuck if it could be fucked
but when it comes to fucking for a revolutionary causes
niggas say fuck revoution
niggas are scared of revolution

niggas are players /are players/are players
niggas play football baseball and basketball
while the white man
is cutting off their balls
when the niggas play aint tight enough
to play with some black thighs
niggers play with white thighs
to see if they still have some play left
when it ain't no white thighs to play with
niggers play with themselves
niggas tell you they're ready to be lilberated
but when you say lets go take our libereation
niggas reply- i was just playin'

144

niggas are playing with revolution and losin
niggas are scared of revolution

niggas do a lot of shootin/ niggas do a lot of shootin
niggers shoot off at the mouth
niggas shoot pool/niggas shoot craps
niggas cut down the corner and shoot down the street
niggas shoot sharp glances at white women
niggas shoot dope into thier arm
niggas shoot guns and rifles on new years eve
a new year is that coming in
the white police will do more shooting at them
where are the niggas when the revolution needs some
shots?
yeah you know /niggas are somewhere shootin the shit
niggas are scared of revolution

niggers are lovers /niggers are lovers are lovers
niggas loved to see clark gable make love to marilyn monroe
niggas love to see tarzan fuck over the natives
niggas love to hear the lone ranger yell/ hi ho silver!
niggas love commercials /niggas love commercials
oh how niggas love commercials

you can take niggas out of the country but/
you can't take the country out of niggas

niggers are lovers are lovers are lovers
niggas loved ot hear malcolm rap
but they didn't love malcolm
niggas love everything but themselves

but i'm a lover too / yes i'm a lover too

i love niggas / i love niggas / i love niggas
cause niggas are me
and i should only love that which is me
i love to see niggas go through changes

i love to see niggas act
i love to see niggas make them plays and shoot the shit
but there is one thing about niggas that i do not love
niggas are scared of revolution....

THE DEAD
Billy Collins

The dead are always looking down on us, they say.
while we are putting on our shoes or making a sandwich,
they are looking down through the glass bottom boats of
heaven as they row themselves slowly through eternity.
They watch the tops of our heads moving below on earth,
and when we lie down in a field or on a couch,
drugged perhaps by the hum of a long afternoon,
they think we are looking back at them,
which makes them lift their oars and fall silent
and wait, like parents, for us to close our eyes.

THE COUNTRY
Billy Collins

I wondered about you
when you told me never to leave
a box of wooden, strike-anywhere matches
lying around the house because the mice

might get into them and start a fire.
But your face was absolutely straight
when you twisted the lid down on the round tin
where the matches, you said, are always stowed.

Who could sleep that night?
Who could whisk away the thought
of the one unlikely mouse
padding along a cold water pipe

behind the floral wallpaper
gripping a single wooden match
between the needles of his teeth?
Who could not see him rounding a corner,

the blue tip scratching against a rough-hewn beam,
the sudden flare, and the creature
for one bright, shining moment
suddenly thrust ahead of his time —

now a fire-starter, now a torchbearer
in a forgotten ritual, little brown druid
illuminating some ancient night.
Who could fail to notice,

lit up in the blazing insulation,
the tiny looks of wonderment on the faces
of his fellow mice, onetime inhabitants
of what once was your house in the country?

SOME DAYS
Billy Collins

Some days I put the people in their places at the table,
bend their legs at the knees,
if they come with that feature,
and fix them into the tiny wooden chairs.

All afternoon they face one another,
the man in the brown suit,
the woman in the blue dress,
perfectly motionless, perfectly behaved.

But other days, I am the one
who is lifted up by the ribs,
then lowered into the dining room of a dollhouse
to sit with the others at the long table.

Very funny,
but how would you like it
if you never knew from one day to the next
if you were going to spend it

striding around like a vivid god,
your shoulders in the clouds,
or sitting down there amidst the wallpaper,
staring straight ahead with your little plastic face?

SIGNIFYING MONKEY
Rudy Ray Moore

Way down in the jungle deep
The badass lion stepped on the signifying monkey's feet
The monkey said, "Muthafucka, can't you see?
Why, you standing on my goddamned feet."
The lion said, "I ain't heard a word you said."
Said, "If you say three more I'll be steppin' on your
muthafuckin' head!"

Now the monkey lived in the jungle in an old oak tree
Bullshitting the lion every day of the week
Well every day before the sun go down
The lion would kick his ass all through the jungle town
But the monkey got wise and started using his wit
Said, "I'm going to put a stop to this ol' ass kicking shit!"

So he ran up on the lion the very next day
Said, "Oh Mr. Lion there's a big, bad muthafucka coming
your way
And when you meet, it's gonna be a goddamn scene
And wherever you meet some ass is bound to bend."
Said, "he's somebody that you don't know
He just broke loose from Ringling Brothers' show."

Said, "Baby, he talked about your people in a helluva way
He talked about your people 'til my hair turned gray
He said your daddy's a freak and your momma's a whore
Said he spotted you running through the jungle
Selling asshole from door to door!

Said your sister did the damndest trick
She got down so low and sucked an earthworm's dick

He said he spotted your niece behind the tree
Screwing a muthafuckin flea
He said he saw your aunt sitting on the fence
Giving a goddamn zebra a French

Then he talked about your mammy and your sister Lou
Then he started talking 'bout how good your grandma
screw
Said your sister's a prostitute and your brother's a punk
And said I'll be damned if you don't eat all the pussy
You see every time you get drunk

He said he cornholed your uncle and fucked your aunty
and your niece
And next time he see your grandma he gonna get him
another good piece
He said your brother died with the whooping cough
And your uncle died with the measles
And your old grandpa died with a rag chunked up in his
ass
Said he was going on home to Jesus

And you know your little sister that you love so dear
I fucked her all day for a bottle of beer
So Mr. Lion, you know that ain't right
So whenever you meet the elephant be ready to fight
So the lion jumped up in a helluva rage
Like a young cocksucker full of gage

He let out a roar, tail shot back like a .44
He went through the jungle knocking down trees
Kicking giraffes to their knees
Then he ran up on the elephant talking to the swine
Said, "All right you big, bad muthafucka, it's gonna be
your ass or mine!"
The elephant looked at him outta the corner of his eye

Said, "Alright go ahead home you little funny-bunny muthafucka
And pick on somebody your own size."

The lion jumped up and made a fancy pass
The elephant side-stepped him and kicked him dead in his ass
He busted up his jaw, fucked up his face
Broke all four legs, snatched his ass outta place
He picked him up, slammed him to the tree
Nothin' but lion shit as far as you could see

He pulled out his nuts, rolled 'em in the sand
And kicked his ass like a natural man
They fought all that night and all the next day
Somehow the lion managed to get away
But he drug his ass back to the jungle more dead than alive
Just to run into that little monkey with some more of his signifying jive

The monkey looked at 'em and said, "Goddamn! Ol' partner
You don't look so swell." Said, "Look like to me you caught a whole lotta hell."
Said, "Your eyes is all red and your asshole is blue
I knew in the beginning it wasn't shit to you
There's one thing you and me gotta get straight
Cause you one ugly cocksucker I sho' do hate!"

"Now when you left, the jungle rung
Now you bring your dog ass back here damn near hung
Look muthafucka, ain't you a bitch
Your face look like you got the Seven Year Itch
I told my wife before you left
I should kicked your ass my muthafuckin' self!"

153

"Why I seen when he threw you into that tree
Cause some of that ol' lion shit got on me
Why every night when me and my wife is trying to get a little bit
Here you come 'round here with some that old 'Aiee-yo' shit
Shut up! Don't you roar!
Cause I'll bail outta this tree and whoop your dog-ass some more!"

"And don't look up here with your sucka-paw case
Cause I'll piss through the bark of this tree in your muthafuckin' face!"
The little monkey got happy, started to jump up and down
His feet missed the limb and his ass hit the ground
Like a streak of lighting and a ball of white heat
That lion was on his ass with all four feet

Dust rolled and tears came into the little monkey's eyes
The little monkey said, "Look Mr. Lion, I apologize!"
Said, "If you let me get my nuts out the sand
Why I'll fight your ass like a natural man
Look muthafucka, ain't you a bitch, you ain't raising no hell
Cause everybody saw you jump on me after I slipped and fell."
Said, "If you'll fight like men should
I'd whoop yo' ass all over these woods!"

This made the lion mad!
It was the boldest challenge he ever had
He squared off for the fight
But that little monkey jumped damn near outta sight
Landed way up in a banana tree and began to grin
Sayin', "Look here you big, bad muthafucka, you been bullshitted again!"

154

Said, "Why, I'll take me one of these bananas
And whoop on your ass 'til it sings the Star-Spangled
Banner!"
And said, "Now if you ever mess with me again
I'm gonna send you back to my elephant friend!"
Said, "The things I told you will never part
But what I'm gonna tell you now is gonna break your
muthafuckin' heart!"

Said, "Your mammy ain't no good and your sister's been a
whore."
Said, "I had that bitch on the corner for a year or more!"
But the lion looked up with a helluva frown
Roared so loud that little monkey fell back to the ground
The little monkey looked up and said "Please, Mr. Lion!
Please don't take my life 'cause I got 13 kids and a very
sickly wife!"

Said, "All my money to you I'll give
Mr. Lion, please just let me live!"
But the lion kicked him in his ass and broke his neck
Left that little monkey in a helluva wreck
The monkey looked up to the sky with tears in his eyes
Nothin' he could see or nothing he could hear
He knew that that was the end
Of his bulllshittin' and signifyin' career

Signifying career…

SALVATION
Langston Huges

I was saved from sin when I was going on thirteen. But not really saved. It happened like this. There was a big revival at my Auntie Reed's church. Every night for weeks there had been much preaching, singing, praying, and shouting, and some very hardened sinners had been brought to Christ, and the membership of the church had grown by leaps and bounds. Then just before the revival ended, they held a special meeting for children, "to bring the young lambs to the fold." My aunt spoke of it for days ahead. That night I was escorted to the front row and placed on the mourners' bench with all the other young sinners, who had not yet been brought to Jesus.

My aunt told me that when you were saved you saw a light, and something happened to you inside! And Jesus came into your life! And God was with you from then on! She said you could see and hear and feel Jesus in your soul. I believed her. I had heard a great many old people say the same thing and it seemed to me they ought to know. So I sat there calmly in the hot, crowded church, waiting for Jesus to come to me.

The preacher preached a wonderful rhythmical sermon, all moans and shouts and lonely cries and dire pictures of hell, and then he sang a song about the ninety and nine safe in the fold, but one little lamb was left out in the cold. Then he said: "Won't you come? Won't you come to Jesus? Young lambs, won't you come?" And he held out his arms to all us young sinners there on the mourners'bench. And the little girls cried. And some of them jumped up and went to Jesus right away. But most of us just sat there.

A great many old people came and knelt around us and prayed, old women with jet-black faces and braided hair, old men with work-gnarled hands. And the church sang a song about the lower lights are burning, some poor sinners to be saved. And the whole building rocked with prayer and song.

Still I kept waiting to *see* Jesus.

Finally all the young people had gone to the altar and were saved, but one boy and me. He was a rounder's son named Westley. Westley and I were surrounded by sisters and deacons praying. It was very hot in the church, and getting late now. Finally Westley said to me in a whisper: "God damn! I'm tired o' sitting here. Let's get up and be saved." So he got up and was saved.

Then I was left all alone on the mourners' bench. My aunt came and knelt at my knees and cried, while prayers and song swirled all around me in the little church. The whole congregation prayed for me alone, in a mighty wail of moans and voices. And I kept waiting serenely for Jesus, waiting, waiting - but he didn't come. I wanted to see him, but nothing happened to me. Nothing! I wanted something to happen to me, but nothing happened.

I heard the songs and the minister saying: "Why don't you come? My dear child, why don't you come to Jesus? Jesus is waiting for you. He wants you. Why don't you come? Sister Reed, what is this child's name?"

"Langston," my aunt sobbed.

"Langston, why don't you come? Why don't you come and be saved? Oh, Lamb of God! Why don't you come?"

Now it was really getting late. I began to be ashamed of myself, holding everything up so long. I began to wonder what God thought about Westley, who certainly hadn't seen Jesus either, but who was now sitting proudly on the platform, swinging his knickerbockered legs and grinning down at me, surrounded by deacons and old women on their knees praying. God had not struck Westley dead for taking his name in vain or for lying in the temple. So I decided that maybe to save further trouble, I'd better lie, too, and say that Jesus had come, and get up and be saved.

So I got up.

Suddenly the whole room broke into a sea of shouting, as they saw me rise. Waves of rejoicing swept the place. Women leaped in the air. My aunt threw her arms around me. The minister took me by the hand and led me to the platform.

When things quieted down, in a hushed silence, punctuated by a few ecstatic "Amens," all the new young lambs were blessed in the name of God. Then joyous singing filled the room.

That night, for the first time in my life but one for I was a big boy twelve years old - I cried. I cried, in bed alone, and couldn't stop. I buried my head under the quilts, but my aunt heard me. She woke up and told my uncle I was crying because the Holy Ghost had come into my life, and because I had seen Jesus. But I was really crying because I couldn't bear to tell her that I had lied, that I had deceived everybody in the church, that I hadn't seen Jesus, and that now I didn't believe there was a Jesus anymore, since he didn't come to help me.

HERO-VILLAIN ARCHETYPES

Handwritten diagram:
Hero
_____
Lenwol Public
_____
Villain

heroin

he·ro

noun \'hir-(¸)ō\
: a person who is admired for great or brave acts or fine
qualities:: an illustrious warrior *c* : a man admired for his
achievements and noble qualities *a* : the principal male character
in a literary or dramatic work

villain

noun vil·lain \'vi-lən\
: a character in a story, movie, etc., who does bad things:
someone or something that is blamed for a particular problem or
difficulty: an uncouth person : boor : a deliberate scoundrel or
criminal

ar·che·type

noun \'är-ki-¸tīp\
: a perfect example of something: the original pattern or model
of which all things of the same type are representations or copies
: PROTOTYPE; *also* : a perfect example

A villain (also known in film and literature as the "antagonist,"
"baddie," "bad guy," "heavy" or "black hat") is an "evil"
character in a story, whether a historical narrative or, especially, a
work of fiction. The villain usually is the antagonist (though can
be the protagonist), the character who tends to have a negative

159

effect on other characters. A female villain is occasionally called a villainess (often to differentiate her from a male villain). *Random House Unabridged Dictionary* defines villain as "a cruelly malicious person who is involved in or devoted to wickedness or crime; scoundrel; or a character in a play, novel, or the like, who constitutes an important evil agency in the plot".

As a literary device, a hero can be defined as the principal character of a literary work. The term hero has been applied not only in the classical sense, but also in the modern literature for the principal character of a story, play or novel.

EIGHT HERO ARCHETYPES

The CHIEF: a dynamic leader, he has time for nothing but work. He might have been born to lead, or perhaps he conquered his way to the top, but either way, he's tough, decisive, goal-oriented. That means he is also a bit overbearing and inflexible. Think William Shatner in *Star Trek*; Harrison Ford in *Sabrina*, or Marlon Brando in *The Godfather*.

The BAD BOY: dangerous to know, he walks on the wild side. This is the rebel, or the boy from the wrong side of the tracks. He's bitter and volatile, a crushed idealist, but he's also charismatic and street smart. Think James Dean in *Rebel Without a Cause*, Matt Damon in *Good Will Hunting*, Patrick Swayze in *Dirty Dancing*.

The BEST FRIEND: sweet and safe, he never lets anyone down. He's kind, responsible, decent, a regular Mr. Nice Guy. This man doesn't enjoy confrontation and can sometimes be unassertive because he doesn't want to hurt anyone's feelings. But he'll always be there. Think Jimmy Stewart in *It's a Wonderful Life*, Adam Sandler in *The Wedding Singer*, Hugh Grant in *Four Weddings & a Funeral*, Kevin Spacey in *American Beauty*.

The CHARMER: more than a gigolo, he creates fantasies. He's fun, irresistible, a smooth operator, yet not too responsible or dependable. He might be a playboy or a rogue, but he's doesn't commit to a woman easily. Think Leonardo DiCaprio in *Titanic*, James Garner/Mel Gibson in *Maverick*, Don Johnson in *Nash Bridges*, Dustin Hoffman in *Midnight Cowboy*.

The LOST SOUL: a sensitive being, he understands. Tortured, secretive, brooding, and unforgiving. That's this man. But he's also vulnerable. He might be a wanderer or an outcast. In work he's creative, but probably also a loner. Think Mel Gibson in *Lethal Weapon*, David Duchovny in *The X-Files*, Beast in *Beauty and the Beast*, Shrek.

The PROFESSOR: coolly analytical, he knows every answer. He's logical, introverted, and inflexible, but genuine about his feelings. At work, he likes cold, hard facts, thank you very much, but he's also honest and faithful, and won't let you down. Think Leonard Nimoy in *Star Trek*, Robin Williams in *Flubber*, Kelsey Gramner in *Frasier*, Russell Crowe in *A Beautiful Mind*.

The SWASHBUCKLER: Mr. Excitement, he's an adventure. This guy is action, action, and more action. He's physical and daring. Fearless, he's a daredevil, or an explorer. He needs thrills and chills to keep him happy. Think Antonio Banderas in *The Mask of Zorro*, Michael Douglas in *Romancing the Stone*, Harrison Ford in *Raiders of the Lost Ark*.

The WARRIOR: a noble champion, he acts with honor. This man is the reluctant rescuer or the knight in shining armor. He's noble, tenacious, relentless, and he always sticks up for the underdog. If you need a protector, he's your guy. He doesn't buckle under to rules, and he doesn't go along just to get along. Think Clint Eastwood in *Dirty Harry*, Russell Crowe in *Gladiator*, Mel Gibson in *Braveheart*.

THE SIXTEEN VILLIAN ARCHETYPES

The TYRANT: the bullying despot, he wants power at any price. He ruthlessly conquers all he surveys, crushing his enemies beneath his feet. People are but pawns to him, and he holds all the power pieces. Hesitate before getting in this man's way – he'll think nothing of destroying you.

The BASTARD: the dispossessed son, he burns with resentment. He can't have what he wants, so he lashes out to hurt those around him. His deeds are often for effect – he wants to provoke action in others. He proudly announces his rebellious dealings. Don't be fooled by his boyish demeanor – he's a bundle of hate.

The DEVIL: the charming fiend, he gives people what he thinks they deserve. Charisma allows him to lure his victims to their own destruction. His ability to discover the moral weaknesses in others serves him well. Close your ears to his cajolery – he'll tempt you to disaster.

The TRAITOR: the double agent, he betrays those who trust him most. No one suspects the evil that lurks in his heart. Despite supportive smiles and sympathetic ears, he plots the destruction of his friends. Never turn your back on him -- he means you harm.

The OUTCAST: the lonely outsider, he wants desperately to belong. Tortured and unforgiving, he has been set off from others, and usually for good cause. He craves redemption, but is willing to gain it by sacrificing others. Waste no sympathy on him - he'll have none for you.

The EVIL GENIUS: the malevolent mastermind, he loves to show off his superior intelligence. Intellectual inferiors are contemptible to him and that includes just about everyone. Elaborate puzzles and experiments are his trademark. Don't let him pull your strings – the game is always rigged in his favor.

The SADIST: the savage predator, he enjoys cruelty for its own sake. Violence and psychological brutality are games to this man; and he plays those games with daring and skill. Run, don't walk, away from this man – he'll tear out your heart, and laugh while doing it.

The TERRORIST: the dark knight, he serves a warped code of honor. Self-righteous, he believes in his own virtue, and judges all around him by a strict set of laws. The end will always justify his nefarious means, and no conventional morality will give him pause. Don't try to appeal to his sense of justice – his does not resemble yours.

The BITCH: the abusive autocrat, she lies, cheats, and steals her way to the top. Her climb to success has left many a heel mark on the backs of others. She doesn't care about the peons around her – only the achievement of her dreams matters. Forget expecting a helping hand from her – she doesn't help anyone but herself.

The BLACK WIDOW: the beguiling siren, she lures victims into her web. She goes after anyone who has something she wants, and she wants a lot. But she does her best to make the victim want to be deceived. An expert at seduction of every variety, she uses her charms to get her way. Don't be fooled by her claims of love – it's all a lie.

The BACKSTABBER: the two-faced friend, she delights in duping the unsuspecting. Her sympathetic smiles enable her to learn her victims' secrets, which she then uses to feather her nest. Her seemingly helpful advice is just the thing to hinder. Put no faith in her – she'll betray you every time.

The LUNATIC: the unbalanced madwoman, she draws others into her crazy environment. The drum to which she marches misses many a beat, but to her, it is the rest of the world that is out of step. Don't even try to understand her logic – she is unfathomable.

The PARASITE: the poisonous vine, she collaborates for her own comfort. She goes along with any atrocity, so long as her own security is assured. She sees herself as a victim who had no choice, and blames others for her crimes. Expect no mercy from her – she won't lift a finger to save anyone but herself.

The SCHEMER: the lethal plotter, she devises the ruin of others. Like a cat with a mouse, she plays with lives. Elaborate plans, intricate schemes; nothing pleases her more than to trap the unwary. Watch out for her complex designs – she means you no good.

The FANATIC: the uncompromising extremist, she does wrong in the name of good. She justifies hers action by her intent, and merely shrugs her shoulders at collateral damage. Anyone not an ally is an enemy, and therefore, fair game. Give up any hope of showing her the error of her ways – she firmly believes you are wrong, wrong, wrong.

The MATRIARCH: the motherly oppressor, she smothers her loved ones. She knows what's best and will do all in her power to controls the lives of those who surround her – all for their own good. A classic enabler, she sees no fault with her darlings, unless they don't follow her dictates. Don't be lured into her family nest – you'll never get out alive.

[handwritten notes]

Chip " Tyrant
– a dick
– manic,
– doesn't care about any

Person " The matriarch
– bitch
– motherly things
– old

Matt " The Entity
– doesn't like himself
– he can bless him
– manic

165

CAPTAIN PLANET VS. BATMAN
Vincent Yedlin

Robert Paulson awakes to the sound of dishes banging in another room. He pulls the sheets off of himself and sits up in bed, the sun shining through the blinds makes it appear that he's wearing a white and black striped prison jump suit. A pleasant aroma is in the air. French toast. Inhaling deeply, Robert lets the smell fill his nostrils.

"God I love Sundays," he says to himself. Robert stands up and stretches. After putting on his robe he walks out of the bedroom and down the hall.

Entering the kitchen, he sees his wife and his two young children. His wife Jen looks up from the stove, "Good morning honey!"

"Good morning, babe! Come here and give your man a kiss." Jen runs up to Robert and jumps into his arms. They share a deep passionate lip-lock. The kids cover their eyes in disgust. After they exchange fluids, Jen goes back to cooking breakfast. Robert kisses his children Max and Alexandra on the tops of their heads and sits down at the table.

"Here dad, I got you the paper," Alexandra says as Robert takes the paper out of her hands.

"Thanks sweety." Robert picks up his Exxon-Mobil coffee mug that's on the table and takes a swig before unfolding the newspaper. The sun from the window behind him illuminates the front page headline: "PLANETEERS

166

STRIKE AGAIN!" accompanied by a picture of SUVs burning at a car lot.

"Those fucking Planeteers!" Robert says in anger.

"Robert! Not in front of the kids!" Jen scolds him.

"Daddy said a bad word," Max points out.

"Sorry, but this eco-terrorism has got to stop. The police aren't doing a thing. How am I supposed to put food on the table when these Planeteers are running wild, destroying everything they feel is a threat to the earth?"

Jen tries to calm him down. "Try to relax Rob, you're doing the best you can, and we're proud of you. Now let's have a nice breakfast, and try to forget about this for today." Jen takes the paper away and replaces it with a hot plate of French toast, syrup, and bacon.

"You're the be…" before Robert can finish his sentence, his face explodes in a mess of flesh, blood, and bone. His wife and kids are covered in a shower of muscle strands, bits of teeth, and tiny flaps of skin. They scream as what's left of Robert's head falls forward into the French toast.

Outside the house on a grassy knoll, a mysterious figure disassembles the sniper rifle and puts it neatly away in its case. The figure walks away having completed the mission.

***

In a damp dark cave, a man in a black cowl and cape looks on a giant computer screen. The body of Robert Paulson is displayed. He pushes a key on the computer. Another image flashes on the screen. His eyes narrow to slits.

"Friend of yours, Master Wayne?" It is Alfred, Bruce Wayne's (aka Batman's) trusted servant and friend.

"His name is Robert Paulson." Batman replies in a guttural growl. "He was an executive at Exxon-Mobil. He's the third executive of that company to be killed in the last two months. They were killed by a Lobaev SVLK-14S Sniper Rifle, made in Russia."

Batman presses more buttons on his super computer. A blonde woman appears. "This is Linka. A member of the Planeteers. And a Russian."

"Are you going after her?" Alfred inquires.

"Yes....and I know where she'll be next."

***

"I'll have a burrito bowl to go please." Linka tells the worker at Chipotle. "Brown rice, chicken, pico de gallo, sour cream, and cheese."

The worker assembles the bowl, and brings it to the cashier. "That will be $8.50 ma'am." Linka digs through her pocket and pulls out a ten dollar bill. She hands it to the cashier and takes the bowl. "Keep the change."

Outside the store in the darkness, Linka gets into her Toyota Prius. Taking out a flashlight, she looks at a paper with a woman's face on it, a name, and an address. She types the address into her GPS. Once the directions pop up, she drives off.

Some minutes later she arrives at an apartment building, parking in the garage across the street. She consumes the delicious Chipotle while studying her target: another Exxon-Mobil executive. "After all these years, we'll finally get revenge for the Exxon-Valdez disaster." she says to herself.

The food consumed, she gets out of her car, opens the trunk and grabs the case containing her sniper rifle. Making sure no one sees her she goes up the stairs to the roof. Once at the roof she sets up the gun and waits for her prey to arrive home across the street. An hour goes by. Finally she sees the door open, and the light turn on. The executive kicks off her shoes and grabs something from the kitchen. It is a bottle of wine. She goes back to the living room and sits on the couch.

Linka steadies herself for the shot. She grips the gun and puts her finger on the trigger. She takes a deep breath and exhales. She takes another deep breath and holds it.

CLANK! Something black and metallic comes out of nowhere and hits the sniper rifle out of her hand. "What the hell?!" She picks up the small black object. It is in the shape of a bat. Just then Batman swoops down from the shadows. Batman is a towering muscular figure that makes Linka look tiny. She just stares at him.

"Your killing is at an end, Linka. You and the Planeteers are finished."

Linka tries to run, but Batman is too fast for her. He grabs her by the shirt and with a few steps he is holding her over the edge of the building. "Who are you!?" she asks, scared to death.

"I'm Batman!" he says as he lets Linka go. She falls screaming at she goes. Right before she is about to be a ketchup stain on the pavement, she uses the power of her ring.

"Wind!" Air rushes out from her ring, slowing down her fall. She lands safely on her feet. She whistles, and the other 4 Planeteers come out from hiding. "You didn't think I'd go on a mission without some backup, did you?"

Batman jumps off the building and lands in between them. "Let's see how you handle Captain Planet!"

The five all raise their rings into the air, and say their respective powers. "Earth, Fire, Wind, Water, Heart!" In a flash of lightning and thunder, a being is formed, appearing before the five and Batman. "By your powers combined, I am Captain Planet!"

Batman looks at this floating blue figure before him, unimpressed. "Tell me Captain…do you bleed?"

The Planeteers scatter as Captain Planet launches a fireball at Batman sending him flying backwards into the concrete, cracking it. Batman responds by throwing a wired batarang around the Captain's ankles and pulling him to the ground. Batman leaps onto the Captain, sitting on his stomach and punches his face. Left, right, left right, left, right. Batman's fists are a storm of hate.

Finally the Captain gets his hands up and holds onto Batman's fists. His legs still tied, he manages to get them up together and kick Batman off him. The Captain takes off in flight. Batman is looking around trying to figure out where he went. Captain Planet swoops down. "Looking for me?" the Captain says as he sucker punches Batman right in the jaw. Batman is reeling, but he gathers his bearing.

Batman tosses golf ball sized bombs at the Captain. They explode throwing a white powder into his eyes, blinding him. Batman runs full speed at him, spearing him into a parked car. The sound of twisting metal and glass shattering echoes through the street.

"Time to end this" Batman grabs the Captain's neck and begins to squeeze. Harder and harder he squeezes. The Captain is now gasping for breath. He feels is trachea being crushed. The light of his life growing dimmer. Captain Planet reaches up to Batman's face and sends a huge bolt of electricity through it. Batman now has holes where his cheeks used to be. You can see right through his face like a window. Batman collapses in pain.

He pushes a button on his utility belt and the Batmobile comes roaring down the street. It stops and twin Gatling guns pop up from the hood. Captain Planet is engulfed in a hailstorm of bullets. Both combatants are on the ground. Both of their bodies racked with pain. After a minute Batman is able to crawl into his car. Just as he is about to drive off, Captain Planet stands up.

The Captain walks up to the Batmobile and rips the roof off it. Batman is in shock. That many bullets should have killed him. Batman tries to speak through his mutilated face. "Why can't I kill you?" Captain Planet grabs Batman by his cape and rips him out of the car, tossing him to the ground. "You can't kill Mother Nature" the Captain responds.

In a last ditch effort to get away, Batman grabs his grappling hook off his utility belt. He shoots it up the building. It latches onto something. Batman is going higher, and higher away from the fight. Or so he thought. Captain Planet grabbed his utility belt after his feet left the ground. He pulls Batman back down to earth. Batman is on his knees, beaten and defeated.

The Captain gets behind him grabbing his head. "Tell me, do you bleed?" With a twist of the head, Batman's is ripped clean from his neck. Blood shoots from his neck as his body falls to the cold, hard asphalt. The Dark Knight is no more.

Batman Wasn't a Punk
Rohan Ranasinghe

It was dark and Hell was hot. Batman awaited his judgement, amber and orange hellfire licking his face. He spent his entire life fighting crime, avenging the memory of his parents, following a strict moral code. This was not the final destination he expected his soul to be delivered to. The sounds of anguished screams and discord filled the air, a cacophony of chains clinking and flames erupting. This was truly hellish. A slender figure of a man in a tight black suit, with waxy tight red skin and small horns on his forehead approached Batman through the flames.

"Brucccce Wayne, so unexpected to see you here! Welcome to the first layer of Hell, I will usher to your soul's eternal punishment," cackled the shiny demon.

" What did I do to deserve this?" growled Batman through his cowl

"Did you accept Jesus as your lord and personal savior, Bruce?" the demon paused, before letting out an obnoxious laugh, exposing his many rows of shark-like teeth.

" Sorry," he continued snortling, "that's a running gag of mine with people who ironically end up here. This is hell; we keep a running count on your character down here. A lot of Christians think they can be a total dick and are totally surprised that they still make it out here.

Bruce sneered through his mask. The demon continued.

"In the moments leading up to your death, it seems like you gave up your moral code to take down the rogue champion of the Pagan Goddess Gaia, the environmental crusader Captain Planet. This puts you in a grey area. You, a mortal, tried to kill what was essentially a demigod with his team of trained eco-assassins. For being one of the world's greatest detectives and strategists, you failed to see that dispatching the team that summons this supernatural force was key to stopping them? Like five kids. Really."

The demon's tone had almost taken a disappointed turn, half lecturing the once dark knight.

"Linka drove a friggin' prius, like a hybrid. How many mods did you have in the batmobile?"
Batman kept silent in his trademark stoicism.

"Like they have elemental power rings, how hard would it to have been to use knockout gas and taken all five rings from them?" the demon was really just scolding him now, as if watching the entire fight that ended Bruce Wayne's life was as bad as paying for Pay Per View for Ronda Rousesy's last three championship fights.

"Come ON," the demon was full on fanboy mode, pacing around the silent Caped Crusader.

"Can you guess what was two major weakness of Captain friggin' Planet?" fumed the demon.

"Pollution is probably on the list," Batman calmly muttered

" FUCKING POLLUTION YES. But also, a LACK OF SUNLIGHT. YOU OPERATE PRIMARILY AT NIGHT. HOW IN THE HELL DID YOU NOT HAPPEN TO GET SOME RADIOACTIVE POLLUTION OR EVEN YES... KRYPONITE TO USE FOR THIS FIGHT. WHO ARE YOU EVEN? YOU AINT SHIT BATMAN. WHAT CRAPPY ALTERNATE UNIVERSE DID YOU COME FROM." the demon had clearly lost all of his shit. Maybe he was a Batman fan, or maybe he was a stickler for continuity, who could tell. Hell was hot and chaotic. Maybe being a demon gave him powers to see through the fourth wall.

The demon took in a slow controlled breath through his mouth, as if to gain composure. Then he shot two railroad spike streams of smoke through his nostrils. Nope, not calm.

"YOU HAVE SMOKE BOMBS IN YOUR UTILITY BELT! FUCKING SUFFOCATE THAT BLUE BITCH!" exploded the slim demon. "FUCCCCCCKKKKK."
He rubbed his horns in frustration.

" Look I can't deal with you being here, your soul still has merit and it's only sin was being a dumbass trying to take on the CAPTAIN PLANET like a noob without a game plan."

The demon looked at his crispy hell-burnt clipboard.

" Anyways I got the go ahead. We can't keep you here, but you can't go to heaven either. Not after that piss poor display. God and Satan were equally disappointed in you. So I hope you feel special Heaven AND Hell have come to an agreement, the world's "greatest" (the demon used air quotes) gets one freebie. We will resurrect you back to earth to avenge your own death against," the demon sighs,"Captain Planet,"

The demon had a real pained look on his face, the kind your parents make after finding out you crashed the car or got suspended from school. The demon made a spinny motion with his hands and sent the soul of Bruce Wayne back to the surface, with the speed of a world ending meteor.

"Fucker," muttered the demon.

Batman awoke in the alley where he died, head reattached. His body was sore, as I would have if it had with such a beating and resurrection. Batman stood up, brush himself off and in a moment of pure, beautiful copyright infringement muttered,

"IT'S CLOBBERING TIME!!!"

VENGEANCE
Rockella Renee

A man sits slouched in a giant chair in front of a large
computer panel. He leans against the armrest, the weight
of his weary head propped up by his arm and elbow. The
glow of the four monitors in front of him, create a haze in
the dark room. Dressed in a gold, satin robe, pink fuzzy
bunny slippers and two giant rollers parallel to each other
in his golden hair, he's ready for bed. He lightly drums a
finger on the other armrest and sings quietly to himself.

"Tomorrow, tomorrow...I love ya tomorrow...you're
only a day away!"

Suddenly he pushes his chair backwards. Standing to his
feet, he spins dramatically around and bursts out in song.

"The sun will come out, tomorrow, bet your bottom
dollar that tomorrow, they'll be..."

In mid sentence, he is cut off by a loud, echoing bang at
the door. He gasps and holds his hand to his heart. He
runs back to the monitors and looks at the one displaying
the front door. A man stands pitifully in full view of the
camera. He has on a sparkling black, skin-tight, latex body
suit with a giant star on the chest. His silver gloves look
like two small sharks gnawing at his elbows. His boots are
thick and buckled; spray-painted silver to match the
gloves. To top off the ensemble, he wears a black mask that
partially covers his face with two silver wings on each side
of his head. It is Mr. Galaxy. Unnerved by the presence of
his guest, Vengeance presses the speaker box button on the
panel.

"What do you want?"

Mr. Galaxy's deep voice, rumbles back a reply, "I need to
speak with you. It is very important."

"Not so fast! I need a better explanation than that. The last time you were here, I had to replace the entire left wing…it cost me a fortune. Do you really expect me to just open my door to you…let alone, at this hour?"

Mr. Galaxy sighs and hangs his head. Deflated, he answers. "No. You shouldn't…but I really need to speak with you. Vengeance, please open the door."

Vengeance carefully watches Mr. Galaxy on the monitor. He can see that there is something legitimately wrong with his foe. Curious and slightly jealous that he was not the one to cause such grief in Mr. Galaxy, he answers him.

"I'll just be a moment."

Vengeance takes off his robe revealing a dark green and gold spandex suit that accentuates his long and slender frame. He removes the rollers from his hair and restyles it into curved devil horns. Finally, he reapplies his black eyeliner and green lipstick.

Mr. Galaxy waits patiently outside. He notices that he can see his breath. He looks around a moment then pretends to smoke a cigarette. The door buzzes and he quickly "puts out" his cigarette butt. Slowly, the heavy metal door rises and reveals Vengeance standing behind it. Surrounded by shadows, he waves Mr. Galaxy towards him.

"This way please."

Unquestioning, Mr. Galaxy follows Vengeance down a dim lit hallway into a large room. As they reach the center of the room an ear-piercing alarm goes off. Mr. Galaxy looks around the room like a startled cat. Suddenly a large metal cage crashes down around him.

"Like that? I just had it installed." Vengeance laughs a desperately evil laugh then sneers at Mr. Galaxy. "Did you really think, I would just allow you to waltz in here…my home…my lair…you can't fool me, Mr. Galaxy."

Again Mr. Galaxy sighs. "I'm not trying to fool you. Honestly. I need help."

Vengeance laughs harder. "You? Need Me? Ha, ha, ha...what a laugh."

"I'm serious. I don't know what to do," Mr. Galaxy whines at Vengeance. "I know our relationship over the years has been tense...but you know me better than anyone."

Bumfuzzled, Vengeance crosses his arms. "Hmmph...You know, you are really draining all the fun out of this!"

"I know," He replies, "but I really need your advice."

Vengeance looks surprised. "Well...you've got my attention now. However, I hope you don't mind me being a little cautious. If it's alright with you, I'd feel much safer with you in there."

As Mr. Galaxy clasps his hands together in praise. "Thank you, thank you, thank you."

Vengeance rolls his eyes, "One's enough." He then motions for Mr. Galaxy to sit on the floor. Mr. Galaxy plops down and crosses his legs like a wide-eyed kindergartener at story-time.

Vengeance pushes his giant chair in front of the cage and sits down. "Go on then. What has you so pathetic these days?"

"The Government!"

"Nothing new there," Vengeance interrupts.

Mr. Galaxy looks up at Vengeance, frowns, then continues. "I was working with the Department of Defense on implementing new security measures to demobilize terrorists before they attack. While at the Pentagon, a close friend of mine pulled me into her office and spoke with me on some new policies being proposed to the white house. She said that the government is trying to create heavier regulations on Heroes. No more masks. No cool weapons and suits...they will be government issue only. Heroes will have to sign a contract with the government just like regular military personnel. Finally, whatever damage is incurred during the restraint of an enemy will result in a fine; 30% of the total cost of damages. If we don't comply to these new policies, we get thrown in jail."

"Wow! That's fantast…I mean, that's absolutely horrific! However, I fail to see the relevance. Why have you come to me?"

Mr. Galaxy tips his eyebrow at Vengeance then answers, "Ever since I was a little boy, I dreamed of becoming a superhero. I could see myself running around the city, saving people from fires…criminals…mastermind villains…like yourself. And sure, when I started out, people were happy. I was happy. But as time went on, they began using me. They'd call me to do menial jobs like taking out the garbage when they forgot it was trash day or flying them across town just to miss rush hour. I don't even get thank you's anymore. Now on top of that…all the Heroes are going to get fines that will send us spiraling into debt. We have to sign our lives away or else face ridiculous consequences. It's just not worth it anymore…but what do I do? There is no way I could live a normal life. I mean, could you see me bagging groceries or sitting behind a desk in a collared shirt and tie. I like my sparkly black suit way too much to give it up."

Mr. Galaxy looks deep into Vengeance's eyes for an answer but he just sits quietly staring back. "Well? What do I do?"

Vengeance abruptly stands to his feet. "Did you forget your big boy underwear today? Am I even talking to Mr. Galaxy right now? Who are you?"

Mr. Galaxy is taken aback. "I…I…I…"

"I…I…I…what?!" Vengeance yells at him. "Stand up!.

Mr. Galaxy jumps to his feet. Vengeance glares directly into his eyes. "Now listen and listen good."

"Well." Mr. Galaxy interjects. Vengeance furls his lip and reaches his hand through the bars, grabbing Mr. Galaxy by the neck. "Listen well, smart ass. I've lived my entire life on the outside. I've watched people…these people you and all your hero friends idolize so much. They are crazy, disgusting pigs. I know I'm diabolical and all, but I'm nothing like them. At least I have real reasons for the way I act. They hate each other for completely asinine reasons like religion, race and status. Who cares? None of those things really matter. In the end, we are all the same…WE DIE! They are greedy, selfish and only care about what new tech is going to fit in their designer jeans. It makes me want to hurl.

Do you see the streets? Do you see how filthy they are? Look what they've done to the planet: Global warming…smog…pollution! Religion. Race. Status. Who cares…none of it matters. In the end, we all die. Then there's the government, controlling its people with an invisible hand…tricking them into believing that any of those issue are actually issues that are credible. A house divided can't stand…I guess that's what they're going for. Then there are the wars. Wars for oil. Wars on terrorists. Wars for peace. Disgusting! You say I'm the bad guy, ha! These are the reasons I am the way I am. This is why I'm angry. This is why I hide up here on my mountain and seek vengeance on the world. So, don't bring your pity party to me."

Tears begin to well up in Mr. Galaxy's eyes. Vengeance notices and sighs. "Oh my god! Really? I thought you were a superhero."

Vengeance paces around then begins to speak again. "Listen, we are who we are and we shouldn't feel the need to change that. I like chaos…I like to hear people scream…I like to watch them run. Do you think for one minute that I'm going to give that up just because idiots are saying that I can't?

Mr. Galaxy shakes his head and weakly replies. "No."

"Do you think I'm going to stop blowing shit up just because someone says it's dangerous?
Again Mr. Galaxy shakes his head again. "No."

"Then why should you?" Vengeance walks up to the bars of the cage. "Look at me! Pull your shit together and get out there. Do what you do best because I can't do what I do without you."

Mr. Galaxy nods and smiles.

"Now get out of my house!" Vengeance yells and clap-claps his hands together. The cage rises and Mr. Galaxy runs out towards the hallway.

Vengeance calls to him and Mr. Galaxy stops dead in his tracks. "Are we still meeting at the top of the empire state building tomorrow? I was planning on throwing the mayor off the top."

"What time?" He asks.

"Uh...I don't know. I was thinking like twelve or so." Mr. Galaxy thinks for a moment. "That kind of cuts into my lunch. What about two o'clock?"

"Sounds good." Vengeance gives him a thumbs up.

"Oh, by the way," Mr. Galaxy adds, "Love the slippers!" Vengeance looks down at his feet and laughs.
After Mr. Galaxy leaves, Vengeance goes back to his room, gets dressed for bed and sits back down in his chair.
"Tomorrow...you're only a day away!"

THE BLACK CAT
Edgar Allan Poe

FOR the most wild, yet most homely narrative which I am about to pen, I neither expect nor solicit belief. Mad indeed would I be to expect it, in a case where my very senses reject their own evidence. Yet, mad am I not -- and very surely do I not dream. But to-morrow I die, and to-day I would unburthen my soul. My immediate purpose is to place before the world, plainly, succinctly, and without comment, a series of mere household events. In their consequences, these events have terrified -- have tortured -- have destroyed me. Yet I will not attempt to expound them. To me, they have presented little but Horror -- to many they will seem less terrible than barroques. Hereafter, perhaps, some intellect may be found which will reduce my phantasm to the common-place -- some intellect more calm, more logical, and far less excitable than my own, which will perceive, in the circumstances I detail with awe, nothing more than an ordinary succession of very natural causes and effects.

From my infancy I was noted for the docility and humanity of my disposition. My tenderness of heart was even so conspicuous as to make me the jest of my companions. I was especially fond of animals, and was indulged by my parents with a great variety of pets. With these I spent most of my time, and never was so happy as when feeding and caressing them. This peculiarity of character grew with my growth, and, in my manhood, I derived from it one of my principal sources of pleasure. To those who have cherished an affection for a faithful and sagacious dog, I need hardly be at the trouble of explaining the nature or the intensity of the gratification thus derivable. There is something in the unselfish and self-sacrificing love of a brute, which goes directly to the heart of him who has had frequent occasion to test the paltry friendship and gossamer fidelity of mere Man.

I married early, and was happy to find in my wife a disposition not uncongenial with my own. Observing my partiality for domestic pets, she lost no opportunity of procuring those of the most agreeable kind. We had birds, gold-fish, a fine dog, rabbits, a small monkey, and a cat.

This latter was a remarkably large and beautiful animal, entirely black, and sagacious to an astonishing degree. In speaking of his intelligence, my wife, who at heart was not a little tinctured with superstition, made frequent allusion to the ancient popular notion, which regarded all black cats as witches in disguise. Not that she was ever *serious* upon this point -- and I mention the matter at all for no better reason than that it happens, just now, to be remembered.

Pluto -- this was the cat's name -- was my favorite pet and playmate. I alone fed him, and he attended me wherever I went about the house. It was even with difficulty that I could prevent him from following me through the streets.

Our friendship lasted, in this manner, for several years, during which my general temperament and character -- through the instrumentality of the Fiend Intemperance -- had (I blush to confess it) experienced a radical alteration for the worse. I grew, day by day, more moody, more irritable, more regardless of the feelings of others. I suffered myself to use intemperate language to my wife. At length, I even offered her personal violence. My pets, of course, were made to feel the change in my disposition. I not only neglected, but ill-used them. For Pluto, however, I still retained sufficient regard to restrain me from maltreating him, as I made no scruple of maltreating the rabbits, the monkey, or even the dog, when by accident, or through affection, they came in my way. But my disease grew upon me -- for what disease is like Alcohol ! -- and at length even Pluto, who was now becoming old, and consequently somewhat peevish -- even Pluto began to experience the effects of my ill temper.

One night, returning home, much intoxicated, from one of my haunts about town, I fancied that the cat avoided my presence. I seized him; when, in his fright at my violence, he inflicted a slight wound upon my hand with his teeth. The fury of a demon instantly possessed me. I knew myself no longer. My original soul seemed, at once, to take its flight from my body; and a more than fiendish malevolence, gin-nurtured, thrilled every fibre of my frame. I took from my waistcoat-pocket a pen-knife, opened it, grasped the poor beast by the throat, and deliberately cut one of its eyes from the socket ! I blush, I burn, I shudder, while I pen the damnable atrocity.

When reason returned with the morning -- when I had slept off the fumes of the night's debauch -- I experienced a sentiment half of horror, half of remorse, for the crime of which I had been guilty; but it was, at best, a feeble and equivocal feeling, and the soul remained untouched. I again plunged into excess, and soon drowned in wine all memory of the deed.

In the meantime the cat slowly recovered. The socket of the lost eye presented, it is true, a frightful appearance, but he no longer appeared to suffer any pain. He went about the house as usual, but, as might be expected, fled in extreme terror at my approach. I had so much of my old heart left, as to be at first grieved by this evident dislike on the part of a creature which had once so loved me. But this feeling soon gave place to irritation. And then came, as if to my final and irrevocable overthrow, the spirit of PERVERSENESS. Of this spirit philosophy takes no account. Yet I am not more sure that my soul lives, than I am that perverseness is one of the primitive impulses of the human heart -- one of the indivisible primary faculties, or sentiments, which give direction to the character of Man. Who has not, a hundred times, found himself committing a vile or a silly action, for no other reason than because he knows he should *not*? Have we not a perpetual inclination, in the teeth of our best judgment, to violate that which is Law, merely because we understand it to be such? This spirit of perverseness, I say, came to my final overthrow. It was this unfathomable longing of the soul to vex itself -- to offer violence to its own nature -- to do wrong for the wrong's sake only -- that urged me to continue and finally to consummate the injury I had inflicted upon the unoffending brute. One morning, in cool blood, I slipped a noose about its neck and hung it to the limb of a tree; -- hung it with the tears streaming from my eyes, and with the bitterest remorse at my heart; -- hung it *because* I knew that it had loved me, and because I felt it had given me no reason of offence; -- hung it *because* I knew that in so doing I was committing a sin -- a deadly sin that would so jeopardize my immortal soul as to place it -- if such a thing were possible -- even beyond the reach of the infinite mercy of the Most Merciful and Most Terrible God.

On the night of the day on which this cruel deed was done, I was aroused from sleep by the cry of fire. The curtains of my bed were in flames. The whole house was blazing. It was with great difficulty that my wife, a servant, and myself, made our escape from the conflagration. The destruction was complete. My entire worldly wealth was swallowed up, and I resigned myself thenceforward to despair.

I am above the weakness of seeking to establish a sequence of cause and effect, between the disaster and the atrocity. But I am detailing a chain of facts -- and wish not to leave even a possible link imperfect. On the day succeeding the fire, I visited the ruins. The walls, with one exception, had fallen in. This exception was found in a compartment wall, not very thick, which stood about the middle of the house, and against which had rested the head of my bed. The plastering had here, in great measure, resisted the action of the fire -- a fact which I attributed to its having been recently spread. About this wall a dense crowd were collected, and many persons seemed to be examining a particular portion of it with very minute and eager attention. The words "strange!" "singular!" and other similar expressions, excited my curiosity. I approached and saw, as if graven in *bas relief* upon the white surface, the figure of a gigantic *cat*. The impression was given with an accuracy truly marvellous. There was a rope about the animal's neck.

When I first beheld this apparition -- for I could scarcely regard it as less -- my wonder and my terror were extreme. But at length reflection came to my aid. The cat, I remembered, had been hung in a garden adjacent to the house. Upon the alarm of fire, this garden had been immediately filled by the crowd -- by some one of whom the animal must have been cut from the tree and thrown, through an open window, into my chamber. This had probably been done with the view of arousing me from sleep. The falling of other walls had compressed the victim of my cruelty into the substance of the freshly-spread plaster; the lime of which, with the flames, and the ammonia from the carcass, had then accomplished the portraiture as I saw it.

Although I thus readily accounted to my reason, if not altogether to my conscience, for the startling fact just detailed, it did not the less fail to make a deep impression upon my fancy. For months I could not rid myself of the phantasm of the cat; and, during this period, there came back into my spirit a half-sentiment that seemed, but was not, remorse. I went so far as to regret the loss of the animal, and to look about me, among the vile haunts which I now habitually frequented, for another pet of the same species, and of somewhat similar appearance, with which to supply its place.

One night as I sat, half stupified, in a den of more than infamy, my attention was suddenly drawn to some black object, reposing upon the head of one of the immense hogsheads of Gin, or of Rum, which constituted the chief furniture of the apartment. I had been looking steadily at the top of this hogshead for some minutes, and what now caused me surprise was the fact that I had not sooner perceived the object thereupon. I approached it, and touched it with my hand. It was a black cat -- a very large one -- fully as large as Pluto, and closely resembling him in every respect but one. Pluto had not a white hair upon any portion of his body; but this cat had a large, although indefinite splotch of white, covering nearly the whole region of the breast.

Upon my touching him, he immediately arose, purred loudly, rubbed against my hand, and appeared delighted with my notice. This, then, was the very creature of which I was in search. I at once offered to purchase it of the landlord; but this person made no claim to it -- knew nothing of it -- had never seen it before.

I continued my caresses, and, when I prepared to go home, the animal evinced a disposition to accompany me. I permitted it to do so; occasionally stooping and patting it as I proceeded. When it reached the house it domesticated itself at once, and became immediately a great favorite with my wife.

For my own part, I soon found a dislike to it arising within me. This was just the reverse of what I had anticipated; but -- I know not how or why it was -- its evident fondness for myself rather disgusted and annoyed. By slow degrees, these feelings of disgust and annoyance rose into the bitterness of hatred. I avoided the creature; a certain sense of shame, and the remembrance of my former deed of cruelty, preventing me from physically abusing it. I did not, for some weeks, strike, or otherwise violently ill use it; but gradually -- very gradually -- I came to look upon it with unutterable loathing, and to flee silently from its odious presence, as from the breath of a pestilence.

What added, no doubt, to my hatred of the beast, was the discovery, on the morning after I brought it home, that, like Pluto, it also had been deprived of one of its eyes. This circumstance, however, only endeared it to my wife, who, as I have already said, possessed, in a high degree, that humanity of feeling which had once been my distinguishing trait, and the source of many of my simplest and purest pleasures.

With my aversion to this cat, however, its partiality for myself seemed to increase. It followed my footsteps with a pertinacity which it would be difficult to make the reader comprehend. Whenever I sat, it would crouch beneath my chair, or spring upon my knees, covering me with its loathsome caresses. If I arose to walk it would get between my feet and thus nearly throw me down, or, fastening its long and sharp claws in my dress, clamber, in this manner, to my breast. At such times, although I longed to destroy it with a blow, I was yet withheld from so doing, partly by a memory of my former crime, but chiefly -- let me confess it at once -- by absolute *dread* of the beast.

This dread was not exactly a dread of physical evil -- and yet I should be at a loss how otherwise to define it. I am almost ashamed to own -- yes, even in this felon's cell, I am almost ashamed to own -- that the terror and horror with which the animal inspired me, had been heightened by one of the merest chimæras it would be possible to conceive. My wife had called my attention, more than once, to the character of the mark of white hair, of which I have spoken, and which constituted the sole visible difference between the strange beast and the one I had destroyed. The reader will remember that this mark, although large, had been originally very indefinite; but, by slow degrees -- degrees nearly imperceptible, and which for a long time my Reason struggled to reject as fanciful -- it had, at length, assumed a rigorous distinctness of outline. It was now the representation of an object that I shudder to name -- and for this, above all, I loathed, and dreaded, and would have rid myself of the monster had I dared -- it was now, I say, the image of a hideous -- of a ghastly thing -- of the GALLOWS ! -- oh, mournful and terrible engine of Horror and of Crime -- of Agony and of Death !

And now was I indeed wretched beyond the wretchedness of mere Humanity. And *a brute beast* -- whose fellow I had contemptuously destroyed -- *a brute beast* to work out for me -- for me a man, fashioned in the image of the High God -- so much of insufferable wo! Alas! neither by day nor by night knew I the blessing of Rest any more! During the former the creature left me no moment

188

alone; and, in the latter, I started, hourly, from dreams of unutterable fear, to find the hot breath of the thing upon my face, and its vast weight -- an incarnate Night-Mare that I had no power to shake off -- incumbent eternally upon my heart !

Beneath the pressure of torments such as these, the feeble remnant of the good within me succumbed. Evil thoughts became my sole intimates -- the darkest and most evil of thoughts. The moodiness of my usual temper increased to hatred of all things and of all mankind; while, from the sudden, frequent, and ungovernable outbursts of a fury to which I now blindly abandoned myself, my uncomplaining wife, alas! was the most usual and the most patient of sufferers.

One day she accompanied me, upon some household errand, into the cellar of the old building which our poverty compelled us to inhabit. The cat followed me down the steep stairs, and, nearly throwing me headlong, exasperated me to madness. Uplifting an axe, and forgetting, in my wrath, the childish dread which had hitherto stayed my hand, I aimed a blow at the animal which, of course, would have proved instantly fatal had it descended as I wished. But this blow was arrested by the hand of my wife. Goaded, by the interference, into a rage more than demoniacal, I withdrew my arm from her grasp and buried the axe in her brain. She fell dead upon the spot, without a groan.

This hideous murder accomplished, I set myself forthwith, and with entire deliberation, to the task of concealing the body. I knew that I could not remove it from the house, either by day or by night, without the risk of being observed by the neighbors. Many projects entered my mind. At one period I thought of cutting the corpse into minute fragments, and destroying them by fire. At another, I resolved to dig a grave for it in the floor of the cellar. Again, I deliberated about casting it in the well in the yard -- about packing it in a box, as if merchandize, with the usual arrangements, and so getting a porter to take it from the house. Finally I hit upon what I considered a far better expedient than either of these. I determined to wall it up in the cellar -- as the monks of the middle ages are recorded to have walled up their victims.

For a purpose such as this the cellar was well adapted. Its walls were loosely constructed, and had lately been plastered throughout with a rough plaster, which the dampness of the atmosphere had prevented from hardening. Moreover, in one of the walls was a projection, caused by a false chimney, or fireplace, that had been filled up, and made to resemble the rest of the cellar. I made no doubt that I could readily displace the bricks at this point, insert the corpse, and wall the whole up as before, so that no eye could detect any thing suspicious.

And in this calculation I was not deceived. By means of a crow-bar I easily dislodged the bricks, and, having carefully deposited the body against the inner wall, I propped it in that position, while, with little trouble, I re-laid the whole structure as it originally stood. Having procured mortar, sand, and hair, with every possible precaution, I prepared a plaster which could not be distinguished from the old, and with this I very carefully went over the new brick-work. When I had finished, I felt satisfied that all was right. The wall did not present the slightest appearance of having been disturbed. The rubbish on the floor was picked up with the minutest care. I looked around triumphantly, and said to myself -- "Here at least, then, my labor has not been in vain."

My next step was to look for the beast which had been the cause of so much wretchedness; for I had, at length, firmly resolved to put it to death. Had I been able to meet with it, at the moment, there could have been no doubt of its fate; but it appeared that the crafty animal had been alarmed at the violence of my previous anger, and forebore to present itself in my present mood. It is impossible to describe, or to imagine, the deep, the blissful sense of relief which the absence of the detested creature occasioned in my bosom. It did not make its appearance during the night -- and thus for one night at least, since its introduction into the house, I soundly and tranquilly slept; aye, slept even with the burden of murder upon my soul!

The second and the third day passed, and still my tormentor came not. Once again I breathed as a freeman. The monster, in terror, had fled the premises forever! I should behold it no more! My happiness was supreme! The guilt of my dark deed disturbed me but little. Some few inquiries had been made, but these had been readily answered. Even a search had been instituted -- but of course nothing was to be discovered. I looked upon my future felicity as secured.

Upon the fourth day of the assassination, a party of the police came, very unexpectedly, into the house, and proceeded again to make rigorous investigation of the premises. Secure, however, in the inscrutability of my place of concealment, I felt no embarrassment whatever. The officers bade me accompany them in their search. They left no nook or corner unexplored. At length, for the third or fourth time, they descended into the cellar. I quivered not in a muscle. My heart beat calmly as that of one who slumbers in innocence. I walked the cellar from end to end. I folded my arms upon my bosom, and roamed easily to and fro. The police were thoroughly satisfied and prepared to depart. The glee at my heart was too strong to be restrained. I burned to say if but one word, by way of triumph, and to render doubly sure their assurance of my guiltlessness.

"Gentlemen," I said at last, as the party ascended the steps, "I delight to have allayed your suspicions. I wish you all health, and a little more courtesy. By the bye, gentlemen, this -- this is a very well constructed house." (In the rabid desire to say something easily, I scarcely knew what I uttered at all.) -- "I may say an *excellently* well constructed house. These walls -- are you going, gentlemen? -- these walls are solidly put together;" and here, through the mere phrenzy of bravado, I rapped heavily, with a cane which I held in my hand, upon that very portion of the brick-work behind which stood the corpse of the wife of my bosom.

But may God shield and deliver me from the fangs of the Arch-Fiend ! No sooner had the reverberation of my blows sunk into silence, than I was answered by a voice from within the tomb! -- by a cry, at first muffled and broken, like the sobbing of a child, and then quickly swelling into one long, loud, and continuous scream, utterly anomalous and inhuman -- a howl -- a wailing shriek, half of horror and half of triumph, such as might have arisen only out of hell, conjointly from the throats of the dammed in their agony and of the demons that exult in the damnation.

Of my own thoughts it is folly to speak. Swooning, I staggered to the opposite wall. For one instant the party upon the stairs remained motionless, through extremity of terror and of awe. In the next, a dozen stout arms were toiling at the wall. It fell bodily. The corpse, already greatly decayed and clotted with gore, stood erect before the eyes of the spectators. Upon its head, with red extended mouth and solitary eye of fire, sat the hideous beast whose craft had seduced me into murder, and whose informing voice had consigned me to the hangman. I had walled the monster up within the tomb!

ENJAMBMENT

Enjambment is the continuation of a sentence or clause over a line-break. If a poet allows all the sentences of a poem to end in the same place as regular line-breaks, a kind of deadening can happen in the ear, and in the brain too, as all the thoughts can end up being the same length. Enjambment is one way of creating audible interest; others include caesurae, or having variable line-lengths.

Line

A line is a subdivision of a poem, specifically a group of words arranged into a row that ends for a reason other than the right-hand margin. This reason could be that the lines are arranged to have a certain number of syllables, a certain number of stresses, or of metrical feet; it could be that they are arranged so that they rhyme, whether they be of equal length or not. But it is important to remember that the poet has chosen to make the line a certain length, or to make the line-break at a certain point. This line-break, where a reader has to turn back to the start of the next line, was known in Latin as the *versus*, which translates as "turn", and is where the modern English term "verse" comes from. It is one of the strongest points of a line, which means that words that fall at the end of a line seem more important to a reader (an effect that rhyme can intensify); other strong points are the start of a line, and either side of a caesura.

THE CRAFTSMAN
Marcus B. Christian

I ply with all the cunning of my art
this little thing, and with consummate care
I fashion it — so that when I depart,
those who come after me shall find it fair
and beautiful. It must be free of flaws —
pointing no laborings of weary hands;
And there must be no flouting of the laws
of beauty — as the artist understands.

Through passion, yearnings infinite — yet dumb —
I lift you from the depths of my own mind
and gild you with my soul's white heat to plumb
the souls of future men. I leave behind
this thing that in return this solace gives:
"He who creates true beauty ever lives."

THE LOSS OF LOVE
Countee Cullen

All through an empty place I go,
And find her not in any room;
The candles and the lamps I light
Go down before a wind of gloom.
Thick-spraddled lies the dust about,
A fit, sad place to write her name
Or draw her face the way she looked
That legendary night she came.

The old house crumbles bit by bit;
Each day I hear the ominous thud
That says another rent is there
For winds to pierce and storms to flood.

My orchards groan and sag with fruit;
Where, Indian-wise, the bees go round;
I let it rot upon the bough;
I eat what falls upon the ground.

The heavy cows go laboring
In agony with clotted teats;
My hands are slack; my blood is cold;
I marvel that my heart still beats.

I have no will to weep or sing,
No least desire to pray or curse;
The loss of love is a terrible thing;
They lie who say that death is worse.

THE SPADE
Dance Aoki

I use this page; I use this pen.
They are my tools:
My spade, my plow.

I turn these words
like land.
I dig the Earth:
A solid mass of
packed down Everydays
and Nice-To-Meet-Yous.
I pick, choose and reconcile phrases,
Turn words over
Turn them again.
 I pry the spade into the Earth
I sweat into these wounds.
Soon, I've plowed a field.
It stretches out like a corduroy plain
blooming something like
Mysteries.

I taste the crop.
It rolls comfortably on my tongue
I squeeze the fruit between my toes.
I peel the hard skin of pomegranate
and pluck shiny red beads.
I twirl the fruit in the kaleidoscope
of my hand.
Persephone did the same
when she married Death.

Mulled over and cultivated
these words are words.

String the seeds together to form a necklace
and thoughts dissolve the image,
like acid to flesh.
Thoughts contain no verbal boundary.
Death and Demeter are not
Dictators to a goddess.
She transcends her mythology.
Now the myth dissolves into a mystery:
thought in mystery and the abundance thereof
until nothing becomes everything.

 That is the crop
That is the poem.

EKPHRASIS

: writing that comments upon another art form, for instance a poem about a photograph or a novel about a film. Keats' "Ode on a Grecian Urn" is a prime example of this type of writing, since the entire poem concerns the appearance and meaning of an ancient piece of pottery.

Ekphrasis has been considered generally to be a rhetorical device in which one medium of art tries to relate to another medium by defining and describing its essence and form, and in doing so, relate more directly to the audience, through its illuminative liveliness. A descriptive work of prose or poetry, a film, or even a photograph may thus highlight through its *rhetorical* vividness what is happening, or what is shown in, say, any of the visual arts, and in doing so, may enhance the original art and so take on a life of its own through its brilliant description. When creating ekphrastic work, it is important to consider the assumptions and inferences relative to what we see and interpret.

AGAIN, THE FIELDS
Natasha Tretheway

the dead they lay long the lines like sheaves of Wheat I
could have walked on the boddes all most from one end too
the other

No more muskets, the bone-drag
weariness of marching, the trampled
grass, soaked earth red as the wine

of sacrament. Now, the veteran
turns toward a new field, bright
as domes of the republic. Here,

he has shrugged off the past—his jacket
and canteen flung down in the corner.
At the center of the painting, he anchors

the trinity, joining earth and sky.
The wheat falls beneath his scythe--
a language of bounty—the swaths

like scripture on the field's open page.
Boundless, the wheat stretches beyond
the frame, as if toward a distant field--

the white canvas where sky and cotton
meet, where another veteran toils,
his hands the color of dark soil.

WE GOT THE JAZZ
Derek Brown

I found love in the melted brass of a setting desert sun
With or without a nose, we'll always know what we knows
You can't deform or dismiss truth
from the face of the womb
that birthed all of yesterday's tomorrows

Puffed cheeks
Pursed lips
Conquering hourglass understanding
Chiming sand and brown sugar
into granules of gratitude
as we inhale this quintessential symphony.

The genius of pyramid construct
pales in comparison
to the organics of us just being us
Cause there's no blueprint for this infinite slow dance
Only footprints surrendering to tribe and tradition
to the blare of a horn courting quicksand til firm

Smiling eyes hypnotize
the float of these notes
Mixing melodies and melanin
into this baritone duet

ARMOR FOR DREAMS
Hiram Sims

Dreams are for the dreamer, treasures of the mind.
Hopes are from the healer, vision for the blind.
Peace is for the mobile, trudging toward the goal.
Life is for ambition, motive for the soul.

Doubt is for the listener, foreign to the dream
Tearing down the vision, ripping at the seam
Seeking redirection, prudence in the claim
Void of understanding, poisoning the aim…

But

Dreams are for the patient, conquering the fear
Trusting without ceasing, mastering the gear
Shield the aspirations, shun the doubtful tones
Let the hopes unrealized, triumph in your bones.

DIALOGUE

---

di·a·logue \ˈdī-ə-ˌlȯg, -ˌläg\
: the things that are said by the characters in a story, movie, play, etc.: a written composition in which two or more characters are represented as conversing : an exchange of ideas and opinions

c : a discussion between representatives of parties to a conflict that is aimed at resolution <a constructive *dialogue* between loggers and environmentalists>

Dialogue is a conversation between two or more people in a work of literature. Dialogue can be written or spoken. It is found in prose, some poetry, and makes up the majority of plays. Dialogue is a literary device that can be used for narrative, philosophical, or didactic purposes. The Ancient Greek philosopher Socrates was a chief proponent of dialogue, and the Socratic Method that is named after him involves a great deal of asking and pondering over questions.The word dialogue comes from the Greek word διάλογος (*dialogos*), which means "conversation," and is a compound of words meaning "through" and "reason or speech." Thus, the definition of dialogue developed as a way of creating meaning through speech. Great dialogue creates characterization.

JALONDRA DAVIS BROWN, M.P.W.
Dialogue

Dialogue gives life to a story or novel. Though many authors are very spare with dialogue and it is possible to have a good story or poem without much of it, that makes it even more important that it is effective, natural, impactful, and smart when it appears. Some things to think about with dialogue:

☐   Character-One of the major ways we usually learn about characters is through dialogue, through what they say and through what others say about them. It is important to know who your characters are by your final draft, and for their dialogue to reflect that. According to playwright Lajos Egri, "Really fine dialogue is impossible unless it follows clearly and validly from the character that uses it; unless it serves to show, naturally and without strain, what has happened to the characters that is important to the action of the play...Dialogue must reveal character. Every speech should be the product of the speaker's three dimensions, telling us what he is, hinting at what he will be."

☐   Voice-Each character should have a voice, and that voice should have some relationship to the tone of the novel. That doesn't mean that the voices of the characters are the voice of the narrator, but that their voices should feel as if they belong in the story/novel. Each character's voice should be consistent enough that we can ascertain, for major characters at least, who is speaking from their voice and their positioning in the conflict or situation driving the dialogue. Dialogue should make sense in the context of the socio-historical-cultural setting of the novel.

☐   Related to Voice-Naturalness-Characters speak in different ways, as do people in real life, so one person's natural may be another's unnatural. But generally, try to make sure your dialogue feels like something a person would actually say. Think about this in terms of the amount of information each portion of dialogue holds, rhythm, and patterns of human breath. Always try your dialogue out loud, placing yourself within that character for a moment, and test how it sounds and feels.

☐   Related to Naturalness-Avoid speechifying and talkiness. In older novels (I am thinking of nineteenth century and earlier) characters often told long stories and spoke in long speeches without interruption. I am not saying there is not a possibility for exception to this, but generally that is anachronistic today. Humans tend to interrupt each other and have short attention spans, and they do things while they are talking. Use action, interruptions, exchange to break up long portions of talking. Be selective about your words. People rarely say everything they are thinking and characters don't have to either.

☐   Related to speechifying and talkiness—Show not tell. Do not replace exposition, action, or storytelling with dialogue. Don't use dialogue to deliver a lot of information which can come out in more creative and active ways. Don't have characters tell each other lots of things they already know. And don't tell us everything through dialogue. People often talk around things they already know or don't want to state directly. Because information and back story isn't in the dialogue does not mean that it is not there, informing the conversation, slipping out in small pieces. Think about your dialogue as a way to show us what is happening between characters and in their world through the way they are interacting with one another rather than telling us everything explicitly.

☐   Related to Show not Tell-Background. Though you don't want to tell us everything explicitly through dialogue, dialogue should always be informed by background of the story, and should tell us something about that background.

☐ Conflict-Usually (there are exceptions to everything) dialogue, like the action in a story, is driven by conflict or tension. The conflict could be big or subtle. There should be some kind of push-pull happening between the characters and the conversation should have somewhere to go. Even in a case of friendly banter between a salesperson and a customer, there is conflict in the attempt to match wits. The conflict might be between the two characters, or it might be something else happening in the story which informs their interaction. One way to approach scenes of dialogue is to think of your characters as wanting two different things, or as wanting the same thing but going about it in different ways. How does thinking about dialogue in this way make even a simple conversation between spouses about who drank the last of the milk much richer and more interesting?

☐ Flesh-flesh it out. A bunch of dialogue going back and forth can work sometimes, but for the most part, it should be fleshed out with things in between that give depth and background and also keep us rooted with who is speaking when. What is your point of view character thinking and observing throughout the conversation? What are people doing as they talk?

☐ Verbs-try to change up your verb use in people talking, as appropriate and natural to the story and your language style: said, stated, started, exclaimed, whispered, growled, etc.

EXERCISE

Scene of dialogue, with at least four lines of dialogue from each of two characters. No one portion of dialogue should be over two lines long. Be conscious of point of view and of the rules of dialogue above. Make sure that there is some kind of conflict, some kind of tension between desires, and some kind of story background which is informing the conversation. Flesh it out with reactions, interior thoughts, and actions.

THE PEDESTRIAN
Ray Bradbury

To enter out into that silence that was the city at eight o'clock of a misty evening in November, to put your feet upon that buckling concrete walk, to step over grassy seams and make your way, hands in pockets, through the silences, that was what Mr Leonard Mead most dearly loved to do. He would stand upon the corner of an intersection and peer down long moonlit avenues of pavement in four directions, deciding which way to go, but it really made no difference; he was alone in this world of A.D., 2053 or as good as alone, and with a final decision made, a path selected, he would stride off, sending patterns of frosty air before him like the smoke of a cigar.

Sometimes he would walk for hours and miles and return only at midnight to his house. And on his way he would see the cottages and homes with their dark windows, and it was not unequal to walking through a graveyard where only the faintest glimmers of firefly light appeared in flickers behind the windows. Sudden grey phantoms seemed to manifest upon inner room walls where a curtain was still undrawn against the night, or there were whisperings and murmurs where a window in a tomb-like building was still open.

Mr Leonard Mead would pause, cock his head, listen, look, and march on, his feet making no noise on the lumpy walk. For long ago he had wisely changed to sneakers when strolling at night, because the dogs in intermittent squads would parallel his journey with barkings if he wore hard heels, and lights might click on and faces appear and an entire street be startled by the passing of a lone figure, himself, in the early November evening.

On this particular evening he began his journey in a westerly direction, towards the hidden sea. There was a good crystal frost in the air; it cut the nose and made the lungs blaze like a Christmas tree inside; you could feel the cold light going on and off, all the branches filled with invisible snow. He listened to the faint push of his soft shoes through autumn leaves with satisfaction, and whistled a cold quiet whistle between his teeth, occasionally picking up a leaf as he passed, examining its skeletal pattern in the infrequent lamplights as he went on, smelling its rusty smell.

'Hello, in there,' he whispered to every house on every side as he moved. 'What's up tonight on Channel 4, Channel 7, Channel 9? Where are the cowboys rushing, and do I see the United States Cavalry over the next hill to the rescue?'

The street was silent and long and empty, with only his shadow moving like the shadow of a hawk in mid-country. If he closed his eyes and stood very still, frozen, he could imagine himself upon the centre of a plain, a wintry, windless Arizona desert with no house in a thousand miles, and only dry river beds, the streets, for company.

'What is it now?' he asked the houses, noticing his wrist watch. 'Eight-thirty p.m.? Time for a dozen assorted murders? A quiz? A revue? A comedian falling off the stage?'

Was that a murmur of laughter from within a moon-white house? He hesitated, but went on when nothing more happened. He stumbled over a particularly uneven section of pavement. The cement was vanishing under flowers and grass. In ten years of walking by night or day, for thousands of miles, he had never met another person walking, not one in all that time.

He came to a clover-leaf intersection which stood silent where two main highways crossed the town. During the day it was a thunderous surge of cars, the petrol stations open, a great insect rustling and a ceaseless jockeying for position as the scarab-beetles, a faint incense puttering from their exhausts, skimmed homeward to the far directions. But now these highways, too, were like streams in a dry season, all stone and bed and moon radiance.

He turned back on a side street, circling around towards his home. He was within a block of his destination when the lone car turned a corner quite suddenly and flashed a fierce white cone of light upon him. He stood entranced, not unlike a night moth, stunned by the illumination, and then drawn towards it.

A metallic voice called to him:

'Stand still. Stay where you are! Don't move!' He halted.

'Put up your hands!' 'But-' he said.

'Your hands up! Or we'll shoot!'

The police, of course, but what a rare, incredible thing; in a city of three million, there was only *one* police car left, wasn't that correct? Ever since a year ago, 2052, the election year, the force had been cut down from three cars to one. Crime was ebbing; there was no need now for the police, save for this one lone car wandering and wandering the empty streets.

'Your name?' said the police car in a metallic whisper. He couldn't see the men in it for the bright light in his eyes.

'Leonard Mead,' he said.

'Speak up!'

'Leonard Mead!'

'Business or profession?'

'I guess you'd call me a writer."

"No profession,' said the police car, as If talking to itself. The light held him fixed, like a museum specimen, needle thrust through chest.

'You might say that,' said Mr Mead. He hadn't written in years. Magazines and books didn't sell any more. Everything went on in the tomb-like houses at night now, he thought, continuing his fancy. The tombs, ill-lit by television light, where the people sat like the dead, the grey or multi-coloured lights touching their faces, but never really touching them.

'No profession,' said the phonograph voice, hissing. 'What are you doing out?'

'Walking,' said Leonard Mead.

'Walking!'

'Just walking,' he said simply, but his face felt cold.

'Walking, just walking, walking?'

'Yes, sir.'

'Walking where? For what?'

'Walking for air. Walking to *see*.'

'Your address!'

'Eleven South Saint James Street.'

'And there is air *in* your house, you have an air *conditioner*, Mr Mead?'

'Yes.'

'And you have a viewing screen in your house to see with?'

'No.'

'No?' There was a crackling quiet that in itself was an accusation.

'Are you married, Mr Mead?'

'No.'

'Not married,' said the police voice behind the fiery beam. The moon was high and clear among the stars and the houses were grey and silent.

'Nobody wanted me,' said Leonard Mead with a smile.

'Don't speak unless you're spoken to!'

Leonard Mead waited in the cold night.

"Just *walking,* Mr Mead?'

'Yes.'

'But you haven't explained for what purpose.'

'I explained; for air, and to see, and just to walk.'

'Have you done this often?'

'Every night for years.'

The police car sat in the centre of the street with its radio throat faintly humming.

'Well, Mr Mead,' it said.

'Is that all?' he asked politely.

'Yes,' said the voice. 'Here.' There was a sigh, a pop. The back door of the police car sprang wide.

'Get in.'

'Wait a minute, I haven't done anything!'

'Get in.'

'I protest!'

'Mr Mead.'

He walked like a man suddenly drunk. As he passed the front window of the car he looked in. As he had expected, there was no-one in the front seat, no-one in the car at all.

'Get in.'

He put his hand to the door and peered into the back seat, which was a little cell, a little black jail with bars. It smelled of riveted steel. It smelled of harsh antiseptic; it smelled too clean and hard and metallic. There was nothing soft there.

'Now if you had a wife to give you an alibi,' said the iron voice. 'But - '

'Where are you taking me?'

The car hesitated, or rather gave a faint whirring click, as if information, somewhere, was dropping card by punch-slotted card under electric eyes. 'To the Psychiatric Centre for Research on Regressive Tendencies. '

He got in. The door shut with a soft thud. The police car rolled through the night avenues, flashing its dim lights ahead.

They passed one house on one street a moment later, one house in an entire city of houses that were dark, but this one particular house had all of its electric lights brightly lit, every window a loud yellow illumination, square and warm in the cool darkness.

'That's *my* house,' said Leonard Mead.

No-one answered him.

The car moved down the empty river- bed streets and off away, leaving the empty streets with the empty pavements, and no sound and no motion all the rest of the chill November night.

THE WHALE WATCHERS
Wendy Rainey

The three men set out from San Pedro Harbor at 8 a.m. in a small motor boat, armed with a cooler full of beer and sandwiches. All three had Tuesday off from their production jobs in Hollywood. Danny took the helm, putting on his Dodger's baseball cap, his iPod blasting Jimi Hendrix , while Hank snapped photographs of the U.S.S. Iowa and various cargo ships docked along the port. Steve was already drinking a beer and Danny (steering the wheel with his elbows) was rolling a joint that he planned on smoking once they got out of the harbor and into prime whale watching territory. "This is the life, man. This is the fuckin' life," Steve said as he lay back in his seat, adjusting his sun visor, his right hand skimming the water. He reached for the can in his drink caddy and chugged it down. "So, what happened last week?" Hank asked Steve. "We saw two Grays just off Portuguese Bend," Hank said, still snapping shots of the harbor boats. "Fuck! I wish I hadn't missed that," Steve said, throwing back his brew. "Last week I was stuck with another director who thinks he's Stanley Kubrick. Forty takes to get a couple of dumb models to step out of a car in front of a green screen." Steve pulled out a pair of binoculars, studying a flock of seagulls on the horizon. "Those Honda people really opened their wallets for this one. Golden hours but it knocked me on my ass," Steve said. Finishing his beer, he let out a belch, and grabbed another can from the ice chest. "That's the last time I'm ever dealing with *that* shit again," Steve sighed and chugged down more of his beer." "Sucks, man, but the money's worth it." Danny said, putting his joint kit away. "No," Steve said. "It's not worth it

220

anymore." Steve slouched down in his seat looking off into the distance. The binoculars hung from his neck. Danny, spotting Hank's plumber's ass, grabbed his Smartphone and took a shot of Hank bending over to get a photo of a tug boat. "Dude," Danny called out to Hank, "I just sent a shot of your ass to Marie!" Without turning around, Hank gave Danny the finger. Danny snapped a shot of that too.

They slowly made their way out of the harbor. Hours passed while Hank took photos of boats and marine life. Danny stayed at the helm blasting Otis Redding and Cream from his iPod. Steve was quiet as he drank one beer after another. Danny fired up the weed, handing joints to Hank and Steve. Steve smiled, inhaling deeply. He let the smoke linger in his lungs for as long as he could before exhaling and then taking another long, deep drag. He played air guitar during a rift in Cream's Strange Brew. Danny picked up an imaginary guitar and joined in for a few moments but then cut the music as they approached a buoy with several sea lions sunning themselves. The baby sea lions had flopped on the backs and bellies of their mothers and fathers in a blubbery, drunken sleep, their wet skins glistening in the sun. Two adult males were hoisting themselves up on their front fins eyeing the boat. Hank focused the camera in on the babies and managed to get several expert shots. Danny maneuvered the boat so that they continuously circled the buoy at a fifty-foot radius for the next five minutes. Steve inhaled the aroma of the sea lions. They smelled of fish, sea weed, and salt. He noticed the way one of the mothers had her left front fin protectively around her cub. He looked at all the cubs as they slept, their twitching whiskers, their tiny fins, the way their half sleeping mothers caressed them with their noses. "I had a dog once. Looked just like that. A really great dog." Just then, one of the slumbering pups woke up and looked at Steve with drowsy eyes. He barked several times as he slid off of his mother's back, waddled to the edge of the buoy, and dove into the ocean. The father sea lion followed him. Hank and Danny hadn't noticed that Steve had started to cry. When they finally did notice they looked at each other, then looked away. They both thought the moment would quickly pass but it didn't. Danny, confused, navigated away from the buoy. Hank, smiling, sat down next to Steve and said, "Hey, buddy, you okay?" He reached into the cooler and pulled out a sandwich. "Why don't you go a little easy on the weed and sop up some of the suds with this?" Steve put his joint down, took the sandwich and started eating it. "Hank, you ever wonder why we spend most of our time doing things we don't wanna do? I never thought about it until a few months ago. But now it just eats at me all the time." Hank looked at Steve as he reached into his bag, pulled out a water bottle with some pink liquid in it and took a sip. "This is for my ulcer," he said, belching. "Jesus, it tastes like shit." He had stopped crying by then. " Ya know, you guys, it would be epic to see some whales, or even a pod of dolphins," Steve said, chomping on his sandwich to get the chalky aftertaste out of his mouth. No more than five minutes had passed when Hank saw a dozen fins break the surface of the water. He motioned for Danny to cut the motor. He turned around to Steve and said, "Look Stevo, dolphins!" There were a hundred dolphins surrounding the boat. Steve threw his sandwich down, grabbed the bottle of pink liquid and downed it. He climbed to the bow of The Boston Whaler. Peering over the handrail, he let out a yelp as the dolphins swam in front of the boat. Some of them sprang out of the water. Steve yelped again when he saw the leaping dolphins. "This is the greatest, you guys! This is fuckin' awesome!" He ripped off his shorts, underwear, and t-shirt. He threw his shoes, socks, visor, and binoculars on the deck and jumped into the ocean.

Hank and Danny looked at each other and ran to the side of the boat, staring at Steve swimming nude with the dolphins. "Steve," Hank screamed, "What the hell are ya doing?" Steve kept repeating, "I'm free. I'm free. I'm free." Hank and Danny looked at each other again, "Look buddy, we know you've been going through some shit," Hank screamed to Steve, "Grab my hand. C'mon now." Hank had his hand extended toward Steve, but Steve kept swimming further out into the ocean. Danny, back at the helm, started the motor up again and followed Steve as he swam with the dolphins. Hank and Danny smiled nervously at each other, shrugging their shoulders, staring at Steve. After a few minutes, Hank called out to Steve, "Stevo, time to come in now buddy." "No! I'm staying out here," Steve said. "Hank, get your camera. I have something to say." "What the hell is this all about, Steve?" Hank screamed. "Get your ass back in the boat right now. You're drunk and you're high." "I'll get back in the boat if you could just film the speech I want to make. It won't take long. Get your camera, Hank. I'll wait." Hank picked up his camera, switched it to video, and as instructed began filming Steve. "To whom it may concern," Steve said, looking directly into the lens. "I drank a cocktail of oxy and sleeping pills a few minutes ago, enough to kill three horses. I'll be gone soon. I want to die today with the dolphins in the ocean. These two guys are my best friends," he pointed to Hank and Danny, whose mouths had fallen open at the same time. "They have nothing to do with this. It's all my idea. I have pancreatic cancer and I've only got about six months left anyway. Six months of shit." Hank put the camera down while it was still rolling and both men extended their hands to Steve, shouting at him to get the fuck back on board. Danny threw him a life preserver. Steve picked it up and flung it away from him. Danny, looking at Hank said, "Hank, get over here and hold the wheel." Hank who had picked up his camera again, managed to keep the camera rolling with one hand while grabbing the wheel with the other. Danny had already jumped into the ocean and was swimming toward Steve. "Is it true Steve? What you said? Is it true?" Danny asked, out of breath. "Yes, it's true." The two men looked at each other. "It's cold out here. Come back on the boat." "No. This is the way I want to go. Swimming with the dolphins. Maybe finding a Gray." "Is there anything I can do for you?" "Nothing. Just let me go," Steve said. "C'mon, man. Get back up on deck. We can come up with a better solution to this uh, this, you know, this predicament." Steve let out a laugh. He threw his hands up in the air. They landed back down in the water with a splash. "Predicament? This is not a little predicament. I'm dying, goddamn it. I'm gonna be dead in six months. I'm not getting back up on deck. Why should I? So I can work myself to death for a little bit longer? For what? For my stupid job? And for a woman who doesn't respect me? Is that how we die?" The three men stared at each other for several moments. "What was any of it ever for? What the fuck was any of it ever for?" Steve shouted to Hank and Danny. Hank and Danny looked at each other. Hank let out a heavy sigh, shaking his head, "It's what we do, Steve." "Well, it's not what I do anymore. I am now a free man!" Steve shouted, smiling. He turned around and dove into the ocean. Hank and Danny could see his bare behind just before it became submerged by the dark water. They stared at the bubbles that surfaced as he swam several feet away from the boat. When he came up for air he said, " Hank, I'm gonna finish up here! Put your goddamned camera on me" Hank picked up his camera and looked at Steve. "What are ya waitin' for motherfucker? Put your goddamned camera on me now!" Hank put his eye up to the camera lens and focused in on Steve. "There is a sealed envelope to my lawyer in my safe deposit box at the bank." Steve swam closer to the camera. "Fuck you, Carol. You soul-sucking leech. I supported you for thirty years and all you do is go on Facebook and Twitter and bitch

about how stupid men are with all your feminist pals who are also living off their husbands. Well, you'll soon be doing a new dance, honey. It's called WORKING. The gravy train has stopped, baby. Consider yourself liberated! And by the way, I know all about that asshole pool man." Steve splashed sea water on his face and stared into the camera one last time, letting out a measured
F-U-C-K Y-O-U!

Steve looked at Hank and Danny. Danny extended his hand to Steve. Steve, smiling, nodded his head, no. "Listen, you two assholes have been my only real friends for the past twenty-five years." he said, smiling at Hank and Danny. "You're the only ones I give a shit about." Steve looked at his friends one last time. He then focused his gaze at the ocean's distant horizon. "I'm sorry to put this on you," Steve shook his head. Hank and Danny looked at each other again and then at Steve. "Danny, crank up Hendrix," Steve said. "You know the song I wanna hear." Danny found the song he knew Steve loved the most and blasted it from the small boat. Steve sang the words, "Purple haze all in my brain. Lately things don't seem the same. Actin' funny but I don't know why. 'Scuse me while I kiss the sky." He threw his head back and howled in the air. "Now I'm gonna go find me some of those Gray's," he slurred. Steve felt his muscles relax. He let the current carry him away from the boat. Smiling, he gave a slow wave to Hank and Danny, who only half raised their hands to him, while Hendrix belted out, "You got me blowin' blowin' my mind. Is it tomorrow or the end of time?" He turned around and swam further and further out into the ocean. Hank and Danny watched their friend swim away from them until he was barely a dot on the surface of the sea.

Hank turned off the camera and put it down, unable to speak. Danny turned the Boston Whaler around and headed back to the port. Both men were silent as they cracked open fresh beers and ate their sandwiches. Afterward, they each lit up a joint. They leaned back in their seats with their sunglasses on, taking their hats and shirts off to let the afternoon sun shine on their faces and warm their bodies. They inhaled the marine air and watched the seagulls flying above them. In the distance they heard the bark of sea lions on a buoy. They had never felt more alive.

DESCRIPTIVE LANGUAGE

: Language intended to create a mood, person, place, thing, event, emotion, or experience. Descriptive language uses images that appeal to the reader's senses, helping the reader to imagine how a subject looks, sounds, smells, tastes, or feels. *Descriptive* language is vivid and specific, and helps someone imagine a scene he didn't witness.

- **sight:** including colors, shapes, sizes (e.g. green, red, brown, square, round, large, small)
- **sound:** including types and volume (rattling, scraping, blowing, loud, soft)
- **smell:** including scents and strengths (putrid, sweet, foul, pungent, strong, faint)
- **taste:** including flavors and strengths (sweet, sour, spicy, bland, strong, weak)
- **touch:** including textures and temperatures (smooth, rough, soft, hard, cool, cold, warm, hot)
- **emotions and subjective reactions:** (happy, excited, ecstatic, sad, lonely, beautiful, ugly)
- **states**: (tired, angered, labored, smart, rich, hungry, lonely, friendly)

1) A Friendly Clown

On one corner of my dresser sits a smiling toy clown on a tiny unicycle--a gift I received last Christmas from a close friend. The clown's short yellow hair, made of yarn, covers its ears but is parted above the eyes. The blue eyes are outlined in black with thin, dark lashes flowing from the brows. It has cherry-red cheeks, nose, and lips, and its broad grin disappears into the wide, white ruffle around its neck. The clown wears a fluffy, two-tone nylon costume. The left side of the outfit is light blue, and the right side is red. The two colors merge in a dark line that runs down the center of the small outfit. Surrounding its ankles and disguising its long black shoes are big pink bows. The white spokes on the wheels of the unicycle gather in the center and expand to the black tire so that the wheel somewhat resembles the inner half of a grapefruit. The clown and unicycle together stand about a foot high. As a cherished gift from my good friend Tran, this colorful figure greets me with a smile every time I enter my room.

2) The Blond Guitar by Jeremy Burden

My most valuable possession is an old, slightly warped blond guitar--the first instrument I taught myself how to play. It's nothing fancy, just a Madeira folk guitar, all scuffed and scratched and finger-printed. At the top is a bramble of copper-wound strings, each one hooked through the eye of a silver tuning key. The strings are stretched down a long, slim neck, its frets tarnished, the wood worn by years of fingers pressing chords and picking notes. The body of the Madeira is shaped like an enormous yellow pear, one that was slightly damaged in shipping. The blond wood has been chipped and gouged to gray, particularly where the pick guard fell off years ago. No, it's not a beautiful instrument, but it still lets me make music, and for that I will always treasure it.

THE POET'S OBLIGATION

Pablo Neruda

To whoever is not listening to the sea
this Friday morning, to who ever is cooped up
in house or office, factory or woman
or street or mine or dry prison cell,
to him I come, and without speaking or looking
I arrive and open the door of his prison,
and a vibration starts up, vague and insistent,
a long rumble of thunder adds itself
to the weigh of the planet and the foam,
the groaning rivers of the ocean rise,
the star vibrates quickly in its corona
and the sea beats, dies, and goes on beating.

So. Drawn on by my destiny,
I ceaselessly must listen to and keep
the sea's lamenting in my consciousness,
I must feel the crash of the hard water
and gather it up in a perpetual cup
so that, wherever those in prison may be,
wherever they suffer the sentence of the autumn,
I may be present with an errant wave,
I may move in and out of the windows,
and hearing me, eyes may lift themselves,
asking "How can I reach the sea?"
And I will pass to them, saying nothing,
the starry echoes of the wave,
a breaking up of foam and quicksand,
a rustling of salt withdrawing itself,
the gray cry of sea birds on the coast.

So, through me, freedom and the sea
will call in answer to the shrouded heart.

AN ODE TO UNSUSPECTING REJECTION

Anony

I knew you would come eventually
but not with this girl.
Not with this morbidly obese
frog baptized in imperfections.
Not with this troll living under her ostracized bridge
of sheer unworthiness. I swear I didn't see you coming
hiding under her scaly, calloused skin warted over with
boils oozing of a lower class.

I knew you were coming, but not like this.
It is a mystery to me
How did you jump into her calloused lips
and utter the words,"I don't want you?"
How did infect her plaque infested gums
To help her say, "I'm not interested?"
How on earth did you force her to unclench
those dirt yellow teeth with the gall to tell me,
 Me of all people, to "Leave me alone?"

Do you know who I am?
Do you know what I've accomplished
in my few arrogant years living?
Do you know my lineage?
And more importantly. No. Most importantly,
did you tell her what she would miss?
Did you tell her the pedigree she could obtain on my arm?
I bet you didn't, but you should have. You should have.

Next time you break me, break me with someone I can
respect.

THIS IS JUST TO SAY
William Carlos Williams

I have eaten

the plums
that were in the icebox

and which
you were probably
saving for breakfast

Forgive me
they were delicious
so sweet
and so cold

MIKE CHECK
Suhier Hammad

one two one two can you
hear me mic check one two
mike checked
my bags at the airport

 in a random
routine check

i understand mike i do
you too were altered
that day and most days
most folks operate on
fear often hate this
is mic check your
job and i am
always random

i understand it was
folks who looked smelled
maybe prayed like me

can you hear me mike
ruddy blonde buzz
cut with corn flower
eyes and a cross
round your neck

mike check
folks who looked like
you stank so bad the
indians smelled them
mic chcek before they landed

they murdered one two
one two as they prayed
spread small pox as alms

mic check yes i
packed my own
bags can you hear
me no they have not
been out of my possession

thanks mike you
have a good day too one
two mike check mike
check mike
a-yo mike
whose gonna
check you?

CINDERELLA'S RATS
Hiram Sims

For this is the miracle that I'd been dreaming of...This is...

.

"Blood.." A sharp, elderly voice echoed behind Cinderella as she spun around to discover who had intruded into her private chamber. Cinderella was holding her bruised left hand over the space between her upper lip and lower nose, which was oozing, quite terribly, with dark red blood. Cinderella had already covered the dark purple bruise on the side of her right eye with taupe foundation, but the hemorraging of the skin permeated through the poorly applied makeup.

"What are you doing in here. No one is allowed in the Queen's Private Chamber. Get Out..Get o..."Cinderella paused only long enough for the elderly woman to notice how quickly the blood coated Cinderella's brilliantly white teeth. "It's You...It's you. Fairy Godmother Its you."

"Yes my Child. Sit down my dear. Let's have a look at you."

"I'm sorry I yelled. I didn't recognize you with your... clothes." Cinderella lifted the dark Black cloak that surrounded the woman, which was in stark contrast to the beautiful light blue gown she wore last time with red ribbon.

"Enough about me dearest. What has happened to you?" The woman brushed Cinderella's hair back to reveal two deep blue bruises on the right side of her forehead. Cinderella buried her head in the woman's chest.

"He's terrible. Absolutely terrible Godmother. After we got married, he starting beating me. When he's stressed out, he beats me. When he gets angry he beats me. After the death of his father, when he became King, he had so much pressure on him. So many problems with the Kingdom....so he takes it out on me. "

Cinderella sobbed uncontrollably as the woman caressed her scalp.

"Now, now," said the old woman rolling her eyes in disgust.

"I'm the laughing stock of this castle. Everyone knows he sleeps with all of the chambermaids. Every single one of them."

"How terrible," the woman said with no surprise at all in her voice.

"And...he shares me." The woman stopped rubbing her. Every molecule in her body stopped.

"Well surely a King must share his young queen with the whole kingdom, that the people might love and adore you and...."

"No Fairy Godmother. He shares me. With the generals of his army. When they visit, he gives me to them." At the sound of these words, Cinderella felt the woman grow extraordinarily hot. She pulled away from her slowly, backing up into the corner. The elderly woman stood up and walk walked toward Cinderella, eyes glowing a steamy, fiery orange.
"You're so weak. In all my days I've never seen a woman of such power so pathetically weak."

"I'm sorry fairy God mother. I'm sorry for everything…"

"Yes you are sorry…absolutely.."The elderly woman saw that Cinderella was paralyzed with fear. She stood still and calmed down, eyes returning from a fiery orange to a brilliant blue.

"Cinderella…Cinderella. Do you know who I am?"

"Of course. You're my fairy Godmother."

"Stop calling me that. That name is weak. Tired. Timid, and doesn't at all reflect the true nature of my power. Do you know what everyone has called me for the past 500 years?

"No. What do they call you?'

"Witch. They call me witch. They called your mom a witch too."
"You knew my mother. How come you didn't tell me?"
"She was my daughter. Sweet little Elizabeth. My only child. so strong and honorable. Not at all like you."
Cinderella put her hand back over her mouth.

"So that makes you my…"

"Yes my dear. Not your godmother, your grandmother."
Cinderella paused and crouched down on the floor, head in between her knees.

"Why did you do this to me Grandmother? The pumpkin into a carriage…the mice into horses…the dress, the glass slippers…this is all your fault."

"You ungrateful little bitch. I gave you exactly what you wanted. Exactly who you wanted. Did I tell you to marry a man after you only danced with him for five minutes. Any man who chooses a wife solely based on her beauty is bound to cheat on her. Stand up."

Cinderella didn't budge. "Stand up," the woman said while gritting her teeth." Cinderella stood up with her eyes still closed as the old woman yanked her hand open.
"You must live up to your full potential. You must rise above this shame and claim the power you were destined to acquire. You must use your gift." Cinderella opened her eyes to see a white wand glowing in her pale palm.

"Use your power." And with that, the elderly woman vanished into black vapor. Cinderella looked at the sundial clock, then headed toward the kitchen.

***

The King pushed the two broad doors open into the dining room chamber. He was followed by the 7 generals of his Royal Army.

"Cinderella! Cinderella!! Get in her now!" The king bellowed through the large, hollow hall as his subjects giggled close behind him. Cinderella burst into the dining carrying 8 huge mugs full of water. The generals took their seats at the table, which left no open seat for Cinderella.

"I'm certain that you have prepared dinner, yes?"

"Yes, My King. I just wanted to bring you drink first so that..."Just then the king took one of the large mugs off of the tray, looked into the contents, and threw the glass mug onto the ground. He then took his large brown hand, and smacked the tray containing the remaining 7 mugs, sending them crashing to the ground.

"Water? Bring us beer. And hurry up, you ignorant peasant." The soldiers nodded in agreement. As she ran back into the kitchen, three other chambermaids rushed in with 8 hot plates of food. The plates steamed of hot mashed potatoes, corn, yams, and a strange looking meat. The women placed the meat in front of the military generals. Cinderella re-emerged carrying 8 new mugs full to the brim with beer. She placed the drinks on the table in front of each general, then in front of the King last.
When she was in arm's reach, the king put his large fingers around Cinderella's throat.
"What the hell is this mystery meat you have placed before me?"

"It's grounghog. Your favorite,"she muttered, choking on her words. The King looked down at his plate, then he slammed Cinderella's head into the side of the table.

"Does this look like groundhog to you?"

Cinderella could feel her warm blood spreading on the dark oak table underneath her face. His hands still firmly around her throat, she whispered, "I baked it this time, that's why it's a little small," she said gulping small rivlets of blood. The King loosened his grip slightly, but did not release her.

"Eat" he commanded his generals, and they eagerly began gulping yams and mashed potatoes in their mouths. "Not the trimmings. The meat. Eat the meat." The men paused, then slowly dug their forks into the soft flesh covered in gravy.The King looked at Cinderella with squinted eyes. She knew he was using the soldiers as guinea pigs to make sure the meat was not poisoned before he ate it. She also knew that if any of them so much as coughed, she was a dead woman. The men ate all of the meat with no problem. After the King felt it wa safe, he lifted Cinderella's neck from the table, and thrusted her small frame onto the floor.

"Sit there like a good little dog while your master enjoys his dinner. "The King sank his large fork into the meat, lifted it into his enormous mouth, and swallowed it whole. He immediately started on the corn, when he noticed out of the corner of his eye, something white and small shaking at him.
Cinderella was pointing her wand directly at the King. "What is that stick you carry wench?"

"You were right" She said as she wiped blood from the side of her face. It was not groundhog you ate. It was a rat."
The King stood up and began walking toward her. He drew his sword, lifted it over his head, as he quietly heard Cinderella say, "Biboty…boboty…booo." She pointed the wand directly at his stomach. He felt a bubbling then a gurgling, than an expanding. It grew rapidly within him, as he watched his stomach move violently as if something within in it was emerging. He felt his skin rip and something large pushed through the front of his clothing. He lifted his shirt and screamed…"It's a ..Its a.."
"A Hoof," shouted one of the generals. It's a bloody hoof."The King fell, and from his limp body, slowly emerged a beautiful white horse. Just as beautiful as the horse that carried her to the ball where she met her shining prince. Just as beautiful as the horse her grandmother had created from a small, loving, diseased rat, only this horse was covered in the King's Blood.
The generals shrieked in panic, knowing they had eaten the same meat, and were probably about to share the same

fate. Several of them sobbed, cried, and began to beg for their lives as they watched Cindrella walk over to the king's mangled frame, remove the crown from his head, and place it firmly on her own.

One solider ran over to her, bowed very humbly and shouted. "Long live the Queen, Ruler of all England."

When the remaining soldiers saw her smile at this phrase, they all ran over to her, bowed, and shouted the same enchanting phrase. "Long live the queen...long live the queen..long live the queen...Long Live the queen...Long live Queen Cinderella."

The smile faded quickly from her face. She stared at the group of cowering men.

"Don't ever call me that again. That name is tired, timid, weak and doesn't at all reflect the true nature of my power. I shall take my mother's name. I shall hence forward and forever be called Queen Elizabeth."

LOS VENDIDOS
Luis Valdez

Characters:
Honest Sancho
Secretary
Farmworker
Pachuco
Revolucionario
Mexican-American
Scene: HONEST SANCHO's *Used Mexican Lot and Mexican Curio Shop. Three models are on display in* HONEST SANCHO *'s shop. To the right, there is a* REVOLUCIONARIO, *complete with sombrero, carrilleras and carabina 30-30. At center, on the floor, there is the* FARMWORKER, *under a broad straw sombrero. At stage left is the* PACHUCO, *filero in hand.* HONEST SANCHO *is moving among his models, dusting them off and preparing for another day of business.*

SANCHO: Bueno, bueno, mis monos, vamos a ver a quién vendemos ahora, ¿no? (*To audience.*) ¡Quihubo! I'm Honest Sancho and this is my shop. Antes fui contratista, pero ahora logré tener mi negocito. All I need now is a customer. (*A bell rings offstage.*) Ay, a customer!

SECRETARY: (*Entering.*) Good morning, I'm Miss Jimenez from …

242

SANCHO: Ah, una chicana! Welcome, welcome Señorita Jiménez.

SECRETARY: (*Anglo pronunciation.*) JIM-enez.

SANCHO: ¿Qué?

SECRETARY: My name is Miss JIM-enez. Don't you speak English? What's wrong with you?

SANCHO: Oh, nothing, Señorita JIM-enez. I'm here to help you.

SECRETARY: That's better. As I was starting to say, I'm a secretary from Governor Reagan's

office, and we're looking for a Mexican type for the administration.

SANCHO: Well, you come to the right place, lady. This is Honest Sancho's Used Mexican Lot,

and we got all types here. Any particular type you want?

SECRETARY: Yes, we were looking for somebody suave

…

SANCHO: Suave.

SECRETARY: Debonaire.

SANCHO: De buen aire.

SECRETARY: Dark.

SANCHO: Prieto.

SECRETARY: But of course, not too dark.

SANCHO: No muy prieto.

SECRETARY: Perhaps, beige.

SANCHO: Beige, just the tone. Asi como cafecito con leche, ¿no?

SECRETARY: One more thing. He must be hard-working.

SANCHO: That could only be one model. Step right over here to the center of the shop, lady.

(*They cross to the* FARMWORKER.) This is our standard farmworker model. As you can see, in the

words of our beloved Senator George Murphy, he is "built close to the ground." Also, take

special notice of his 4-ply Goodyear huaraches, made from the rain tire. This wide-brimmed sombrero is an extra added feature; keeps off the sun, rain and dust.

SECRETARY: Yes, it does look durable.

SANCHO: And our farmworker model is friendly. Muy amable. Watch. (*Snaps his fingers.*)

FARMWORKER: (*Lifts up head.*) Buenos días, señorita. (*His head drops.*)

SECRETARY: My, he is friendly.

SANCHO: Didn't I tell you? Loves his patrones! But his most attractive feature is that he's hardworking. Let me show you. (*Snaps fingers. FARMWORKER stands.*)

FARMWORKER: ¡El jale! (*He begins to work.*)

SANCHO: As you can see he is cutting grapes.

SECRETARY: Oh, I wouldn't know.

SANCHO: He also picks cotton. (*Snaps. FARMWORKER begins to pick cotton.*)

SECRETARY: Versatile, isn't he?

SANCHO: He also picks melons. (*Snaps. FARMWORKER picks melons.*) That's his slow speed for late in the season. Here's his fast speed. (*Snap. FARMWORKER picks faster.*)

SECRETARY: Chihuahua … I mean, goodness, he sure is a hardworker.

SANCHO: (*Pulls the FARMWORKER to his feet.*) And that isn't the half of it. Do you see these little holes on his arms that appear to be pores? During those hot sluggish days in the field when the vines or the branches get so entangled, it's almost impossible to move, these holes emit certain grease that allows our model to slip and slide right through the crop with no trouble at all.

SECRETARY: Wonderful. But is he economical?

SANCHO: Economical? Señorita, you are looking at the Volkswagen of Mexicans. Pennies a day

is all it takes. One plate of beans and tortillas will keep him going all day. That, and chile. Plenty
of chile. Chile jalapeños, chile verde, chile colorado. But, of course, if you do give him chile,
(*Snap.* FARMWORKER *turns left face. Snap.*
FARMWORKER *bends over.*) then you have to change his oil filter once a week.
SECRETARY: What about storage?
SANCHO: No problem. You know these new farm labor camps our Honorable Governor Reagan
has built out by Parlier or Raisin City? They were designed with our model in mind. Five, six,
seven, even ten in one of those shacks will give you no trouble at all. You can also put him in old
barns, old cars, riverbanks. You can even leave him out in the field over night with no worry!
SECRETARY: Remarkable.
SANCHO: And here's an added feature: every year at the end of the season, this model goes back
to Mexico and doesn't return, automatically, until next Spring.
SECRETARY: How about that. But tell me, does he speak English?
SANCHO: Another outstanding feature is that last year this model was programmed to go out on
STRIKE! (*Snap.*)
FARMWORKER: ¡Huelga! ¡Huelga! Hermanos, sálganse de esos files. (*Snap. He stops.*)
SECRETARY: No! Oh no, we can't strike in the State Capitol.
SANCHO: Well, he also scabs. (*Snap.*)
FARMWORKER: Me vendo barato, ¿y qué? (*Snap.*)
SECRETARY: That's much better, but you didn't answer my question. Does he speak English?
SANCHO: Bueno … no, pero he has other …
SECRETARY: No.

SANCHO: Other features.

SECRETARY: No! He just won't do!

SANCHO: Okay, okay, pues. We have other models.

SECRETARY: I hope so. What we need is something a little more sophisticated.

SANCHO: Sophisti-qué?

SECRETARY: An urban model.

SANCHO: Ah, from the city! Step right back. Over here in this corner of the shop is exactly what you're looking for. Introducing our new 1969 JOHNNY PACHUCO model! This is our fast-back model. Streamlined. Built for speed, low-riding, city life. Take a look at some of these features. Mag shoes, dual exhausts, green chartruese paint-job, dark-tint windshield, a little poof on top. Let me just turn him on. (*Snap.* JOHNNY *walks to stage center with a* PACHUCO *bounce.*)

SECRETARY: What was that?

SANCHO: That, señorita, was the Chicano shuffle.

SECRETARY: Okay, what does he do?

SANCHO: Anything and everything necessary for city life. For instance, survival: he knife fights. (*Snaps.* JOHNNY *pulls out a switchblade and swings at* SECRETARY. SECRETARY *screams.*) He dances. (*Snap.*)

JOHNNY: (*Singing.*) "Angel Baby, my Angel Baby ..." (*Snap.*)

SANCHO: And here's a feature no city model can be without. He gets arrested, but not without resisting, ofcourse. (*Snap.*)

JOHNNY: En la madre, la placa. I didn't do it! I didn't do it! (JOHNNY *turns and stands up against an imaginary wall, legs spread out, arms behind his back.*)

SECRETARY: Oh no, we can't have arrests! We must maintain law and order.

SANCHO: But he's bilingual.

SECRETARY: Bilingual?

SANCHO: Simón que yes. He speaks English! Johnny, give us some English. (*Snap.*)

JOHNNY: (*Comes downstage.*) Fuck-you!

SECRETARY: (*Gasps.*) Oh! I've never been so insulted in my whole life!

SANCHO: Well, he learned it in your school.

SECRETARY: I don't care where he learned it.

SANCHO: But he's economical.

SECRETARY: Economical?

SANCHO: Nickels and dimes. You can keep Johnny running on hamburgers, Taco Bell tacos,
Lucky Lager beer, Thunderbird wine, yesca …

SECRETARY: Yesca?

SANCHO: Mota.

SECRETARY: Mota?

SANCHO: Leños … marijuana. (*Snap.* JOHNNY *inhales on an imaginary joint.*)

SECRETARY: That's against the law!

JOHNNY: (*Big smile, holding his breath.*) Yeah.

SANCHO: He also sniffs glue. (*Snap.* JOHNNY *inhales glue, big smile.*)

JOHNNY: Tha's too much man, ese.

SECRETARY: No, Mr. Sancho, I dont' think this …

SANCHO: Wait a minute, he has other qualities I know you'll love. For example, an inferiority complex. (*Snap.*)

JOHNNY: (*To* SANCHO.) You think you're better than me, huh, ese? (*Swings switchblade.*)

SANCHO: He can also be beaten and he bruises. Cut him and he bleeds, kick him and he … (*He beats, bruises and kicks PACHUCO.*) Would you like to try it?

247

SECRETARY: Oh, I couldn't.

SANCHO: Be my guest. He's a great scape goat.

SECRETARY: No really.

SANCHO: Please.

SECRETARY: Well, all right. Just once. (*She kicks* PACHUCO.) Oh, he's so soft.

SANCHO: Wasn't that good? Try again.

SECRETARY: (*Kicks* PACHUCO.) Oh, he's so wonderful! (*She kicks him again.*)

SANCHO: Okay, that's enough, lady. You'll ruin the merchandise. Yes, our Johnny Pachuco model can give you many hours of pleasure. Why, the LAPD just bought 20 of these to train their rookie cops on. And talk about maintenance. Señorita, you are looking at an entirely selfsupporting machine. You're never going to find our Johnny Pachuco model on the relief rolls.

No, sir, this model knows how to liberate.

SECRETARY: Liberate?

SANCHO: He steals. (*Snap.* JOHNNY *rushes to* SECRETARY *and steals her purse.*)

JOHNNY: ¡Dame esa bolsa, vieja! (*He grabs the purse and runs. Snap by* SANCHO, *he stops.*

SECRETARY *runs after* JOHNNY *and grabs purse away from him, kicking him as she goes.*)

SECRETARY: No, no, no! We can't have any more thieves in the State Administration. Put him back.

SANCHO: Okay, we still got other models. Come on, Johnny, we'll sell you to some old lady.

(SANCHO *takes* JOHNNY *back to his place.*)

SECRETARY: Mr. Sancho, I don't think you quite understand what we need. What we need is something that will attract the women voters. Something more traditional, more romantic.

SANCHO: Ah, a lover. (*He smiles meaningfully.*) Step right over here, señorita. Introducing our
standard Revolucionario and/or Early California Bandit type. As you can see, he is well-built,
sturdy, durable. This is the International Harvester of Mexicans.

SECRETARY: What does he do?

SANCHO: You name it, he does it. He rides horses, stays in the mountains, crosses deserts,
plains, rivers, leads revolutions, follows revolutions, kills, can be killed, serves as a martyr, hero,
movie star. Did I say movie star? Did you ever see *Viva Zapata*? *Viva Villa, Villa Rides, Pancho
Villa Returns, Pancho Villa Goes Back, Pancho Villa Meets Abbott and Costello*?

SECRETARY: I've never seen any of those.

SANCHO: Well, he was in all of them. Listen to this. (*Snap.*)

REVOLUCIONARIO: (*Scream.*) ¡Viva Villaaaaa!

SECRETARY: That's awfully loud.

SANCHO: He has a volume control. (*He adjusts volume. Snap.*)

REVOLUCIONARIO: (*Mousey voice.*) Viva Villa.

SECRETARY: That's better.

SANCHO: And even if you didn't see him in the movies, perhaps you saw him on TV. He makes
commercials. (*Snap.*)

REVOLUCIONARIO: Is there a Frito Bandito in your house?

SECRETARY: Oh yes, I've seen that one!

SANCHO: Another feature about this one is that he is economical. He runs on raw horsemeat
and tequila!

SECRETARY: Isn't that rather savage?

SANCHO: Al contrario, it makes him a lover. (*Snap.*)

REVOLUCIONARIO: (*To* SECRETARY.) Ay, mamasota, cochota, ven pa 'ca! (*He grabs*
SECRETARY *and folds her back, Latin-lover style.*)
SANCHO: (*Snap.* REVOLUCIONARIO *goes back upright.*) Now wasn't that nice?
SECRETARY: Well, it was rather nice.
SANCHO: And finally, there is one outstanding feature about this model I know the ladies are
going to love: he's a genuine antique! He was made in Mexico in 1910!
SECRETARY: Made in Mexico?
SANCHO: That's right. Once in Tijuana, twice in Guadalajara, three times in Cuernavaca.
SECRETARY: Mr. Sancho, I thought he was an American product.
SANCHO: No, but …
SECRETARY: No, I'm sorry. We can't buy anything but American made products. He just
won't do.
SANCHO: But he's an antique!
SECRETARY: I don't care. You still don't understand what we need. It's true we need Mexican
models, such as these, but it's more important that he be American.
SANCHO: American?
SECRETARY: That's right, and judging from what you've shown me, I don't think you have what
we want. Well, my lunch hour's almost over, I better …
SANCHO: Wait a minute! Mexican but American?
SECRETARY: That's correct.
SANCHO: Mexican but … (*A sudden flash.*) American! Yeah, I think we've got exactly what you
want. He just came in today! Give me a minute. (*He exits. Talks from backstage.*) Here he is in
the shop. Let me just get some papers off. There. Introducing our new 1970 Mexican-American!

250

Ta-ra-ra-raaaa! (SANCHO *brings out the* MEXICAN-AMERICAN *model, a clean-shaven middle class type in a business suit, with glasses.*)

SECRETARY: (*Impressed.*) Where have you been hiding this one?

SANCHO: He just came in this morning. Ain't he a beauty? Feast you eyes on him! Sturdy U.S. Steel frame, streamlined, modern. As a matter of fact, he is built exactly like our Anglo models, except that he comes in a variety of darker shades: naugahide, leather or leatherette.

SECRETARY: Naugahide.

SANCHO: Well, we'll just write that down. Yes, señorita, this model represents the apex of American engineering! He is bilingual, college educated, ambitious! Say the word "acculturate" and he accelerates. He is intelligent, well-mannered, clean. Did I say clean? (*Snap.* MEXICANAMERICAN *raises his arm.*) Smell.

SECRETARY: (*Smells.*) Old Sobaco, my favorite.

SANCHO: (*Snap.* MEXICAN-AMERICAN *turns toward* SANCHO.) Eric? (*To* SECRETARY.) We call him Eric García. (*To* ERIC.) I want you to meet Miss JIM-enez, Eric.

MEXICAN-AMERICAN: Miss JIM-enez, I am delighted to make your acquaintance. (*He kisses her hand.*)

SECRETARY: Oh, my, how charming!

SANCHO: Did you feel the suction? He has seven especially engineered suction cups right behind his lips. He's a charmer all right!

SECRETARY: How about boards, does he function on boards?

SANCHO: You name them, he is on them. Parole boards, draft boards, school boards, taco quality control boards, surf boards, two by fours.

SECRETARY: Does he function in politics?

SANCHO: Señorita, you are looking at a political machine. Have you ever heard of the OEO, EOC, COD, WAR ON POVERTY? That's our model! Not only that, he makes political speeches.

SECRETARY: May I hear one?

SANCHO: With pleasure. (*Snap.*) Eric, give us a speech.

MEXICAN-AMERICAN: Mr. Congressman, Mr. Chairman, members of the board, honored guests, ladies and gentlemen. (SANCHO *and* SECRETARY *applaud.*) Please, please. I come before you as a Mexican-American to tell you about the problems of the Mexican. The problems of the Mexican stem from one thing and one thing only: he's stupid. He's uneducated. He needs to stay in school. He needs to be ambitious, foward-looking, harder-working. He needs to think American, American, American, American, American! God bless America! God bless America! God bless America! (*He goes out of control. SANCHO snaps frantically and the* MEXICAN-AMERICAN *finally slumps forward, bending at the waist.*)

SECRETARY: Oh my, he's patriotic too!

SANCHO: Sí, señorita, he loves his country. Let me just make a little adjustment here. (*Stands* MEXICAN-AMERICAN *up.*)

SECRETARY: What about upkeep? Is he economical?

SANCHO: Well, no, I won't lie to you. The Mexican-American costs a little bit more, but you get what you pay for. He's worth every extra cent. You can keep him running on dry Martinis, Langendorf bread …

SECRETARY: Apple pie?

SANCHO: Only Mom's. Of course, he's also programmed to eat Mexican food at ceremonial functions, but I must warn you, an overdose of beans will plug up his exhaust.

SECRETARY: Fine! There's just one more question. How much do you want for him?

SANCHO: Well, I tell you what I'm gonna do. Today and today only, because you've been so

sweet, I'm gonna let you steal this model from me! I'm gonna let you drive him off the lot for

the simple price of, let's see, taxes and license included, $15,000.

SECRETARY: Fifteen thousand dollars? For a Mexican!!!!

SANCHO: Mexican? What are you talking about? This is a Mexican-American! We had to melt

down two pachucos, a farmworker and three gabachos to make this model! You want quality, but

you gotta pay for it! This is no cheap run-about. He's got class!

SECRETARY: Okay, I'll take him.

SANCHO: You will?

SECRETARY: Here's your money.

SANCHO: You mind if I count it?

SECRETARY: Go right ahead.

SANCHO: Well, you'll get your pink slip in the mail. Oh, do you want me to wrap him up for up?

We have a box in the back.

SECRETARY: No, thank you. The Governor is having a luncheon this afternoon, and we need a

brown face in the crowd. How do I drive him?

SANCHO: Just snap your fingers. He'll do anything you want. (SECRETARY *snaps*. MEXICANAMERICAN *steps forward*.)

MEXICAN-AMERICAN: ¡Raza querida, vamos levantando armas para liberarnos de estos desgraciados gabachos que nos explotan! Vamos …

SECRETARY: What did he say?

SANCHO: Something about taking up arms, killing white people, etc.

SECRETARY: But he's not supposed to say that!

SANCHO: Look, lady, don't blame me for bugs from the factory. He's your Mexican-American,
you bought him, now drive him off the lot!

SECRETARY: But he's broken!

SANCHO: Try snapping another finger. (SECRETARY *snaps.* MEXICAN-AMERICAN *comes to life again.*)

MEXICAN-AMERICAN: Esta gran humanidad ha dicho basta! ¡Y se ha puesto en marcha! ¡Basta! ¡Basta! ¡Viva la raza! ¡Viva la causa! ¡Viva la huelga! ¡Vivan los brown berets! ¡Vivan los estudiantes! ¡Chicano power!(*The* MEXICAN-AMERICAN *turns toward the* SECRETARY, *who gasps and backs up. He keeps turning toward the* PACHUCO, FARMWORKER *and* REVOLUCIONARIO, *snapping his fingers and turning each of them on, one by one.*)

PACHUCO: (*Snap. To* SECRETARY.) I'm going to get you, baby! ¡Viva la raza!

FARMWORKER: (*Snap. to* SECRETARY.) ¡Viva la huelga! ¡Viva la ¡huelga! ¡Viva la huelga!

REVOLUCIONARIO: (*Snap. To* SECRETARY.) ¡Viva la revolución! (*The three models join together and advance toward the* SECRETARY, *who backs up and runs out of the shop screaming.* SANCHO *is at the other end of the shop holding his money in his hand. All freeze. After a few seconds of silence, the* PACHUCO *moves and stretches, shaking his arms and loosening up. The* FARMWORKER *and* REVOLUCIONARIO *do the same.* SANCHO *stays where he is, frozen to his spot.*)

JOHNNY: Man, that was a long one, ese. (*Others agree with him.*)

FARMWORKER: How did we do?

JOHNYY: Pretty good, look at all that lana, man! (*He goes over to* SANCHO *and removes the money from his hand.* SANCHO *stays where he is.*)

REVOLUCIONARIO: En la madre, look at all the money.

JOHNNY: We keep this up, we're going to be rich.

FARMWORKER: They think we're machines.

REVOLUCIONARIO: Burros.

JOHNNY: Puppets.

MEXICAN-AMERICAN: The only thing I don't like is how come I always get to play the goddamn Mexican-American?

JOHNNY: That's what you get for finishing high school.

FARMWORKER: How about our wages, ese?

JOHNNY: Here it comes right now. $3,000 for you, $3,000 for you, $3,000 for you and $3,000 for me. The rest we put back into the business.

MEXICAN-AMERICAN: Too much, man. Heh, where you vatos going tonight?

FARMWORKER: I'm going over to Concha's. There's a party.

JOHNNY: Wait a minute, vatos. What about our salesman? I think he needs an oil job.

REVOLUCIONARIO: Leave him to me. (*The* PACHUCO, FARMWORKER *and* MEXICANAMERICAN *exit, talking loudly about their plans for the night. The* REVOLUCIONARIO *goes over to* SANCHO, *removes his derby hat and cigar, lifts him up and throws him over his shoulder.* SANCHO *hangs loose, lifeless. To audience.*) He's the best model we got! ¡Ajúa!

(*Exit.*)

TRAGEDY

noun trag·e·dy \ˈtra-jə-dē\
: a very bad <u>event</u> that causes great sadness and often involves someone's death: a very sad, unfortunate, or upsetting situation : something that causes strong feelings of sadness or regret : a serious drama typically describing a conflict between the protagonist and a superior force (as destiny) and having a sorrowful or disastrous conclusion that elicits pity or terror
b : the literary genre of <u>tragic</u> dramas

In literature, the concept of tragedy refer to a series of unfortunate events by which one or more of the literary characters in the story undergo several misfortunes, which finally culminate into a disaster of 'epic proportions'. Tragedy is generally built up in 5 stages: a) happy times b) the introduction of a problem c) the problem worsens to a crisis or dilemma d) the characters are unable to prevent the problem from taking over e) the problem results in some catastrophic, grave ending, which is the tragedy culminated.
In literary terms, tragedy is a form of drama in which there is a display of human suffering and often <u>catharsis</u> for the audience. Tragedy, as we know it in Western culture, has its foundation in ancient Greece about 2,500 years ago. It has evolved over the millennia and had an important role in many different cultures and eras, such as in the time of the Roman Republic, in Elizabethan England, and including up until the present day.

Modern theories of Tragedy: Most modern theorists build upon the Aristotelian notions of tragedy. Two examples are the Victorian critic A.C. Bradley (*Shakespearean Tragedy*, 1904) and Northrop Frye (*The Anatomy of Criticism*, 1957). Keep these theories in mind as you read; consider whether and how they are helpful in understanding Shakespeare's work.

- **A. C. Bradley** divides tragedy into an *exposition* of the state of affairs; the beginning, growth, and vicissitudes of the *conflict*; and the final *catastrophe* or tragic outcome. Bradley emphasizes the Aristotelian notion of the *tragic flaw*: the tragic hero errs by action or omission; this error joins with other causes to bring about his ruin. According to Bradley, "This is always so with Shakespeare. The idea of the tragic hero as a being destroyed simply and solely by external forces is quite alien to him; and not less so is the idea of the hero as contributing to his destruction only by acts in which we see no flaw." Bradley's emphasis on the tragic flaw implies that Shakespeare's characters bring their fates upon themselves and thus, in a sense, deserve what they get. It should however be noted that in some of Shakespeare's plays (e.g. *King Lear*), the tragedy lies less in the fact that the characters "deserve" their fates than in how much more they suffer than their actions (or flaws) suggest they should.

- **Northrop Frye** distinguishes five stages of action in tragedy: **1)** *Encroachment.* Protagonist takes on too much, makes a mistake that causes his/her "fall." This mistake is often unconscious (an act blindly done, through over-confidence in one's ability to regulate the world or through insensitivity to others) but still violates the norms of human conduct. **2)** *Complication.* The building up of events aligning opposing forces that will lead inexorably to the tragic conclusion. "Just as comedy often sets up an arbitrary law and then organizes the action to break or evade it, so tragedy presents the reverse theme of narrowing a comparatively free life into

258

a process of causation." **3) *Reversal*.** The point at which it becomes clear that the hero's expectations are mistaken, that his fate will be the reverse of what he had hoped. At this moment, the vision of the dramatist and the audience are the same. The classic example is Oedipus, who seeks the knowledge that proves him guilty of murdering his father and marrying his mother; when he accomplishes his objective, he realizes he has destroyed himself in the process. **4) *Catastrophe*.** The catastrophe exposes the limits of the hero's power and dramatizes the waste of his life. Piles of dead bodies remind us that the forces unleashed are not easily contained; there are also elaborate subplots (e.g. Gloucester in *King Lear*) which reinforce the impression of a world inundated with evil. **5) *Recognition*.** The audience (sometimes the hero as well) recognizes the larger pattern. If the hero does experience recognition, he assumes the vision of his life held by the dramatist and the audience. From this new perspective he can see the irony of his actions, adding to the poignancy of the tragic events.

POEM FOR SOME WOMEN
Sonia Sanchez

Huh,
I'm alright.
I say, I'm alright.
What you looking at?
I say, I'm alright.
doing okay,
I-I-I'm still writing, producing
on the radio.
Who I foolin?
I'm a little ill.
Now I just got a little jones,
Jones, jones, habit, habit.

Took my seven-year-old to the crack house with me on
Thursday.
beautiful little girl,
prettiest little girl her mama done ever seen.
Took her so she understands
why I late sometimes
with her breakfast, dinner, bedtime
needings, bedtime love.
Wanted her to know how hard it is for me.
You know, a single woman,
out here on her own.

You know, so I took her to the crack house
where this man, this dog, this former friend of mine lived.
Wouldn't give me no crack,
no action.
Even when I offered my thighs
to give him some again for the umpteenth time,

260

he said no.
All the while,
looking at my baby,
my pretty little baby.
And he said,
"I want her. I need a virgin.
Yo' pussy's too loose.
You had so much traffic up your pussy,
you could park a truck up there
and still have room for something else."
And he laughed,
this loooonnng laugh.
And I looked at him
and the stuff he was holding in his hand.
You know, I couldn't remember my baby's name.
He held out the stuff to me,
and I couldn't remember her birthday.
I couldn't remember my daughter's face.
And I cried as I walked out that door.
What's her name?
Pudd'n'Tang.
Ask me again,
I'll tell you the same thing.
Couldn't even hear her screaming my name,
as he tore into her pretty little panties.
Prettiest girl you done ever seen.
Prettiest little mama's baby you done ever seen.

Bought my baby this pretty little leather jacket off the
street.
When I went to pick her up on Sunday,
seven days later,
walked right up to the house,
opened the door,
saw her sitting on the floor.
She said,

"Mama! Where you been? Mama, I called for you.
Mama! Mama! Mama! Mama!
They hurt me something bad.
I wanna go home!
Mamaaaa!"

Mama's little baby
loves shortening, shortening.
Mama's little baby loves shortening bread.
Put on the jacket.
Put on the jacket.
Mama's little baby loves shortening bread.

When we got home
she wouldn't talk to me.
She just sat and stared,
wouldn't even watch the TV
when I turned it on.
When we got home,
She just stared at me with her eyes,
dog-like,
just sat and looked at me with her eyes
'til I had to get out of there.

You know,
my baby ran away from home last week.
My sweet little shortening bread
ran away from home last night.
And I dreamed she was dead,
dreamed she was surrounded by panthers
who tossed her back and forth,
nibbling and biting,
and tearing her up.
My little shortening bread
ran away from home last week.

Peek-a-boo.
Peek-a-boo.
Peek-a-boo.
I see you
and you
and you
and yoooou.

I Can't Read
Lamont Carey

I'm eleven years old in the sixth grade and I can't read.
The class is so full that the teacher doesn't notice me but I
can't read. And when she finally asks me to come to the
head of the class,I do everything in my power to make the
class laugh. What would you do if you knew that they all
would laugh at you.

But I can't read and I can't write and I can't spell and most
of the time,I don't know my left from my right

but they keep on passing me
because I can dribble a ball and I can hit a three pointer
y'all and I am guaranteed to get you 13 points.

But I can't read and I can't right, I can't spell most of the
time I don't know my left form my right.

The teachers aid says it's the teachers fault and the
teacher says it's the board of education and the board of
education says its my parents fault and y'all my parents
blame me.

But I still can't read, I can't write and most of the time
 I don't know my left from my right.

But on the biggest game of the year,I was coming down
the lane and I was doing my thing when number 13
crashed into me. At the same time that I heard
my knee snap, I heard my family dream shatter.
See, they depended on me to get us out of the ghetto,

so when I hit the ground I did everything in my power not to frown. But it was just to much pain and ran straight to my brain and the last thing I remember is the doctor saying that I would never run again.
So now I'm asking y'all what are my options,

I can't read.

FINAL MATCH
Lindsay Shorters

As blood trickled down the side of my face, I could taste my salted tears. I could feel my heart fighting to maintain a steady, controlled beat. My body was so heavy, I felt like I had lived a thousand lives that had led to this very point. I began to take deeper breaths, and I could feel the rage building inside as I watched this slyly, murderous man sit on *my* couch like he hadn't done anything. I could see my little brother's dead body on the floor not too far from me. His body was tangled up like a lifeless rag doll. His legs were intertwined, and his arm hung from its socket. Around his body was the eeriest lake I had seen my entire life. *Lake Blood.* When I looked down at my ripped clothing and exposed body, my chest began to pump air like a mad man. It was like I could feel my eyes turning red, and the personification of anger, hatred, rage, humiliation, despair, and every other terrible word you could think of -- rose up inside me. My eyes shot around the room like fiery darts in an attempt to look for a weapon. As I cautiously stood up, my mind was slow, but my thoughts were clear.

"My brother should not have died like this; and I refuse to die, while these filthy scum bags get to live. They might have won round one, but I'm going to win the final match."

***

As she shimmied out of her red Jessica Rabbit evening gown and heels, Laci remembered the vow she took almost seven years ago. Lately, she had been dreaming about Jacen, her little brother who was murdered by robbers when their home was invaded. The men who

266

broke into the house, the perps, were never found. Out of all the blood spilled and broken items in her childhood home, the police had not a single fingerprint or blood sample to go on. As she thought back, she couldn't remember Bryan or the other two guys wearing gloves. Eventually the case went cold, and she and her family were forced to move forward with their lives, despite the loss of the youngest member of the family.

Today was Jacen's birthday, and also the day she planned to carry out her mission. Leaving the bedroom area of the hotel, she went to the bathroom sink and began to wipe off the make-up she had worn for the Police Department's Annual Banquet. As she watched water mix with the make-up on the towel, she imagined the mask she had been wearing for two years. She saw it slowly folding and melting down the drain. Quickly refocusing herself, she began to count down the fifteen minutes she had to transform herself from the reserved girlfriend of police chief, Chris Donaldsin, to the real her -- a cold hearted revenge seeker. Standing in front of the hotel's full length mirror, she looked at herself. She was much stronger than the dark haired, teenager who watched her brother die years ago. She was beautiful with mocha skin and long red hair curled to perfection. Picking up a brush, she began to comb out the curls Chris' stylist had spent hours creating. She swooped her hair up into a sleek bun, and applied red lipstick to her lips. Chris hated red lipstick, so she never got to wear it anymore. He despised when other men looked at her. After today, none of that would matter, and she wouldn't have to pretend anymore.

As she stepped into leather tights, her smooth legs slid against the material like she had bathed in baby oil. Next she pulled on a deep red, leather jacket, zipping it up just enough to show a good amount of cleavage. *"This will get to Chris,"* she thought chuckling. The leather hugged her twenty three year old curves, and complimented her body.

As she looked at herself in the mirror, she wondered would it all be worth it. *"It will,"* she confirmed in her head.

Walking away from the mirror, she bent down and grabbed both of her heeled boots to put them on. Laci then retrieved her glock, G19, a lightweight little thing and slipped it into the side of her right boot. She put 9mm bullets in the left compartment of her hoister belt. Then she grabbed her real gun, loaded it while it was in her sling, and threw it over her shoulder. It was go time.

***

Laci stood in one of the old service hallways behind the stage. She had a clear, unobstructed view of Chris, her boyfriend. He was supposed to introduce her before she came on stage to give her presentation to the honoree, Chattanooga's Police Hero. She watched as Chris went on and on about how they met. The complete story he told was a lie, but everyone would know that soon enough.

"Ladies and gentlemen, I now present to you, my girlfriend and future wife, Morgan Chaseey."

Everyone clapped as Laci walked to the stage. Immediately murmuring began. She could hear women making comments about what she wearing, and Chris looked instantly furious. She just gave him a cute smile in return.

"Good evening everyone. I'm glad you all could make it out tonight to honor Bryan Donaldsin, who one day I hope will be my brother-in-law." Laci played her role like a long time pro. Tonight I have a special presentation. I know, on your program it says, "Acrobats and Gun Show," but I think I would like to start with the gun show," she said pulling her AK47 out of its' sling on her back and pointing it directly at Bryan. The crowd went nuts, and people began to run to the exits.

"One quick announcement!" she said over the microphone quickly before anyone got to the exits. "All exits have

268

bombs wired to them, and if you push the door everyone in here will die!" she said in a pleasant, helpful tone. Laci watched as the hysteria grew to another level. Women were crying and screaming, while men looked for ways out other than the doors. The countdown for the door bombs showed all around the room on the projectors.

"Now that you have gotten your screams out, would everyone return to their *assigned seats!* It's very important to stay in your assigned seats!" she said like a mother. "Now calm down! This little tirade is only going to last a little while. So just sit down, be quiet, and watch the presentation I have planned for you."

"Let me check the time real quick...okay we have eighteen minutes left." she said over the microphone that was attached to her cheek. "My name is Laci Swime. Seven years ago today--" she was interrupted by three loud beeps. "Dang it!" she said as a sniper rifle shot a deputy who traded seats with his wife to get closer to the door. Everyone screamed, especially the deputy's wife. Laci's voice rang loud on the microphone.

"I told all of you to remain in *your* seats. Everyone look up to balconies above us please," the crowd gasped. "Up above are sniper rifles pointed at selected people. If you move, the retina scan on the gun will detect you're missing from where you're supposed to be. Three beeps will go off, and you will be shot whereever you are standing or sitting. So please follow my rules! I've only planned for one, maybe two causalities." A deafening silence came over the room.

"Now, as I was saying, seven years ago my childhood home was broken into, and my eight year old brother, Jacen Swime was murdered right before my eyes." Now she had the audience's attention. "Today is his birthday, and I plan to honor him with the unveiling of the truth. Now audience, would you clap as Bryan and my wonderful Chris come to the stage?" she said

269

enthusiastically. No one clapped. "Clap!" she yelled like a roaring lioness. The sound of claps sounded like praises from heaven.

"If you cooperate, we can get out of here before your seventeen minutes are up," she said yelling. Chris and Bryan reached the stage at the same time. "Now audience, these brothers are going to tell you what happened seven years ago, and why I am standing before you."

As she was talking, Bryan whispered to Chris, "All this time, I knew this crazy bitch looked familiar." Laci let her sling catch the AK, and as she pulled a knife from her belt and slammed Bryan's hand on a nearby table, chopping off his pinky finger in front of everyone. Bryan screamed like the little bitch he was. He was louder than the entire crowd.

When she released his four fingered hand, she said, "Get to talking;" poking him in the butt with her AK.

Bryan's eyes were watery red, as he held his hand from the pain and gushing blood. Bryan looked at his older brother as if asking what to do. "I don't know what she wants us to say," Chris said to no one in particular. Laci grabbed Bryan's same hand and chopped off his ring finger. Bryan yelled again, and the crowd tried to remain calm as Bryan's gold banned finger flew across the room.

"You guys are wasting these dear people's time, and I'd hate for the Chattanooga police hero right here, not to be able to hold a gun ever again because he's missing all his fingers. So I'll just tell the story." The projectors switched to a picture of a news article printed about what happened to her family.

"Seven years ago, Bryan and a few of his lowlife friends broke into my house and tried to rob the place. Little did they know, my parents decided not to take the kids on their little weekend getaway." Laci flipped to the next slide, a picture of her parents at a vacation resort miles away from Chattanooga.

"My older sister, Milyn had just left the house to go on a nightcap date with a boy from her school. Bryan, here, and his flunkies ransacked my entire house, while Jacen and I were hiding upstairs. After a little time had passed, I figured I should try to get my cell phone to call one of the wonderful policemen in this room today. Only, when I got to cell phone, Bryan's friend found me, and boy did they mess me up." She showed a picture of herself after the attack. She looked worse than Rihanna did after the Chris Brown brawl.

Next she showed pictures of her little brother's body tangled up and lifeless on her old living room floor. The women began weeping and covering their eyes, as husbands tried to comfort them and whisper that "Morgan" had gone crazy.

"The Chattanooga hero and his friends demanded to know where our family safe was, but at first I didn't tell them....that is, until they started hurting my brother. Even after they got the combination to the safe, they shot my brother just as he mouthed he loved me." People were vocally outraged.

Some were saying, "This all is a lie! Bryan wouldn't do that," and "She's crazyyy!" Others were saying "Poor woman," and "How could we let this happen?"

Next Laci put up the police report, and the findings from her rape kit. "These are both images of the police reports that mysteriously were never filed or just disappeared....right Chris?" she said looking into his eyes. He looked physically sick. *He should be,* she thought to herself.

"After I was brutally raped and left for dead, a neighbor found me. Well at least that's what my parents told me after I woke up from five emergency surgeries." Laci began to choke up a bit, but had to quickly pull it together if she was going to complete her mission.

"During that same year, my father died of a stroke. He couldn't get over what had happened to his family." She showed a picture of his obituary. "He blamed himself for the entire ordeal. But it was not his fault." It was so quiet in the room you could hear clocks on the wall ticking.

"Yeah, I know. Sad story, but it gets better. Two years ago I met a wonderful man," she said with a smirk and condescending tone. He gave me access to everything I needed. At the time, I didn't know he was Bryan's brother; I just needed a way to get into the police records easily without being detected. Soon enough, I put two and two together. The reason my family's case was closed was because there was no resounding evidence. No blood, fingerprints, or witnesses." Everyone was staring at Chris now. They had nine minutes till they met their demise.

"Oh wait, a minute," Laci acted like she forgot something, but everything was planned down to the last detail. "I forgot to tell you how Chris and I really first met."

"One night I was leaving a college party in Red Bank, and I met Mr. Police Chief, here," she said pulling her G-19 out of her boot and placing it to Chris' temple. "Mr. Police Chief was pushing some drunk girl out of the backseat of his squad car, when I asked him for a ride." He was definitely drunk while I played the role, and told him I always wanted to ride in the backseat of a police car. So he opened the back door and gave me what he thought was the ride of my life." Laci put up pictures of herself and Chris in the backseat of the police car two years ago. The crowd was so outraged, she had to yell for everyone to be quiet.

"Alright! Alright! I know all of this sounds crazy, but it's true," she said motioning to the nearest projector. Chris tried to quickly tackle her to ground, but she shot him in the knee just as he got his arms around her.

"Did I mention that I went and got trained in defense and weaponry to help me get over the rape?" She asked no one in particular with a smirk returning to her face. The crowd was back screaming. Someone off to the side was yelling, "Jesus help us all! Please God!" God had helped Laci through the pain, but he sure hadn't touched the revenge bones in her body.

With just six minutes left on the clock, the second to last slide on the projector was Chris, Bryan, and Laci from last Thanksgiving. "I infiltrated this entire police department easier than an ant entering a new ant hill. Women, I hope you feel safe, because your husbands clearly aren't doing their jobs. Hopefully when one of your daughters gets raped, they'll bring you some justice....or when your son or brother is murdered, they'll commit to finding the killer. So in conclusion, I'd like to hear from this little piggy," she said pointing at Chris. "--And from Chattanooga's Hero... Side note, don't you just hate that little phrase?" she said leaning forward whispering to the audience like they were her girlfriends.

Chris tried to stand up, but fell yelling in pain as he tried to apply pressure to his knee. A woman close to him got up without thinking to give him her napkin, and the beeping noise returned. She was shot dead. "Just when we were almost done, Mary-Beth," Laci said whining sadly, but sarcastically. People were back in their hysteria. I guess the death of Mary-Beth, a sweet, innocent bystander was just too much. Mary-Beth's husband slammed his head on the table and sobbed loudly. Laci felt for him....but not enough to stop all that she was doing. "As I said in the beginning, today is not supposed to be a day of death, but a day of honoring. Honoring the truth about my brother, Jacen Swime. So Chris and Bryan, it's time to admit your crimes. Sheriffs Jeffries and Thomas, I would like for you to cuff them now, please. Both Sheriffs looked at each other. There was no way they were getting up after what just happened to Mary-Beth.

"Don't worry guys, I don't have the rifles set to track you. I know you're the actual good guys. Your wives will be safe too. Just come forward. The men reluctantly got up and cuffed both guys. Luckily Laci had told the truth and they were not shot on the spot.

"Have you all even wondered why the police department threw this event?" Laci said as if she were having a cool conversation amongst friends, and not hostages. "I got with the wives and told them we should starting honoring our men for the work they do; and the retired police chief's wife gave me the green light! So I nominated Bryan!" Laci said starting to laugh like a crazy person. "I chose this venue, because they had balconies for my guns! I made everyone check-in, in front of the glass window to verify your retina scans I got when I personally delivered your invitations." Laci's eyes were turning red as she laughed more. "I even made you all check in your guns, weapons, and walkie-talkies!" Laci's smile was starting scare everyone and panic began to bubble in their stomachs.

"Okay enough about me," she said straightening up and pulling herself together. She smoothed her leather, bullet proof jacket and said, "Bryan you have the floor. We have three minutes till the building blows."

Bryan was reluctant. He wasn't so sure Laci or Morgan, or whatever her name was, had actually set up the bomb like she said. Bryan refused to say anything, and was willing to let everyone die. He just starred at the ground. Chris even pleaded with him to speak. "Just say something man. None of us believe her anyway." Chris was an actor too, seeing as he was the one who covered for Bryan.

"Oh Bryan," Laci said singing his name in a playful tone. "I've already taken care of Milton and Sam. I saved the best for last!"

With the sound of his old buddies' names, his head shot up. *This bitch isn't playing, he thought.*

"Well let's give Chris a chance," Laci said. She could hear faint sirens. She had left one walkie talkie on one of the guys on purpose. She wanted the boys from out of town to come. "We have three minutes....Chris, either you did it or you didn't."

"I covered up the Swime murder and break in," he said. The people were getting restless and antsy, because the last slide was the timer with a picture of Jacen and a building he made out of cardboard for a science project. Men started yelling at Bryan.

"Tell the truth man!"

"Tell her what she wants to hear!"

"You're going to make us all die cuz you're a coward?"

"Fuck you, Bryan!" All these words were running together in loud chants."Last chance Bryan," Laci said putting the gun to his brother's head. Chris pleaded for him to speak and he wouldn't. Laci shot Chris in the head and he died instantly. The clock read two and a half minutes. Women and men alike were yelling and screaming. They would've probably attacked him if they could leave their seats.

"Fuck it." Laci pistol whipped Bryan and he fell to the floor. She pulled a remote from her pocket and turned off the sniper guns. The guns all rang with beeps. "Exit through the far door on the left! It is the only one that isn't bomb wired!" The people ran for their lives leaving Bryan alone with her.

"Stand up, you filthy bitch!" Bryan slowly rose. "I told you I would win the final match! You are no hero! I am the hero of this story!" She shot him once in the chest. She could hear the SWAT Teams entering the room. She shot him again and again. Then she unloaded all the bullets she had on him. She took her AK-47 and shot him some more. Just as she felt a bullet collide with her own head, she looked up at her brother's smiling face and mouthed, "I love you."

As far as she was concerned, she won the final match.

SATIRE

Satire *noun* sat·ire \'sa-ˌtī(-ə)r\: a way of using humor to show that someone or something is foolish, weak, bad, etc. : humor that shows the weaknesses or bad qualities of a person, government, society, etc.: a literary work holding up human vices and follies to ridicule or scorn: trenchant wit, irony, or sarcasm used to expose and discredit vice or folly

Humor is a literary tool that makes audiences laugh, or that intends to induce amusement or laughter. Its purpose is to break the monotony, boredom and tedium, and make the audience's nerves relaxed. The use of satire in literature refers to the practice of making fun of a human weakness or character flaw. The use of satire is often inclusive of a need or decision of correcting or bettering the character that is on the receiving end of the satire. In general, even though satire might be humorous and may "make fun," its purpose is not to entertain and amuse but actually to derive a reaction of contempt from the reader.

if there is anyone
in the audience
in the entertainment industry
watching me perform,
I want you to keep in mind
that if you are casting any films
and need a Korean grocery store owner,
a computer expert or the random thug
of a yakuza gang,
i'm your man.
if you're making Jackie Chan
knock-off films
and need a stunt double,
that stunt double is me.
if you need a Chinese jay-z,
a Japanese eminem,
or a Vietnamese backstreet boy,
please consider me,
because I am all those things and more.
i come from the house that
step n' fetchit built
and i will broken English my way
to sidekick status
if that's what's expected of me
make an Asian different strokes.
i'll walk around on my knees yelling,
ahso, what you talk about wirris?!
because it's been 23 months and 14 days

since my art has done anything for me,
and i would be noble and toil on,
i swear i would.
live for the art and the art alone,
and all that crapass.
but college loans are monthly up my ass,
my salmon teriyaki habit is getting way out of control,
and i want some
motherfucking cable!
so you can understand where i'm coming from.
when tight verse
exhibiting dynamics
within the text
falls by the wayside
rejoice in its
pretty, packaged, boygroup,
talentless twats
sent from florida
to make me puke
but i'm not preaching. none siree, boss.
i cannot stress how ready i am
to sell out,
wear jiggy clothes,
and yell from the top of my lungs
any hook i am told to sing.
if you want the caricature
of a caricature,
then i am that caricature.
if you want an exotic dragon lady
like lucy liu,
who fucks like a kama sutra
come to life,
just tell my ass where ya want it,

and i will bend over.
if you need a voice-over artist,
just tell me
where you want the,
hi-ya's! to go
and i will be there,
because i am all that more,
i am a pop culture whore,
i am a co-sponsored world tour,
an i am
an appropriated culture at my core.
i've been noticed, acclaimed, and funny
and now all i want
is a beach front house to paint in
and a range rover
to listen to my music in,
cuz struggling fucking sucks hard
after the ninth package of ramen noodle soup.
i'm beau sia.
give me a chance,
and i'll
change the world.

STANK BREATH
Helena D. Lewis

Imagine the worst smell you ever smelled
multiply that by 10
Homeboy's breath was so bad
I could smell it through his cheeks.
The odor singed my nose hairs
and cleared my nasal passages of mucus.
I was in a no-win situation.
He did purchase one of my CDs
But how do you tell someone you barely know
their breath has more kicks than
Crouching Tiger Hidden Dragon.
In an effort to be kind,
instead of speaking my mind,
I offered him a stick of gum
and he declined.
Oblivious to the fact that his breath combined with a
match can set the whole world on fire.

Okay, so I cut the conversation short,
pretending that someone across the room was calling
me, thinking he would catch the hint
and let a sista be.
But he didn't.
He followed me across the room,
like a predator after prey,
like a fat man after a sandwich,
like R. Kelly after a 12 year old.
Asking me,
asking me questions about my poetry,
the motivation for my free verse,
how often did I rehearse

and he kept using words that began with the letter 'H'
like, 'Hey...'
And then,
and then it happened.

Something so hideous,
it would make the devil say, 'Mama.'
A stray piece of spit torpedoed from his mouth
and landed on my forehead
and I'm not talking about a little piece of spit
I'm talking about a piece of spit so big
I actually saw it coming.
But for some strange reason
I could not move.
If only I had rented the movie Matrix one more time,
then maybe I could have dodged it.
And that was the straw that broke this poet's back.

Well, I had to say what I was thinking.
I, I had to say what I was feeling.
I had to say, 'Colgate,
Ultra Brite,
Aim,
Liquid Plumber,
Tide with Bleach my brotha.
Don't you know, brushing your teeth 3 times a day,
combined with flossing,
gargling,
regular visits to your dentist,
and prescription tictacs can help you.
Please
give
tartar control a try,
and take this stick of gum.
Get the Fuck! Out! Of! My! Face!

PALE KID
Morgan Dwyer

I'm a pale kid, I talk fast,
 Never been arrested, but I used to cut class,
 Always smoking chronic, speaking in ebonics,
And I'm really, really, really, really, really good at rap.

Yeah, okay, I'm white, but I can still rap!
I sold weed once, that counts as "the trap."
I can say funny words with misogynistic twists,
Like, "A tisket, a tasket, my dick is in yo ass, bitch!" 'Cause
that's all I can see hiphop to be,
What's the big deal? This shit seems easy,
I can relate to black music, dawg, for sheezy,
I mean, I never struggled, but I listened to Jeezy.
          ...once. It was dope.

I'm a pale kid, I talk fast,
Never been arrested, but I used to cut class,
Always smoking chronic, speaking in ebonics,
And I'm really, really, really, really, really good at rap.

Man, white rappers sure get a bad rep.
I can adlib (HANH), I can twostep,
And if I ever end up winning that hiphop Grammy,
I'll just apologize to Kendrick and post it on the 'Gram, G.
So I could spend my whole life tryna get signed with Jigga,
And shoot a music video with finger on the trigger,
Reach a lot of white kids, keep blowing up bigger,
When all I really want is for Kanye to say, "That's my n -
new friend, he's really good at rap."

 I'm a pale kid, I talk fast,

282

Never been arrested, but I used to cut class,
Always smoking chronic, speaking in ebonics, And I'm
really, really, really, really, really good at rap.

A SPECIAL THANK YOU...
Tracy Walton

First off, I'd like to thank those who "protect & serve"
For being a wonderful example of those 2 verbs
Protecting eachother, upholding their code
Serving the law as they oversee the road
And you can tell they just love serving the community
That sinister smile & flash of the badge is a warning that
reads "Diplomatic Immunity"
And don't you just love the way they deal with people
Talkin with their hand on their gun as if to say "I will kill
you"
And to the minorities, trust me, they don't mean any harm
It's just that most of you boys look armed
With ya hat brims low & ya tatted up arms
It'd be ludicrous not to sound the alarms
And if you don't pay those fines you will be charged
"But sir I was in class I couldn't move my car"
Question you & me to the 3rd degree
But the rapist down the street?
They let him flee
Quick to place an innocent man at the scene of the crime
But tell us "wrong guy" after they shot my godbrother
numerous times
Oh well, just add it to the mountain of lies
& then let's add that to the mountain of lines
They inhale, once they take em off the streets
Just to put it in a different bag & re-sell

Such great fellows
They love to say hello
Right before they pass by your cell & bellow
Right or wrong, straight or curved
Your demise will incur
Special thanks to those who protect & serve…

WAR OF THE WALKER
Leah Harr

Just another day in Monoville, Iowa. The minivans cruised by. The rows of identical houses, with their green lawns and golden retrievers glistened in the afternoon sun. The Frisbees soared across the neighbor's fences, smoke furled into the blue sky from the backyard barbeques. The world was at peace. But it was all too perfect, the patties on the grill were just too primely sizzled, the blades of green grass were too freshly trimmed, the polo shirts were too exquisitely tucked into the khaki shorts. *Something* must be wrong. Suddenly, there came a scream; it could be heard from at least a house and a half down. Jason, who happened to only be a flight of stairs away, heard it perfectly.

"Mom! Mom! Is everything alright?!" He called as he ran down the stairs and into the kitchen.

"Does it *look* like everything is alright?!" His mother sobbed from the floor where she was crumpled. Laying beside her was a pile of broken glass and macaroni salad. One oven mitt was across the room, the other was barely keeping its place as she flailed in despair.

"Barbara what-" Jason's father ran through the backdoor and stopped upon seeing the scene. "Honey.... Oh.... Oh no! Not the macaroni salad! Ron and his family will be here in a half an hour! Please don't tell me we have to have potato salad *again* god damn it. I HAD ONE REQUEST. Please, please let us not have potato salad as a side dish. Do you know how that makes me look at the office? I CANNOT BE THE POTATO SALAD GUY, BARBARA."

"Dad! Calm down! Look, I'm sure we can work something out," Jason interjected, "Ill run to the store and grab some of that premade stuff, or something." His father paced, looked up at the clock, then rubbed his chin.

"That might be our only option at this point... Quick go now, Barbara, pull yourself together. This isn't damn Target on a Black Friday, no need for the hysteria." His father said.

From the floor, Jason's mother sniffed, "it won't be the same as my famous- "

"We all know you buy it pre made, damn it!" Jason grabbed the keys and left, before he got dragged into this fiasco any further.

***

Jason pulled into the lot at Big Savings Food Depot. As he walked towards the store he heard a feeble cry. "Hello... Young man! Hey! Young man!" He turned around confused, and saw a little old woman with a walker tugging on his sleeve. "Do you mind sparing a moment, and some dollars, on the local Senior Citizens in Desperate Need of Funds Organization?"

"Oh, um, I'm kind of in a hurry-" He began to reply, before he was cut off.

"Did you hear anything I said? Desperate *need*. Please... Just a few dollars will suffice." As he looked into her saggy red rimmed eyes, and saw the light catch in her brilliantly white hair, he felt sympathetic. He watched as one single, dusty, tear rolled down her translucent wrinkled skin, and land on her white collar, that peaked over the fluffy yellow cardigan she wore. "Desperate *need*," she whispered.

"Well... Alright," he said, as he took out his wallet and shuffled through it. "How's... two dollars."

"No, no," she said softly. "Let's see now if you could bump that up to... 80."

"Wait a second, 80 bucks? Don't you think that's a little steep? Look, I'm just here to get some macaroni. What do you even need 80 bucks for anyway?" The instant the words left his mouth, he regretted them. In the once soggy, fogged over eyes, of the little old granny, there was a storm a brewin'.

"Youth," she spat the word like a poison. "No respect for the elders *in need...*" He backed away, startled, but as he did so she began to inch after. Step by rickety old step, she and her walker drew closer. Jason was so taken aback that without a moment's hesitation, he turned and hurriedly walked away, into the store. *Well that ended that,* he thought. *Catch me if you can.*

***

As Jason waited on the tub of macaroni salad from the deli, he couldn't help but think back on the confrontation he had just had. Never in his life had he seen such malice in someone he had only just met. "That'll be $9.95 up front." Said the deli guy, bringing Jason back to reality.

"Thanks!" He grabbed the tub and turned to leave, but something stopped him. He made eye contact with a small boy sitting in a cart. The boy was freckled, with bright red hair, and chocolate stains on the corners of his mouth. Jason was shocked by the intensity of the stare, and as he continued to look, the boy took his small finger from the crevasses of his nostrils, and pointed. Jason followed his gaze, to the end of the aisle. There, now wearing her bifocal lenses, was the little old lady with the walker. She squinted her beady red eyes, then scurried out of sight. Jason was a little nervous at this point. Was she watching him?

***

He was now in line for check out. He still felt uncomfortable from the whole encounter, but he knew he would soon be home. "Youth these days. They're all scum! A bunch of lazy bums piggy backing off the accomplishments of everyone else!" startled, Jason looked up. In the checkout line across from him stood the same feeble bag of bones, draped in that lousy yellow sweater. She stared directly at him and with every insult, came a wrinkled yellow-toothed smirk. *What is her problem?* He thought. Finally, he reached the end of the checkout, and as he went to walk away he heard "Oh no, I'm not buying anything." That was it. This whole time the old goat had waited in line and stood across from him *just* to piss him off.

As she lurched out of line, a dreadful smile on her face, he turned around and said, "Look *ma'am*, I'm not exactly sure why you're so upset with me, but I would appreciate it if you have a problem, deal with it directly. I don't know what this game you're trying to play is, but I have had enough."

Her bitter nostrils flared and her brow furrowed, "*My name is Eunice.* You've had enough have you? Well so have I! I'm sick and tired of you, *youth,* and your snotty behavior. You think you've got it *all* figured out, now don't you. I was young once, young and naive. But now I have power. UNLIMITED POWER!" She threw her head back in an evil cackle. Shocked, Jason stumbled back. He felt a snap at his foot and fell to the floor in pain. He looked down and clasped around his shoe was a set of dentures, squeezing so tightly he thought his toes might break. They had been set there, like a bear trap in the woods, and as the horror began to set in he slowly turned his head to watch as Eunice hobbled out the glass doors. Like military vehicles, come to impose martial law, the senior buses began rolling in. Their doors swung open and out swarmed a plague of liver spotted skin, and white tennis shoes with extreme arch support and Velcro straps. He gazed on in dismay as the countless numbers of old people flooded the parking lot. "My brothers and sisters! They have dropped us off at nursing homes, forgotten about us, left us for dead! Too many old people jokes have slipped between their youthful lips and firmly planted teeth. But no longer!"

Silence permeated the lot. Then suddenly, from the depths of the swarm there was a croak. "What? Can't hear you when you mumble like that"

Slowly, and shakily, Eunice began to lift her walker, like a mighty weapon of war. "I said... ATTACK!" With slow-paced savagery the old began to swarm. They ripped and tore at the hair, skin, and eyes of all the customers they could reach. The buses began to move again, and were poorly maneuvered around the parking lot, causing major damage to the surrounding cars. From out of the windows flew used diapers and colostomy bags; all hell had broken loose.

The people in the store began to panic, "WHAT THE HELL IS HAPPENING?!" "OH GOD NO! NOT MY MERCEDES!" People began racing in circles, some employees attempted to barricade the doors, others tried to phone the authorities. Jason finally managed to pry the dentures off his foot and stood up. *This is my fault; I shouldn't have engaged. I have to stop this.* He searched for some sort of weapon, and finally settled on a plastic Wiffle ball bat. *But what's the plan? I can't beat them all. Not with this anyway... There must be some way I can shut them down...* He looked around hurriedly, and in the midst of the panic inside the store he saw the little ginger boy. He stood, chocolate on mouth, finger in nose, the only solace in this world of disarray. And from his nose, once again, came the finger. Like a prophecy it led Jason's eyes to the flat screen mounted above customer service. The TV was muted but the familiar image still played across the screen. It was like he could hear the cry, drowning out, all the chaos around him. *"I've fallen and I can't get up!"* He would have known those words even in the thickest of deliriums. *I know what I must do.* He thought, *I must destroy Life Alert.*

METAPHOR

noun met·a·phor \ˈme-tə-ˌför *also* -fər\
: a word or phrase for one thing that is used to refer to another thing in order to show or suggest that they are similar: an object, activity, or idea that is used as a symbol of something else

: a figure of speech in which a word or phrase literally denoting one kind of object or idea is used in place of another to suggest a likeness or analogy between them (as in *drowning in money*); *broadly* : figurative language — compare simile

Metaphors are one of the most extensively used literary devices. A metaphor refers to a meaning or identity ascribed to one subject by way of another. In a metaphor, one subject is implied to be another so as to draw a comparison between their similarities and shared traits. The first subject, which is the focus of the sentences is usually compared to the second subject, which is used to convey a degree of meaning that is used to characterize the first. The purpose of using a metaphor is to take an identity or concept that we understand clearly (second subject) and use it to better understand the lesser known element (the first subject).

Metaphor Examples for Intermediate Readers
The slashes indicate line breaks.

1. The detective listened to her tales with a wooden face.
2. She was fairly certain that life was a fashion show.
3. The typical teenage boy's room is a disaster area.
4. What storms then shook the ocean of my sleep.
5. The children were roses grown in concrete gardens, beautiful and forlorn.
6. Kisses are the flowers of love in bloom.
7. His cotton candy words did not appeal to her taste.
8. Kathy arrived at the grocery store with an army of children.
9. Her eyes were fireflies.
10. He wanted to set sail on the ocean of love but he just wasted away in the desert.

Metaphor Examples for Advanced Readers
Here are more challenging examples of metaphors. The slashes indicate line breaks.

1. The light flows into the bowl of the midnight sky, violet, amber and rose.
2. Men court not death when there are sweets still left in life to taste.
3. In capitalism, money is the life blood of society but charity is the soul.
4. Whose world is but the trembling of a flare, / And heaven but as the highway for a shell,
5. Fame is the fragrance of heroic deeds, / Of flowers of chivalry and not of weeds!
6. So I sit spinning still, round this decaying form, the fine threads of rare and subtle thought.

THIS BEACH
Oscar Brown Jr.

And now, I've landed on this beach
It takes sixty odd years to reach
As this generation of mine
is ordered on to life's front line
The targets of a fusillade
that forces us to think of God

Reluctantly we storm this beach
Advancing to fill up the breach
Created by that fallen corp
Of elders who charged here before
While we enjoyed our middle age
We moved from fire, we now engage

A withering barrage rakes this beach
Its bullets bear the names of each
Of those who set foot on these sands
Old general calendar commands
Advancing to a sure defeat
Without The option to retreat

We knew, before we hit this beach
The enemy that we besiege
Has ammunition for us all
Who as casualties must fall
Not one will manage to survive
Nobody leaves this beach alive

For those arriving on this beach
There is no prayer to pray nor preach
To beg us off in any tongue
Since we've outlived dying young

And for surviving, in exchange
Now face the fire at point blank range

The witness we bear on this beach
Has only one lesson to teach
Here the carnage never stops
As everyday another drops
Some classmate, relative, or friend
Whose attack comes to abrupt end

So on into the breach my peers
Who knows how many weeks or years
Remain 'til you and I are hit
As we inch onward bit by bit
We only know our lives will bleach
Eternally out on this beach

THE ROCKING HORSE WINNER
D. H. Lawrence

There was a woman who was beautiful, who started with all the advantages, yet she had no luck. She married for love, and the love turned to dust. She had bonny children, yet she felt they had been thrust upon her, and she could not love them. They looked at her coldly, as if they were finding fault with her. And hurriedly she felt she must cover up some fault in herself. Yet what it was that she must cover up she never knew. Nevertheless, when her children were present, she always felt the centre of her heart go hard. This troubled her, and in her manner she was all the more gentle and anxious for her children, as if she loved them very much. Only she herself knew that at the centre of her heart was a hard little place that could not feel love, no, not for anybody. Everybody else said of her: "She is such a good mother. She adores her children." Only she herself, and her children themselves, knew it was not so. They read it in each other's eyes.

There were a boy and two little girls. They lived in a pleasant house, with a garden, and they had discreet servants, and felt themselves superior to anyone in the neighbourhood.

Although they lived in style, they felt always an anxiety in the house. There was never enough money. The mother had a small income, and the father had a small income, but not nearly enough for the social position which they had to keep up. The father went into town to some office. But though he had good prospects, these prospects never materialised. There was always the grinding sense of the shortage of money, though the style was always kept up.

At last the mother said: "I will see if I can't make something." But she did not know where to begin. She racked her brains, and tried this thing and the other, but could not find anything successful. The failure made deep lines come into her face. Her children were growing up, they would have to go to school. There must be more money, there must be more money. The father, who was always very handsome and expensive in his tastes, seemed as if he never would be able to do anything worth doing. And the mother, who had a great belief in herself, did not succeed any better, and her tastes were just as expensive.

And so the house came to be haunted by the unspoken phrase: There must be more money! There must be more money! The children could hear it all the time though nobody said it aloud. They heard it at Christmas, when the expensive and splendid toys filled the nursery. Behind the shining modern rocking-horse, behind the smart doll's house, a voice would start whispering: "There must be more money! There must be more money!" And the children would stop playing, to listen for a moment. They would look into each other's eyes, to see if they had all heard. And each one saw in the eyes of the other two that they too had heard. "There must be more money! There must be more money!"

It came whispering from the springs of the still-swaying rocking-horse, and even the horse, bending his wooden, champing head, heard it. The big doll, sitting so pink and smirking in her new pram, could hear it quite plainly, and seemed to be smirking all the more self-consciously because of it. The foolish puppy, too, that took the place of the teddy-bear, he was looking so extraordinarily foolish for no other reason but that he heard the secret whisper all over the house: "There must be more money!"

Yet nobody ever said it aloud. The whisper was everywhere, and therefore no one spoke it. Just as no one ever says: "We are breathing!" in spite of the fact that breath is coming and going all the time.

"Mother," said the boy Paul one day, "why don't we keep a car of our own? Why do we always use uncle's, or else a taxi?"

"Because we're the poor members of the family," said the mother.

"But why are we, mother?"

"Well - I suppose," she said slowly and bitterly, "it's because your father has no luck."

The boy was silent for some time.

"Is luck money, mother?" he asked, rather timidly.

"No, Paul. Not quite. It's what causes you to have money."

"Oh!" said Paul vaguely. "I thought when Uncle Oscar said filthy lucker, it meant money."

"Filthy lucre does mean money," said the mother. "But it's lucre, not luck."

"Oh!" said the boy. "Then what is luck, mother?"

"It's what causes you to have money. If you're lucky you have money. That's why it's better to be born lucky than rich. If you're rich, you may lose your money. But if you're lucky, you will always get more money."

"Oh! Will you? And is father not lucky?"

"Very unlucky, I should say," she said bitterly.

The boy watched her with unsure eyes.

"Why?" he asked.

"I don't know. Nobody ever knows why one person is lucky and another unlucky."

"Don't they? Nobody at all? Does nobody know?"

"Perhaps God. But He never tells."

"He ought to, then. And are'nt you lucky either, mother?"

"I can't be, it I married an unlucky husband."

"But by yourself, aren't you?"

"I used to think I was, before I married. Now I think I am very unlucky indeed."

"Why?"

"Well - never mind! Perhaps I'm not really," she said.

The child looked at her to see if she meant it. But he saw, by the lines of her mouth, that she was only trying to hide something from him.

"Well, anyhow," he said stoutly, "I'm a lucky person."

"Why?" said his mother, with a sudden laugh.

He stared at her. He didn't even know why he had said it.

"God told me," he asserted, brazening it out.

"I hope He did, dear!", she said, again with a laugh, but rather bitter.

"He did, mother!"

"Excellent!" said the mother, using one of her husband's exclamations.

The boy saw she did not believe him; or rather, that she paid no attention to his assertion. This angered him somewhere, and made him want to compel her attention.

He went off by himself, vaguely, in a childish way, seeking for the clue to 'luck'. Absorbed, taking no heed of other people, he went about with a sort of stealth, seeking inwardly for luck. He wanted luck, he wanted it, he wanted it. When the two girls were playing dolls in the nursery, he would sit on his big rocking-horse, charging madly into space, with a frenzy that made the little girls peer at him uneasily. Wildly the horse careered, the waving dark hair of the boy tossed, his eyes had a strange glare in them. The little girls dared not speak to him.

When he had ridden to the end of his mad little journey, he climbed down and stood in front of his rocking-horse, staring fixedly into its lowered face. Its red mouth was slightly open, its big eye was wide and glassy-bright.

"Now!" he would silently command the snorting steed. "Now take me to where there is luck! Now take me!"

And he would slash the horse on the neck with the little whip he had asked Uncle Oscar for. He knew the horse could take him to where there was luck, if only he forced it. So he would mount again and start on his furious ride, hoping at last to get there.

"You'll break your horse, Paul!" said the nurse.

"He's always riding like that! I wish he'd leave off!" said his elder sister Joan.

But he only glared down on them in silence. Nurse gave him up. She could make nothing of him. Anyhow, he was growing beyond her.

One day his mother and his Uncle Oscar came in when he was on one of his furious rides. He did not speak to them.

"Hallo, you young jockey! Riding a winner?" said his uncle.

"Aren't you growing too big for a rocking-horse? You're not a very little boy any longer, you know," said his mother.

But Paul only gave a blue glare from his big, rather close-set eyes. He would speak to nobody when he was in full tilt. His mother watched him with an anxious expression on her face.

At last he suddenly stopped forcing his horse into the mechanical gallop and slid down.

"Well, I got there!" he announced fiercely, his blue eyes still flaring, and his sturdy long legs straddling apart.

"Where did you get to?" asked his mother.

"Where I wanted to go," he flared back at her.

"That's right, son!" said Uncle Oscar. "Don't you stop till you get there. What's the horse's name?"

"He doesn't have a name," said the boy.

"Get's on without all right?" asked the uncle.

"Well, he has different names. He was called Sansovino last week."

"Sansovino, eh? Won the Ascot. How did you know this name?"

"He always talks about horse-races with Bassett," said Joan.

The uncle was delighted to find that his small nephew was posted with all the racing news. Bassett, the young gardener, who had been wounded in the left foot in the war and had got his present job through Oscar Cresswell, whose batman he had been, was a perfect blade of the 'turf'. He lived in the racing events, and the small boy lived with him.

Oscar Cresswell got it all from Bassett.

"Master Paul comes and asks me, so I can't do more than tell him, sir," said Bassett, his face terribly serious, as if he were speaking of religious matters.

"And does he ever put anything on a horse he fancies?"

"Well - I don't want to give him away - he's a young sport, a fine sport, sir. Would you mind asking him himself? He sort of takes a pleasure in it, and perhaps he'd feel I was giving him away, sir, if you don't mind.

Bassett was serious as a church.

The uncle went back to his nephew and took him off for a ride in the car.

"Say, Paul, old man, do you ever put anything on a horse?" the uncle asked.

The boy watched the handsome man closely.

"Why, do you think I oughtn't to?" he parried.

"Not a bit of it! I thought perhaps you might give me a tip for the Lincoln."

The car sped on into the country, going down to Uncle Oscar's place in Hampshire.

"Honour bright?" said the nephew.

"Honour bright, son!" said the uncle.

"Well, then, Daffodil."

"Daffodil! I doubt it, sonny. What about Mirza?"

"I only know the winner," said the boy. "That's Daffodil."

"Daffodil, eh?"

There was a pause. Daffodil was an obscure horse

comparatively.

"Uncle!"

"Yes, son?"

"You won't let it go any further, will you? I promised Bassett."

"Bassett be damned, old man! What's he got to do with it?"

"We're partners. We've been partners from the first. Uncle, he lent me my first five shillings, which I lost. I promised him, honour bright, it was only between me and him; only you gave me that ten-shilling note I started winning with, so I thought you were lucky. You won't let it go any further, will you?"

The boy gazed at his uncle from those big, hot, blue eyes, set rather close together. The uncle stirred and laughed uneasily.

"Right you are, son! I'll keep your tip private. How much are you putting on him?"

"All except twenty pounds," said the boy. "I keep that in reserve."

The uncle thought it a good joke.

"You keep twenty pounds in reserve, do you, you young romancer? What are you betting, then?"

"I'm betting three hundred," said the boy gravely. "But it's between you and me, Uncle Oscar! Honour bright?"

"It's between you and me all right, you young Nat Gould," he said, laughing. "But where's your three hundred?"

"Bassett keeps it for me. We're partner's."

"You are, are you! And what is Bassett putting on Daffodil?"

"He won't go quite as high as I do, I expect. Perhaps he'll go a hundred and fifty."

"What, pennies?" laughed the uncle.

"Pounds," said the child, with a surprised look at his uncle. "Bassett keeps a bigger reserve than I do."

Between wonder and amusement Uncle Oscar was silent. He pursued the matter no further, but he determined to take his nephew with him to the Lincoln races.

"Now, son," he said, "I'm putting twenty on Mirza, and I'll put five on for you on any horse you fancy. What's your pick?"

"Daffodil, uncle."

"No, not the fiver on Daffodil!"

"I should if it was my own fiver," said the child.

"Good! Good! Right you are! A fiver for me and a fiver for you on Daffodil."

The child had never been to a race-meeting before, and his eyes were blue fire. He pursed his mouth tight and watched. A Frenchman just in front had put his money on

Lancelot. Wild with excitement, he flayed his arms up and down, yelling "Lancelot!, Lancelot!" in his French accent.

Daffodil came in first, Lancelot second, Mirza third. The child, flushed and with eyes blazing, was curiously serene. His uncle brought him four five-pound notes, four to one.

"What am I to do with these?" he cried, waving them before the boys eyes.

"I suppose we'll talk to Bassett," said the boy. "I expect I have fifteen hundred now; and twenty in reserve; and this twenty."

His uncle studied him for some moments.

"Look here, son!" he said. "You're not serious about Bassett and that fifteen hundred, are you?"

"Yes, I am. But it's between you and me, uncle. Honour bright?"

"Honour bright all right, son! But I must talk to Bassett."

"If you'd like to be a partner, uncle, with Bassett and me, we could all be partners. Only, you'd have to promise, honour bright, uncle, not to let it go beyond us three. Bassett and I are lucky, and you must be lucky, because it was your ten shillings I started winning with ..."

Uncle Oscar took both Bassett and Paul into Richmond Park for an afternoon, and there they talked.

"It's like this, you see, sir," Bassett said. "Master Paul would get me talking about racing events, spinning yarns, you know, sir. And he was always keen on knowing if I'd made or if I'd lost. It's about a year since, now, that I put five shillings on Blush of Dawn for him: and we lost. Then the luck turned, with that ten shillings he had from you: that we put on Singhalese. And since that time, it's been pretty steady, all things considering. What do you say, Master Paul?"

"We're all right when we're sure," said Paul. "It's when we're not quite sure that we go down."

"Oh, but we're careful then," said Bassett.

"But when are you sure?" smiled Uncle Oscar.

"It's Master Paul, sir," said Bassett in a secret, religious voice. "It's as if he had it from heaven. Like Daffodil, now, for the Lincoln. That was as sure as eggs."

"Did you put anything on Daffodil?" asked Oscar Cresswell.

"Yes, sir, I made my bit."

"And my nephew?"

Bassett was obstinately silent, looking at Paul.

"I made twelve hundred, didn't I, Bassett? I told uncle I was putting three hundred on Daffodil."

"That's right," said Bassett, nodding.

"But where's the money?" asked the uncle.

"I keep it safe locked up, sir. Master Paul he can have it any minute he likes to ask for it."

"What, fifteen hundred pounds?"

"And twenty! And forty, that is, with the twenty he made on the course."

"It's amazing!" said the uncle.

"If Master Paul offers you to be partners, sir, I would, if I were you: if you'll excuse me," said Bassett.

Oscar Cresswell thought about it.

"I'll see the money," he said.

They drove home again, and, sure enough, Bassett came round to the garden-house with fifteen hundred pounds in notes. The twenty pounds reserve was left with Joe Glee, in the Turf Commission deposit.

"You see, it's all right, uncle, when I'm sure! Then we go strong, for all we're worth, don't we, Bassett?"

"We do that, Master Paul."

"And when are you sure?" said the uncle, laughing.

"Oh, well, sometimes I'm absolutely sure, like about Daffodil," said the boy; "and sometimes I have an idea; and sometimes I haven't even an idea, have I, Bassett? Then we're careful, because we mostly go down."

"You do, do you! And when you're sure, like about Daffodil, what makes you sure, sonny?"

"Oh, well, I don't know," said the boy uneasily. "I'm sure,

you know, uncle; that's all."

"It's as if he had it from heaven, sir," Bassett reiterated.

"I should say so!" said the uncle.

But he became a partner. And when the Leger was coming on Paul was 'sure' about Lively Spark, which was a quite inconsiderable horse. The boy insisted on putting a thousand on the horse, Bassett went for five hundred, and Oscar Cresswell two hundred. Lively Spark came in first, and the betting had been ten to one against him. Paul had made ten thousand.

"You see," he said. "I was absolutely sure of him."

Even Oscar Cresswell had cleared two thousand.

"Look here, son," he said, "this sort of thing makes me nervous."

"It needn't, uncle! Perhaps I shan't be sure again for a long time."

"But what are you going to do with your money?" asked the uncle.

"Of course," said the boy, "I started it for mother. She said she had no luck, because father is unlucky, so I thought if I was lucky, it might stop whispering."

"What might stop whispering?"

"Our house. I hate our house for whispering."

"What does it whisper?"

"Why - why" - the boy fidgeted - "why, I don't know. But it's always short of money, you know, uncle."

"I know it, son, I know it."

"You know people send mother writs, don't you, uncle?"

"I'm afraid I do," said the uncle.

"And then the house whispers, like people laughing at you behind your back. It's awful, that is! I thought if I was lucky -"

"You might stop it," added the uncle.

The boy watched him with big blue eyes, that had an uncanny cold fire in them, and he said never a word.

"Well, then!" said the uncle. "What are we doing?"

"I shouldn't like mother to know I was lucky," said the boy.

"Why not, son?"

"She'd stop me."

"I don't think she would."

"Oh!" - and the boy writhed in an odd way - "I don't want her to know, uncle."

"All right, son! We'll manage it without her knowing."

They managed it very easily. Paul, at the other's suggestion, handed over five thousand pounds to his uncle, who deposited it with the family lawyer, who was then to inform Paul's mother that a relative had put five thousand pounds into his hands, which sum was to be paid out a thousand pounds at a time, on the mother's birthday, for the next five years.

"So she'll have a birthday present of a thousand pounds for five successive years," said Uncle Oscar. "I hope it won't make it all the harder for her later."

Paul's mother had her birthday in November. The house had been 'whispering' worse than ever lately, and, even in spite of his luck, Paul could not bear up against it. He was very anxious to see the effect of the birthday letter, telling his mother about the thousand pounds.

When there were no visitors, Paul now took his meals with his parents, as he was beyond the nursery control. His mother went into town nearly every day. She had discovered that she had an odd knack of sketching furs and dress materials, so she worked secretly in the studio of a friend who was the chief 'artist' for the leading drapers. She drew the figures of ladies in furs and ladies in silk and sequins for the newspaper advertisements. This young woman artist earned several thousand pounds a year, but Paul's mother only made several hundreds, and she was again dissatisfied. She so wanted to be first in something, and she did not succeed, even in making sketches for drapery advertisements.

She was down to breakfast on the morning of her birthday. Paul watched her face as she read her letters. He knew the lawyer's letter. As his mother read it, her face hardened and became more expressionless. Then a cold, determined look came on her mouth. She hid the letter under the pile of others, and said not a word about it.

"Didn't you have anything nice in the post for your birthday, mother?" said Paul.

"Quite moderately nice," she said, her voice cold and hard and absent.

She went away to town without saying more.

But in the afternoon Uncle Oscar appeared. He said Paul's mother had had a long interview with the lawyer, asking if the whole five thousand could not be advanced at once, as she was in debt.

"What do you think, uncle?" said the boy.

"I leave it to you, son."

"Oh, let her have it, then! We can get some more with the other," said the boy.

"A bird in the hand is worth two in the bush, laddie!" said Uncle Oscar.

"But I'm sure to know for the Grand National; or the Lincolnshire; or else the Derby. I'm sure to know for one of them," said Paul.

So Uncle Oscar signed the agreement, and Paul's mother touched the whole five thousand. Then something very curious happened. The voices in the house suddenly went mad, like a chorus of frogs on a spring evening. There were certain new furnishings, and Paul had a tutor. He was really going to Eton, his father's school, in the following autumn. There were flowers in the winter, and a blossoming of the luxury Paul's mother had been used to.

And yet the voices in the house, behind the sprays of mimosa and almond-blossom, and from under the piles of iridescent cushions, simply trilled and screamed in a sort of ecstasy: "There must be more money! Oh-h-h; there must be more money. Oh, now, now-w! Now-w-w - there must be more money! - more than ever! More than ever!"

It frightened Paul terribly. He studied away at his Latin and Greek with his tutor. But his intense hours were spent with Bassett. The Grand National had gone by: he had not 'known', and had lost a hundred pounds. Summer was at hand. He was in agony for the Lincoln. But even for the Lincoln he didn't 'know', and he lost fifty pounds. He became wild-eyed and strange, as if something were going to explode in him.

"Let it alone, son! Don't you bother about it!" urged Uncle Oscar. But it was as if the boy couldn't really hear what his uncle was saying.

"I've got to know for the Derby! I've got to know for the Derby!" the child reiterated, his big blue eyes blazing with a sort of madness.

His mother noticed how overwrought he was.

"You'd better go to the seaside. Wouldn't you like to go now to the seaside, instead of waiting? I think you'd better," she said, looking down at him anxiously, her heart curiously heavy because of him.

But the child lifted his uncanny blue eyes.

"I couldn't possibly go before the Derby, mother!" he said. "I couldn't possibly!"

"Why not?" she said, her voice becoming heavy when she was opposed. "Why not? You can still go from the seaside to see the Derby with your Uncle Oscar, if that that's what you wish. No need for you to wait here. Besides, I think you care too much about these races. It's a bad sign. My family has been a gambling family, and you won't know till you grow up how much damage it has done. But it has done damage. I shall have to send Bassett away, and ask Uncle Oscar not to talk racing to you, unless you promise to be reasonable about it: go away to the seaside and forget it. You're all nerves!"

"I'll do what you like, mother, so long as you don't send me away till after the Derby," the boy said.

"Send you away from where? Just from this house?"

"Yes," he said, gazing at her.

"Why, you curious child, what makes you care about this house so much, suddenly? I never knew you loved it."

He gazed at her without speaking. He had a secret within a secret, something he had not divulged, even to Bassett or to his Uncle Oscar.

But his mother, after standing undecided and a little bit sullen for some moments, said: "Very well, then! Don't go to the seaside till after the Derby, if you don't wish it. But promise me you won't think so much about horse-racing and events as you call them!"

"Oh no," said the boy casually. "I won't think much about them, mother. You needn't worry. I wouldn't worry, mother, if I were you."

"If you were me and I were you," said his mother, "I wonder what we should do!"

"But you know you needn't worry, mother, don't you?" the boy repeated.

"I should be awfully glad to know it," she said wearily.

"Oh, well, you can, you know. I mean, you ought to know you needn't worry," he insisted.

"Ought I? Then I'll see about it," she said.

Paul's secret of secrets was his wooden horse, that which had no name. Since he was emancipated from a nurse and a nursery-governess, he had had his rocking-horse removed to his own bedroom at the top of the house.

"Surely you're too big for a rocking-horse!" his mother had remonstrated.

"Well, you see, mother, till I can have a real horse, I like to have some sort of animal about," had been his quaint answer.

"Do you feel he keeps you company?" she laughed.

"Oh yes! He's very good, he always keeps me company, when I'm there," said Paul.

So the horse, rather shabby, stood in an arrested prance in the boy's bedroom.

The Derby was drawing near, and the boy grew more and more tense. He hardly heard what was spoken to him, he was very frail, and his eyes were really uncanny. His mother had sudden strange seizures of uneasiness about him. Sometimes, for half an hour, she would feel a sudden anxiety about him that was almost anguish. She wanted to rush to him at once, and know he was safe.

Two nights before the Derby, she was at a big party in town, when one of her rushes of anxiety about her boy, her first-born, gripped her heart till she could hardly speak. She fought with the feeling, might and main, for she believed in common sense. But it was too strong. She had to leave the dance and go downstairs to telephone to the country. The children's nursery-governess was terribly surprised and startled at being rung up in the night.

"Are the children all right, Miss Wilmot?"

"Oh yes, they are quite all right."

"Master Paul? Is he all right?"

"He went to bed as right as a trivet. Shall I run up and look at him?"

"No," said Paul's mother reluctantly. "No! Don't trouble. It's all right. Don't sit up. We shall be home fairly soon." She did not want her son's privacy intruded upon.

"Very good," said the governess.

It was about one o'clock when Paul's mother and father drove up to their house. All was still. Paul's mother went to her room and slipped off her white fur cloak. She had told her maid not to wait up for her. She heard her husband downstairs, mixing a whisky and soda.

And then, because of the strange anxiety at her heart, she

stole upstairs to her son's room. Noiselessly she went along the upper corridor. Was there a faint noise? What was it?

She stood, with arrested muscles, outside his door, listening. There was a strange, heavy, and yet not loud noise. Her heart stood still. It was a soundless noise, yet rushing and powerful. Something huge, in violent, hushed motion. What was it? What in God's name was it? She ought to know. She felt that she knew the noise. She knew what it was.

Yet she could not place it. She couldn't say what it was. And on and on it went, like a madness.

Softly, frozen with anxiety and fear, she turned the door-handle.

The room was dark. Yet in the space near the window, she heard and saw something plunging to and fro. She gazed in fear and amazement.

Then suddenly she switched on the light, and saw her son, in his green pyjamas, madly surging on the rocking-horse. The blaze of light suddenly lit him up, as he urged the wooden horse, and lit her up, as she stood, blonde, in her dress of pale green and crystal, in the doorway.

"Paul!" she cried. "Whatever are you doing?"

"It's Malabar!" he screamed in a powerful, strange voice. "It's Malabar!"

His eyes blazed at her for one strange and senseless second, as he ceased urging his wooden horse. Then he fell with a crash to the ground, and she, all her tormented motherhood flooding upon her, rushed to gather him up.

But he was unconscious, and unconscious he remained, with some brain-fever. He talked and tossed, and his mother sat stonily by his side.

"Malabar! It's Malabar! Bassett, Bassett, I know! It's Malabar!"

So the child cried, trying to get up and urge the rocking-horse that gave him his inspiration.

"What does he mean by Malabar?" asked the heart-frozen mother.

"I don't know," said the father stonily.

"What does he mean by Malabar?" she asked her brother Oscar.

"It's one of the horses running for the Derby," was the answer.

And, in spite of himself, Oscar Cresswell spoke to Bassett, and himself put a thousand on Malabar: at fourteen to one.

The third day of the illness was critical: they were waiting for a change. The boy, with his rather long, curly hair, was tossing ceaselessly on the pillow. He neither slept nor regained consciousness, and his eyes were like blue stones. His mother sat, feeling her heart had gone, turned actually into a stone.

In the evening Oscar Cresswell did not come, but Bassett sent a message, saying could he come up for one moment, just one moment? Paul's mother was very angry at the intrusion, but on second thoughts she agreed. The boy was the same. Perhaps Bassett might bring him to consciousness.

The gardener, a shortish fellow with a little brown moustache and sharp little brown eyes, tiptoed into the room, touched his imaginary cap to Paul's mother, and stole to the bedside, staring with glittering, smallish eyes at the tossing, dying child.

"Master Paul!" he whispered. "Master Paul! Malabar came in first all right, a clean win. I did as you told me. You've made over seventy thousand pounds, you have; you've got over eighty thousand. Malabar came in all right, Master Paul."

"Malabar! Malabar! Did I say Malabar, mother? Did I say Malabar? Do you think I'm lucky, mother? I knew Malabar, didn't I? Over eighty thousand pounds! I call that lucky, don't you, mother? Over eighty thousand pounds! I knew, didn't I know I knew? Malabar came in all right. If I ride my horse till I'm sure, then I tell you, Bassett, you can go as high as you like. Did you go for all you were worth, Bassett?"

"I went a thousand on it, Master Paul."

"I never told you, mother, that if I can ride my horse, and get there, then I'm absolutely sure - oh, absolutely! Mother, did I ever tell you? I am lucky!"

"No, you never did," said his mother.

But the boy died in the night.

And even as he lay dead, his mother heard her brother's

voice saying to her, "My God, Hester, you're eighty-odd thousand to the good, and a poor devil of a son to the bad. But, poor devil, poor devil, he's best gone out of a life where he rides his rocking-horse to find a winner."

CHARACTERIZATION

noun char·ac·ter \'ker-ik-tər, 'ka-rik-\ **a :** one of the attributes or features that make up and distinguish an individual
the detectable <u>expression</u> of the action of a gene or group of genes (3) : the <u>aggregate</u> of distinctive
qualities <u>characteristic</u> of a breed, strain, or type <a wine of great *character*>
c : the <u>complex</u> of mental and ethical traits marking and often individualizing a person, group, or
nation <the *character* of the American people>
d : main or essential nature especially as strongly marked and serving to distinguish <excess sewage gradually changed the *character* of the lake>

Characterization in literature refers to the step by step process wherein an author introduces and then describes a character. The character can be described directly by the author or indirectly through the actions, thoughts, and speech of the character.

THE TELL-TALE HEART
Edgar Allan Poe

TRUE!-NERVOUS--very, very dreadfully nervous I had been and am! but why will you say that I am mad? The disease had sharpened my senses--not destroyed--not dulled them. Above all was the sense of hearing acute. I heard all things in the heaven and in the earth. I heard many things in hell. How, then, am I mad? Hearken! and observe how healthily--how calmly I can tell you the whole story.

It is impossible to tell how first the idea entered my brain; but once conceived, it haunted me day and night. Object there was none. Passion there was none. I loved the old man. He had never wronged me. He had never given me insult. For his gold I had no desire. I think it was his eye! Yes, it was this! One of his eyes resembled that of a vulture--a pale blue eye, with a film over it. Whenever it fell upon me, my blood ran cold; and so by degrees--very gradually--I made up my mind to take the life of the old man, and thus rid myself of the eye forever.

Now this is the point. You fancy me mad. Madmen know nothing. But you should have seen me. You should have seen how wisely I proceeded--with what caution--with what foresight--with what dissimulation I went to work!

I was never kinder to the old man than during the whole week before I killed him. And every night, about midnight, I turned the latch of his door and opened it--oh, so gently! And then, when I had made an opening sufficient for my head, I put in a dark lantern, all closed, closed, so that no light shone out, and then I thrust in my head. Oh, you would have laughed to see how cunningly I thrust it in! I moved it slowly--very, very slowly, so that I might not disturb the old man's sleep. It took me an hour to place my whole head within the opening so far that I could see him as he lay upon his bed. Ha!--would a madman have been so wise as this? And then, when my head was well in the room, I undid the lantern cautiously--oh, so cautiously--cautiously (for the hinges creaked)--I undid it just so much that a single thin ray fell upon the vulture eye. And this I did for seven long nights--every night just at midnight--but I found the eye always closed; and so it was impossible to do the work; for it was not the old man who vexed me, but his Evil Eye. And every morning, when the day broke, I went boldly into the chamber, and spoke courageously to him, calling him by name in a hearty tone, and inquiring how he had passed the night. So you see he would have been a very profound old man, indeed, to suspect that every night, just at twelve, I looked in upon him while he slept.

Upon the eighth night I was more than usually cautious in opening the door. A watch's minute hand moves more quickly than did mine. Never before that night had I felt the extent of my own powers--of my sagacity. I could scarcely contain my feelings of triumph. To think that there I was, opening the door, little by little, and he not even to dream of my secret deeds or thoughts. I fairly chuckled at the idea; and perhaps he heard me; for he moved on the bed suddenly, as if startled. Now you may think that I drew back--but no. His room was as black as pitch with the thick darkness (for the shutters were close fastened, through fear of robbers), and so I knew that he could not see the opening of the door, and I kept pushing it on steadily, steadily.

I had my head in, and was about to open the lantern, when my thumb slipped upon the tin fastening, and the old man sprang up in bed, crying out: "Who's there?"

I kept quite still and said nothing. For a whole hour I did not move a muscle, and in the meantime I did not hear him lie down. He was still sitting up in the bed listening;--

just as I have done, night after night, hearkening to the death watches in the wall.

Presently I heard a slight groan, and I knew it was the groan of mortal terror. It was not a groan of pain or grief--oh no!--it was the low stifled sound that arises from the bottom of the soul when overcharged with awe. I knew the sound well. Many a night, just at midnight, when all the world slept, it has welled up from my own bosom, deepening, with its dreadful echo, the terrors that distracted me. I say I knew it well. I knew what the old man felt, and pitied him, although I chuckled at heart. I knew that he had been lying awake ever since the first slight noise, when he had turned in the bed. His fears had been ever since growing upon him. He had been trying to fancy them causeless, but could not. He had been saying to himself: "It is nothing but the wind in the chimney--it is only a mouse crossing the floor," or "it is merely a cricket which has made a single chirp." Yes, he had been trying to comfort himself with these suppositions; but he had found all in vain. All in vain; because Death, in approaching him. had stalked with his black shadow before him, and enveloped the victim. And it was the mournful influence of the unperceived shadow that caused him to feel--although he neither saw nor heard--to feel the presence of my head within the room.

When I had waited a long time, very patiently, without hearing him lie down, I resolved to open a little--a very, very little crevice in the lantern. So I opened it--you cannot imagine how stealthily, stealthily--until, at length, a single dim ray, like the thread of the spider, shot from out the crevice and full upon the vulture eye.

It was open--wide, wide open--and I grew furious as I gazed upon it. I saw it with perfect distinctness--all a dull blue, with a hideous veil over it that chilled the very marrow in my bones; but I could see nothing else of the old man's face or person: for I had directed the ray, as if by instinct, precisely upon the damned spot.

And now--have I not told you that what you mistake for madness is but over-acuteness of the senses?--now, I say, there came to my ears a low, dull, quick sound, such as a watch makes when enveloped in cotton. I knew that sound well too. It was the beating of the old man's heart. It increased my fury, as the beating of a drum stimulates the soldier into courage.

But even yet I refrained and kept still. I scarcely breathed. I held the lantern motionless. I tried how steadily I could maintain the ray upon the eye. Meantime the hellish tattoo of the heart increased. It grew quicker and quicker' and louder and louder every instant. The old man's terror must have been extreme! It grew louder, I say, louder every moment!--do you mark me well? I have told you that I am nervous: so I am. And now at the dead hour of night, amid the dreadful silence of that old house, so strange a noise as this excited me to uncontrollable terror. Yet, for some minutes longer I refrained and stood still. But the beating grew louder, louder! I thought the heart must burst. And now a new anxiety seized me--the sound would be heard by a neighbor! The old man's hour had come! With a loud yell, I threw open the lantern and leaped into the room. He shrieked once--once only. In an instant I dragged him to the floor, and pulled the heavy bed over him. I then smiled gaily, to find the deed so far done. But, for many minutes, the heart beat on with a muffled sound. This, however, did not vex me; it would not be heard through the wall. At length it ceased. The old man was dead. I removed the bed and examined the corpse. Yes, he was stone, stone dead. I placed my hand upon the heart and held it there many minutes. There was no pulsation. He was stone dead. His eye would trouble me no more.

If still you think me mad, you will think so no longer when I describe the wise precautions I took for the concealment of the body. The night waned, and I worked hastily, but in silence. First of all I dismembered the corpse. I cut off the head and the arms and the legs.

I then took up three planks from the flooring of the chamber, and deposited all between the scantlings. I then replaced the boards so cleverly, so cunningly, that no human eye--not even his--could have detected anything wrong. There was nothing to wash out--no stain of any kind--no blood-spot whatever. I had been too wary for that. A tub had caught all--ha! ha!

When I had made an end of these labors, it was four o'clock--still dark as midnight. As the bell sounded the hour, there came a knocking at the street door. I went down to open it with a light heart--for what had I now to fear? There entered three men, who introduced themselves, with perfect suavity, as officers of the police. A shriek had been heard by a neighbor during the night: suspicion of foul play had been aroused; information had been lodged at the police office, and they (the officers) had been deputed to search the premises.

I smiled--for what had I to fear? I bade the gentlemen welcome. The shriek, I said, was my own in a dream. The old man, I mentioned, was absent in the country. I took my visitors all over the house. I bade them search--search well. I led them, at length, to his chamber. I showed them his treasures, secure, undisturbed. In the enthusiasm of my confidence, I brought chairs into the room, and desired them here to rest from their fatigues, while I myself, in the wild audacity of my perfect triumph, placed my own seat upon the very spot beneath which reposed the corpse of the victim.

The officers were satisfied. My manner had convinced them. I was singularly at ease. They sat, and while I answered cheerily, they chatted familiar things. But, ere long, I felt myself getting pale and wished them gone. My head ached, and I fancied a ringing in my ears: but still they sat and still chatted. The ringing became more distinct:--it continued and became more distinct: I talked more freely to get rid of the feeling: but it continued and gained definiteness--until, at length, I found that the noise was not within my ears.

No doubt I now grew very pale,--but I talked more fluently, and with a heightened voice. Yet the sound increased--and what could I do? It was a low, dull, quick sound--much such a sound as a watch makes when enveloped in cotton. I gasped for breath--and yet the officers heard it not. I talked more quickly--more vehemently; but the noise steadily increased. Why would they not be gone? I paced the floor to and fro with heavy strides, as if excited to fury by the observation of the men-- but the noise steadily increased. Oh, God; what could I do? I foamed--I raved--I swore! I swung the chair upon which I had been sitting, and grated it upon the boards, but the noise arose over all and continually increased. It grew louder--louder --louder! And still the men chatted pleasantly, and smiled. Was it possible they heard not? Almighty God!--no, no! They heard!--they suspected--they knew!--they were making a mockery of my horror!--this I thought, and this I think. But anything was better than this agony! Anything was more tolerable than this derision! I could bear those hypocritical smiles no longer! I felt that I must scream or die!--and now--again!--hark! louder! louder! louder!

"Villains!" I shrieked, "dissemble no more! I admit the deed!--tear up the planks!--here, here!--it is the beating of his hideous heart!"

KURT VONNEGUT:
8 BASICS OF CREATIVE WRITING

With his customary wisdom and wit, Vonnegut put forth 8 basics of what he calls Creative Writing 101:

1. Use the time of a total stranger in such a way that he or she will not feel the time was wasted.
2. Give the reader at least one character he or she can root for.
3. Every character should want something, even if it is only a glass of water.
4. Every sentence must do one of two things—reveal character or advance the action.
5. Start as close to the end as possible.
6. Be a sadist. No matter how sweet and innocent your leading characters, make awful things happen to them—in order that the reader may see what they are made of.
7. Write to please just one person. If you open a window and make love to the world, so to speak, your story will get pneumonia.
8. Give your readers as much information as possible as soon as possible. To heck with suspense. Readers should have such complete understanding of what is going on, where and why, that they could finish the story themselves, should cockroaches eat the last few pages.

2 B R 2 B
Kurt Vonnegut

Got a problem? Just pick up the phone.
It solved them all--and all the same way!

Everything was perfectly swell.

There were no prisons, no slums, no insane asylums, no cripples, no poverty, no wars.

All diseases were conquered. So was old age.

Death, barring accidents, was an adventure for volunteers.

The population of the United States was stabilized at forty-million souls.

One bright morning in the Chicago Lying-in Hospital, a man named Edward K. Wehling, Jr., waited for his wife to give birth. He was the only man waiting. Not many people were born a day any more.

Wehling was fifty-six, a mere stripling in a population whose average age was one hundred and twenty-nine.

X-rays had revealed that his wife was going to have triplets. The children would be his first.

Young Wehling was hunched in his chair, his head in his hand. He was so rumpled, so still and colorless as to be virtually invisible. His camouflage was perfect, since the waiting room had a disorderly and demoralized air, too. Chairs and ashtrays had been moved away from the walls. The floor was paved with spattered dropcloths.

The room was being redecorated. It was being redecorated as a memorial to a man who had volunteered to die.

A sardonic old man, about two hundred years old, sat on a stepladder, painting a mural he did not like. Back in the days when people aged visibly, his age would have been guessed at thirty-five or so. Aging had touched him that much before the cure for aging was found.

The mural he was working on depicted a very neat garden. Men and women in white, doctors and nurses, turned the soil, planted seedlings, sprayed bugs, spread fertilizer.

Men and women in purple uniforms pulled up weeds, cut down plants that were old and sickly, raked leaves, carried refuse to trash-burners.

Never, never, never--not even in medieval Holland nor old Japan--had a garden been more formal, been better tended. Every plant had all the loam, light, water, air and nourishment it could use.

A hospital orderly came down the corridor, singing under his breath a popular song:

If you don't like my kisses, honey,
Here's what I will do:
I'll go see a girl in purple,
Kiss this sad world toodle-oo.
If you don't want my lovin',
Why should I take up all this space?
I'll get off this old planet,
Let some sweet baby have my place.

The orderly looked in at the mural and the muralist. "Looks so real," he said, "I can practically imagine I'm standing in the middle of it."

"What makes you think you're not in it?" said the painter. He gave a satiric smile. "It's called 'The Happy Garden of Life,' you know."

"That's good of Dr. Hitz," said the orderly.

* * * * *

He was referring to one of the male figures in white, whose head was a portrait of Dr. Benjamin Hitz, the hospital's Chief Obstetrician. Hitz was a blindingly handsome man.

330

"Lot of faces still to fill in," said the orderly. He meant that the faces of many of the figures in the mural were still blank. All blanks were to be filled with portraits of important people on either the hospital staff or from the Chicago Office of the Federal Bureau of Termination.

"Must be nice to be able to make pictures that look like something," said the orderly.

The painter's face curdled with scorn. "You think I'm proud of this daub?" he said. "You think this is my idea of what life really looks like?"

"What's your idea of what life looks like?" said the orderly.

The painter gestured at a foul dropcloth. "There's a good picture of it," he said. "Frame that, and you'll have a picture a damn sight more honest than this one."

"You're a gloomy old duck, aren't you?" said the orderly.

"Is that a crime?" said the painter.

The orderly shrugged. "If you don't like it here, Grandpa--" he said, and he finished the thought with the trick telephone number that people who didn't want to live any more were supposed to call. The zero in the telephone number he pronounced "naught."

The number was: "2 B R 0 2 B."

It was the telephone number of an institution whose fanciful sobriquets included: "Automat," "Birdland," "Cannery," "Catbox," "De-louser," "Easy-go," "Good-by, Mother," "Happy Hooligan," "Kiss-me-quick," "Lucky Pierre," "Sheepdip," "Waring Blendor," "Weep-no-more" and "Why Worry?"

"To be or not to be" was the telephone number of the municipal gas chambers of the Federal Bureau of Termination.

* * * * *

The painter thumbed his nose at the orderly. "When I decide it's time to go," he said, "it won't be at the Sheepdip."

"A do-it-yourselfer, eh?" said the orderly. "Messy business, Grandpa. Why don't you have a little consideration for the people who have to clean up after you?"

The painter expressed with an obscenity his lack of concern for the tribulations of his survivors. "The world could do with a good deal more mess, if you ask me," he said.

The orderly laughed and moved on.

Wehling, the waiting father, mumbled something without raising his head. And then he fell silent again.

A coarse, formidable woman strode into the waiting room on spike heels. Her shoes, stockings, trench coat, bag and overseas cap were all purple, the purple the painter called "the color of grapes on Judgment Day."

The medallion on her purple musette bag was the seal of the Service Division of the Federal Bureau of Termination, an eagle perched on a turnstile.

The woman had a lot of facial hair--an unmistakable mustache, in fact. A curious thing about gas-chamber hostesses was that, no matter how lovely and feminine they were when recruited, they all sprouted mustaches within five years or so.

"Is this where I'm supposed to come?" she said to the painter.

"A lot would depend on what your business was," he said. "You aren't about to have a baby, are you?"

"They told me I was supposed to pose for some picture," she said. "My name's Leora Duncan." She waited.

"And you dunk people," he said.

"What?" she said.

"Skip it," he said.

"That sure is a beautiful picture," she said. "Looks just like heaven or something."

"Or something," said the painter. He took a list of names from his smock pocket. "Duncan, Duncan, Duncan," he

332

said, scanning the list. "Yes--here you are. You're entitled to be immortalized. See any faceless body here you'd like me to stick your head on? We've got a few choice ones left."

She studied the mural bleakly. "Gee," she said, "they're all the same to me. I don't know anything about art."

"A body's a body, eh?" he said, "All righty. As a master of fine art, I recommend this body here." He indicated a faceless figure of a woman who was carrying dried stalks to a trash-burner.

"Well," said Leora Duncan, "that's more the disposal people, isn't it? I mean, I'm in service. I don't do any disposing."

The painter clapped his hands in mock delight. "You say you don't know anything about art, and then you prove in the next breath that you know more about it than I do! Of course the sheave-carrier is wrong for a hostess! A snipper, a pruner--that's more your line." He pointed to a figure in purple who was sawing a dead branch from an apple tree. "How about her?" he said. "You like her at all?"

"Gosh--" she said, and she blushed and became humble--"that--that puts me right next to Dr. Hitz."

"That upsets you?" he said.

"Good gravy, no!" she said. "It's--it's just such an honor."

"Ah, You admire him, eh?" he said.

"Who doesn't admire him?" she said, worshiping the portrait of Hitz. It was the portrait of a tanned, white-haired, omnipotent Zeus, two hundred and forty years old. "Who doesn't admire him?" she said again. "He was responsible for setting up the very first gas chamber in Chicago."

"Nothing would please me more," said the painter, "than to put you next to him for all time. Sawing off a limb--that strikes you as appropriate?"

333

"That is kind of like what I do," she said. She was demure about what she did. What she did was make people comfortable while she killed them.

* * * * *

And, while Leora Duncan was posing for her portrait, into the waitingroom bounded Dr. Hitz himself. He was seven feet tall, and he boomed with importance, accomplishments, and the joy of living.

"Well, Miss Duncan! Miss Duncan!" he said, and he made a joke. "What are you doing here?" he said. "This isn't where the people leave. This is where they come in!"

"We're going to be in the same picture together," she said shyly.

"Good!" said Dr. Hitz heartily. "And, say, isn't that some picture?"

"I sure am honored to be in it with you," she said.

"Let me tell you," he said, "I'm honored to be in it with you. Without women like you, this wonderful world we've got wouldn't be possible."

He saluted her and moved toward the door that led to the delivery rooms. "Guess what was just born," he said.

"I can't," she said.

"Triplets!" he said.

"Triplets!" she said. She was exclaiming over the legal implications of triplets.

The law said that no newborn child could survive unless the parents of the child could find someone who would volunteer to die. Triplets, if they were all to live, called for three volunteers.

"Do the parents have three volunteers?" said Leora Duncan.

"Last I heard," said Dr. Hitz, "they had one, and were trying to scrape another two up."

"I don't think they made it," she said. "Nobody made three appointments with us. Nothing but singles going through today, unless somebody called in after I left. What's the name?"

"Wehling," said the waiting father, sitting up, red-eyed and frowzy. "Edward K. Wehling, Jr., is the name of the happy father-to-be."

He raised his right hand, looked at a spot on the wall, gave a hoarsely wretched chuckle. "Present," he said.

"Oh, Mr. Wehling," said Dr. Hitz, "I didn't see you."

"The invisible man," said Wehling.

"They just phoned me that your triplets have been born," said Dr. Hitz. "They're all fine, and so is the mother. I'm on my way in to see them now."

"Hooray," said Wehling emptily.

"You don't sound very happy," said Dr. Hitz.

"What man in my shoes wouldn't be happy?" said Wehling. He gestured with his hands to symbolize carefree simplicity. "All I have to do is pick out which one of the triplets is going to live, then deliver my maternal grandfather to the Happy Hooligan, and come back here with a receipt."

* * * * *

Dr. Hitz became rather severe with Wehling, towered over him. "You don't believe in population control, Mr. Wehling?" he said.

"I think it's perfectly keen," said Wehling tautly.

"Would you like to go back to the good old days, when the population of the Earth was twenty billion--about to become forty billion, then eighty billion, then one hundred and sixty billion? Do you know what a drupelet is, Mr. Wehling?" said Hitz.

"Nope," said Wehling sulkily.

"A drupelet, Mr. Wehling, is one of the little knobs, one of the little pulpy grains of a blackberry," said Dr. Hitz.

"Without population control, human beings would now be

packed on this surface of this old planet like drupelets on a blackberry! Think of it!"

Wehling continued to stare at the same spot on the wall.

"In the year 2000," said Dr. Hitz, "before scientists stepped in and laid down the law, there wasn't even enough drinking water to go around, and nothing to eat but sea-weed--and still people insisted on their right to reproduce like jackrabbits. And their right, if possible, to live forever."

"I want those kids," said Wehling quietly. "I want all three of them."

"Of course you do," said Dr. Hitz. "That's only human."

"I don't want my grandfather to die, either," said Wehling.

"Nobody's really happy about taking a close relative to the Catbox," said Dr. Hitz gently, sympathetically.

"I wish people wouldn't call it that," said Leora Duncan.

"What?" said Dr. Hitz.

"I wish people wouldn't call it 'the Catbox,' and things like that," she said. "It gives people the wrong impression."

"You're absolutely right," said Dr. Hitz. "Forgive me." He corrected himself, gave the municipal gas chambers their official title, a title no one ever used in conversation. "I should have said, 'Ethical Suicide Studios,'" he said.

"That sounds so much better," said Leora Duncan.

"This child of yours--whichever one you decide to keep, Mr. Wehling," said Dr. Hitz. "He or she is going to live on a happy, roomy, clean, rich planet, thanks to population control. In a garden like that mural there." He shook his head. "Two centuries ago, when I was a young man, it was a hell that nobody thought could last another twenty years. Now centuries of peace and plenty stretch before us as far as the imagination cares to travel."

He smiled luminously.

The smile faded as he saw that Wehling had just drawn a revolver.

Wehling shot Dr. Hitz dead. "There's room for one--a great big one," he said.

And then he shot Leora Duncan. "It's only death," he said to her as she fell. "There! Room for two."

And then he shot himself, making room for all three of his children.

Nobody came running. Nobody, seemingly, heard the shots.

The painter sat on the top of his stepladder, looking down reflectively on the sorry scene.

* * * * *

The painter pondered the mournful puzzle of life demanding to be born and, once born, demanding to be fruitful ... to multiply and to live as long as possible--to do all that on a very small planet that would have to last forever.

All the answers that the painter could think of were grim. Even grimmer, surely, than a Catbox, a Happy Hooligan, an Easy Go. He thought of war. He thought of plague. He thought of starvation.

He knew that he would never paint again. He let his paintbrush fall to the dropcloths below. And then he decided he had had about enough of life in the Happy Garden of Life, too, and he came slowly down from the ladder.

He took Wehling's pistol, really intending to shoot himself. But he didn't have the nerve.

And then he saw the telephone booth in the corner of the room. He went to it, dialed the well-remembered number: "2 B R 0 2 B."

"Federal Bureau of Termination," said the very warm voice of a hostess.

"How soon could I get an appointment?" he asked, speaking very carefully.

"We could probably fit you in late this afternoon, sir," she said. "It might even be earlier, if we get a cancellation."

"All right," said the painter, "fit me in, if you please." And he gave her his name, spelling it out.

"Thank you, sir," said the hostess. "Your city thanks you; your country thanks you; your planet thanks you. But the deepest thanks of all is from future generations."

TURBULENCE
Kylee Evans

Looking out from the terminal window in the wee hours of the October morning, the infusion of crimson and lilac colors graced the smoggy sky. The people in the airport were lethargically planted in their seats, while the airline personnel stood dully at their post. My little brother and I were the only ones wide awake from our caffeine wiring, combined with the temporary energy ignition from a McDonalds breakfast. As I awaited to board the flight to Miami, Florida, I listened to the sporadic roll of wheels on the pearly-white speckled floor, and glanced at this quick-tempered woman who continuously twitched at the screams of a young child across the departure lounge. I was entranced by this peculiar lady, because her patience wore thin, like a fragile string on a banjo ready for it's last pluck. Once the staff green-lit us to board, my mother quickly nudged my shoulder to alert our hasty uprising. We were first in line to board the A section, with boarding passes in hand, backpacks zipped, as we smoothly treaded down the hollow tarmac. Right as I walked past the artificially cordial flight attendants, I was adorned by the non-claustrophobic empty isles, and the plushy luminescent baby blue seats. My mother immediately scooted her way into the first aisle as my brother and I closely followed. My brother propped both my mother's and my small carry-on suitcases onto the drably painted shelves as the rest of the passengers piled in behind us. Once we were settled, my brother and I played our favorite airplane game... people watch. As the rest of the passengers stuttered in, the variety of different faces amused us. One man stood in the middle of the aisle allowing people to pass him by, because he was unsure of what seat to sit in. His diaphoretic face was drenched with fear and displacement, as if this was his first time on an airplane. Another woman was as contagious as the Bubonic Plague, she wore a germ-protection mask and latex gloves with a cough that sounded as if parasites were feasting on her fragile lungs. The next noticeable prospect was the disturbed woman from the departure lounge; she was as creepy as a porcelain doll placed in a haunted house. She was definitely in her late forties yet, her face was pulled back far enough it could replace a slingshot. Her body was extremely muscular which downplayed the strained softness in her extremely pale facial appearance. Her hair was bleached blonde which wiped her out completely, leaving her chiseled cheekbones as a shadow to break the harsh arrangement of her highlighted features. The sounds began to build up from the chatter and occasional dings from the pilot channels, and the subtle escalation of noise became seemingly bothersome to the impetuous woman, as her nostrils began to flare and her cheeks broke out into microscopic hives. My brother and I turned to each other in utter discontent, hoping she would not sit adjacent to us... But that, she did. She swiftly hauled up her bags into the shelves and sat down gracefully. She was very agile and flexible but slightly odd once she crossed her legs into a Buddhist praying position. More people began to take their seats, as two scrawny twin men sat beside her. The last members to board happened to consist of the crying baby who agitated the twitching woman's peace, along with his two densely inconsiderate parents, and the only seats that were left, were the ones directly behind the impulsive woman. By this time my mother had already fallen into a deep sleep, which was routinely normal. Once everyone had taken their seats, we immediately prepared for takeoff. While we still remained on the runway, the flight attendants on both sides of the plane held up little pamphlets instructing us of what to do in case of an emergency, and once that humdrum spiel was done with, the plane was near departure. However, soon after the flight attendants left the aisles, the screeching shrill of a naughty brat echoed all the way to the last cabin row. The small child reeked of a stench that only days without a bath could bring. His parents were doe-eyed newbies that seemed as if they gave up on parenting, and just let him holler. And by no surprise, the woman across from me, lit up faster than a kerosene fire in the summertime. She immediately wriggled her way out of her positioning and popped her head over the seat. Her pupils were dilated and the hairs on her head rose from static formulation. She lunged her fist right at the boys jaw, but her swing, thankfully missed. Her chaotic amplification caused a major scene so I decided to alert the nearest flight attendant, and right as I did, she whipped her head in my direction, and screamed at the top of her lungs. My mother jolted awake as this ludicrous crisis that scarred a permanent scowl on her face. As she tried to figure out the situation through my brother. The parents of the child sprung up and called for help. The twins sitting next to her crossed their arms in front of their face and leaned against the window. All of the passengers were alerted by this time, and enraged by this deranged animalistic woman. She would not stop staring at me, alternating a heroin-like scratch of the arm, with an eerie burst of laughter. I decided to look away, as my mother made an effort to share eyes with her. When suddenly she yelled… "Shut up! All of you! You disgusting rats, bleed! And bleed some more!" The place flew up in uproar, as many people cussed at her and alerted the flight crew. One by one, each flight attendant rushed to the scene to deal with this demented head case. The lady was clearly having an out-of-body experience or a mental breakdown at this point. She threw out racial slurs to me as well, as an Indian man across the way. A teenager stood up and yelled, "This lady's on bath salts!" The flight attendants huddled around her until a pilot could call for help. But through the warmbodied flight crew I could still see the woman's eyes piercing directly at me, as she winked uncontrollably. The twin passengers beside her jumped over her and frantically moved into the middle of the isle to get away from her possessed soul. Not long after, the police arrived and escorted the dingbat off the plane, and as she got up she uttered to the officers with a calming voice, "Sorry officers, it must have been the turbulence." And she was gone.

THE GOOD, BAD AND THE JESUS
Penelope Lowder

Reverend Woodson stepped down hard on the floor, shakin' an' quakin' the whole gotdamn building! Colored folks fannin' off the humid heat with white fans. Reverend lookin' ovah the whole congregation. His good eye puttin' the stink on us.

"Gawd would smite thee down!" Behold, I shew you a mystery; we shall not all sleep, but we shall all be changed. I Corinthians 15 –

He looked over at some Negro mesmerized by his preachin'. His brown, bloodshot eyes fillin' with wonderment. The Reverend looked from the man's eyes, down to the man's hands that was clutched around the collection plate. The Reverend drew back in dismay, stomp hop twice on the floor.

"Gawd don't like greedy. He wants all his flock to be generous and giva' to the house of worship to honor His Father!"

The Reverend looked ovah at the mesmerized man hopin' that would shake the man's hands loose but he did not budge. The man's clutch was tight on that collection plate, like the grip of a rabid dog. Ms. Pitts a saintly woman, whose husband was serving time on Captain Bridges farm for havin' his zipper down in front of a white woman, was eagerly awaitin to place her tithin' in the plate. Her husband had about six part time jobs and was haulin' away furniture for some white woman when he went to take a leak in the woods. He come back to move the rest of the furniture an' the woman started screamin' rape. He tried to explain things to her, that he forgot to zip up an' she called Sheriff Fountain. Although there was no evidence of rape or him even thinkin' about rapin', he got six years on Captain Bridges work farm. Ms. Pitts prayed, prayed hard. Where was the church? Where was anybody to save Mr. Pitts? But she loyal to this preacher an' every Sunday got her tithe ready hopin' that the good Lord, Jesus or anybody would return her husband to her in one piece. Her sausage fingers bulging through her delicate pink embroidered glove wavin' her tithin' for Jeesus. Reverend leaned in at the man, took out his holy white handkerchief embroidered with small crosses on each side, wiped the sweat from the sides of his mouth then flashin' all thirty two's toward the man.

" Is you alright brother?"

The man's spell was broke, like he woke up, realizin' he probably wasn't in heaven. He shook off whatever he was thinkin, jumped.

"Uh-uh-uh Yes Reverend."

Reverend grin got even wider; he drew breath, exhaled his annoyance into the microphone.

"Then Brother stop holdin' onto the plate like you the gatekeeper Peter and pass it on to sistah' Pitts.

The man, embarrassed, passed the plate to sistah Pitts who was in the throes of the holy holy. He tapped her on her arm. Startled she slapped the poor man's hand away. She raised up in the name of the Holy Spirit, sendin' the poor man deeper into his seat.

"Don't you know not to tap a woman catchin' the spirit?"

The man got some backbone after seein'the rest of the congregation snicker at his weakness.

"Ah Woman put your envelope in the plate."

The preacher straightened up, took a step forward. Bent down real low like, whisperin' in the man's ear.

"Don't let me have to summon the Deacons."

The man now fully back on earth and not so mesmerized shifted in his seat, tugged at the line of his light brown cassimere trousers. He looked real hard at Ms. Pitts. She stayed sanctified. He rose up, ready to walk, She tugged at his jacket. He jerked back.

"Turn me loose woman."

She held on tighter to him, thinkin' whatever she had shown him in private would work in the daylight.

"Oh come on Elgin, Reverend didn't mean nuthin' by it". Right Reverend?

The congregation in unison drew a huge gasp at a secret they knew wasn't secret but she spoke the indiscretion. A sanctified woman, whose husband doin' time, shackin' up with a new man. A man no one had met only speculated about. He sat back down, his agitation was wearin' that suit.

"See honey this why I don't go to chuuch. Ya' see what all happens."

Sister Pitts lookin' back at the eyes condemnin' her before her round wide bottom could touch the bench. She patted her newfound man, which was gonna be the church's early-afternoon-Sunday-dinner-take-the-children-outta-the-room, gossip story. Man like that he was now apart of the community.

Yeah brother let me put some wisdom on you. Stay anonymous an' pass the plate. That's how you keep yor'self outta trouble. Pass that plate. The Reverend jus' preachin' an' the plate bein' passed. Lonely heart Sandy Clark drop one dollar bills, Horace Hilton droppin' five-dollar bills, Donard Pinkton droppin' ten dollar bills an' I mean it just keep goin', pass the plate.

The plate does some good, it helps some of these niggahs when they get sick, or about to lose they house, or get some niggah out of town, fast, dependin' on the niggah... that money goes to help with the what nots. Well here comes the plate. I drop my dollar in. Lookin' at it sittin on a pile of Lincolns, Washington's, Jackson's. All those dead white men, laughin' lookin' at me. I can hear their voices; say, "Stick 'em up." Then I look at that Reverend, he hollerin' with his mouth an' the whole time got one eye watchin' that collection plate.

A couple of young gals in the back, one light skin wearin' a soft chiffon peach dress an' the other nice brown-red bone lookin' gal in a light green colored dress, was lookin' at Tigner an' me. They whisper somethin' to each other. In the middle of 'em was this young boy, about eight dressed in a dark suit. He never moved, jus sat there starin' at me. Those two gals whisperin' away an' then from time to time look up at the Reverend. I looked at Tigner.

"You know them gals, sittin' behin' us?"

Tigner shifted around and turned back. Straightened himself up.

"No."

I crinkled my brow an' let it go. Passed him the plate.

"Your turn."

Tigner's tight wad self. Reverend gonna be a little light. Tigner rather spend his money on painted up women, fast cars and hard liquor…

"Tigner put your wallet away man I put down a dollar. Fifty cents for both us. You can pay me when we git outta here. "

Tigner didn't hear a word. His hand was on his billfold, his fingers fishin' through rectangular green bills. I stared at him.

Whatchu' gonna do?

"Bill, quiet now."

Bill? I STOPPED. Looked at Tigner. I thought, Tigner this is me, Foots… You don't have ta impress these folks'…I sat back, let Tigner make his tithe of a dollar. Tigner done throwed down a ten-dollar bill in the collection plate!

"Tigner, niggah what's wrong with you!"

He folded his billfold, stuffed it in his pocket an' sat back.

"I can git right with the Lord."

"When you ever been concerned about gittin' right with the Lord?"

The preacher strides on ovah on a string of Yeesah, Jeeeeesus enough of those to land him right in front of us. He whipped that microphone down in front of our faces. He think he gonna make a lesson outta me and Tigner.

I said loudly, "don't give all your money to this man, he ridin' in a brand new Cadillac! And over at the juke..' Well that's all I could git out before the Reverend full baritone voice hugs the mic.

PASS THE PLATE AH!

Tigner bout to pass the plate. I grabbed the plate back.

"Uh hold on a minute."

I fished through a mountain of ten, twenty, five dollar bills and white envelopes. Tigner ovah there lookin' horrified. The congregation was just a chatterin' away at what I was doin'. The Reverend's almightiness disappeared an' the man I knew from over at the juke joint, dancin' it up and liquorin' it down on Saturday nights appeared.

"BOY, YOU BETTAH PASS THAT PLATE!"

I stayed calm, enjoyin' every moment.

In my best Sydney Poitier impression, "Noht until I get my dollah." An' went back to fishin' ever so politely for my dollar.

"BOY PASS THE PLATE. YOU CAN'T TAKE BACK YOUR DOLLAR! GAWD, DONE BRING US DOWN HERE TO FELLOWSHIP WITH HIM. GETAH CLOSE TO HIM!"

A chorus of female voices rang out loud and clear, "AMEN REVEREND!" The words settlin' in on the back of my neck. "AMEN" I hear Tigner's deep-throated croaked voice. He bowin' his head an' carryin' on. This niggah done more wicked shit than anyone I know an' he got us both sittin' in the front pew. When I git outta here gonna bop this niggah in the head. Tigner know he come for the fried chicken.

"Too much money takes you away form Gawd-ah tithin' the only way GAwd-ah will bless you. He will give awl you need. WHATCHU' DOIN', THAT'S GOIN' AGAINST GAWD!"

I sat on the edge of my seat. The hardwood bench cuttin' into the circulation of the back of my legs makin' me move rhythmically back an' forth.

"No It's goin' against the payments you got to make on that Cadillac every month."

The Reverend lurch toward me takin' big gigantic purposeful steps.

"BOY YOU PLAYIN' IN THE DEVIL'S PLAYGROUND."

"Reverend, you brought the ball an' the bat, I'm jes tryin' to git my dollar bill."

The Deacons stood up as the Reverend stepped closer to me.

"BOY THERE ARE PLENTY OF DOLLAR BILLS IN THERE."

"Mines has a red bulls eye on it. It's my lucky dollar."

Tigner spun toward me, tallkin through his grinnin' teeth, tryin' to keep up some kinda' front.

"Foots why you got to act this way?"

"You the one Amenin' an' carryin' on like your baptism took".

Tigner rose up, the blackness of his skin seem to shine brighter, his eyes narrowed, his smile wiped away.

"Niggah it did take!"

"You told me it didn't!"

"You askin' me why I do the things I do, how else you expect me to explain what it is I do."

"You a outlaw Niggah, same as me. End of explanation."

The Preacher had enough. He summoned the Deacons to come deal with us.

"Negro take your dollar out of that plate and git out of my church with your sinnin' ways."

I stopped the Deacons by loadin' the stink eye on 'em. Well I found my dollar. It dropped down to the bottom. I plucked it up out of the plate, passed the plate to the next person who I recognized cuz we play cards together.

"Hey Markus how you doin'?"

Nigga' act like he didn't know me. Thass alright. When he need money to stake him for one more hand, his memory'll come back.

I got up, start to leave. Tigner pulled me back down.

"Man what's wrong with you?" I reshaped my smoked grey flannel suit.

Tigner looked at me with this grin. Oh shit is Tigner gonna hold up the congregation?

He stood up and turned to the congregation.

"Please excuse my friend and me. We been outlawin' for so long. We jes don't know how to act amongst decent folk. Reverend we have been playin' with the devil an' now its time for us to stop, git a jersey an' join the Lawd's team. Bill, stand up and say you sorry."

I jumped back in my seat, "WHAT?!"

Tigner stood straight as an oak tree.

"I said, apologize to these kind people."

My head's spinnin' tryin' to make sense of what's goin' on here. I looked back at all the people in this church many of 'em I know. There was tricky ass Adams who sold watered down liquor but charged full price on the dollar. There was Clarence Pritchard, who lay you away, but don't die on Friday night cuz he'll double his price. Saturday night is card night an' that man can't play cards worth a damn.

351

Sittin' in the third row with his girlfriend is Scotty Anders, brown skin Negro, got a muscle twitch on his right lip. Story goes that he was messin' around with some woman an' her husband cut him above his lip, when he did, cut one 'a the nerves an' that negro been twitchin' since then. I wonder if Mrs. Anders would approve of the new girlfriend? Too bad she livin' a few counties down from us, deep in them back woods. Maybe I'll put that on my list as places to visit. Yeah they were all there. Not all of 'em bad but more than most of these people need more than throwin' money in a plate and sayin' Amen. They need to be thrown in a river. Baptized and pardoned by a system that we live under.

I looked at Tigner lookin' over all the congregation. He nudgin' at me. Annoyed cuz I don't like to be nudged. Okay he want me to speak. I hopped up right side of Tigner. I grabbed a bible out of the hands of Phalba Quarrels. Hell she a good woman, she won't miss it. I held that book out high. On the front cover of her bible was the picture of Jesus in his pale skin, long hair, his gaze locked toward the heavens, hands together in prayer. For the first time, I studied this picture of this man, Jesus the son of God. Everyone starin' at me, Miss Quarrels, near tears cuz she terrified at the thought of the damage I could do to her bible. I lifted the book higher above my head. Turned Jesus in the direction of the Reverend.

"Reverend! Is this the man we all suppose to pray to, the one that's suppose to keep us from harm? I'd like to say somethin' to him: so far you not doin' a good job Jesus, you or your father. Just thought I'd let you know."

Somethin' came up in me. All the frustration that I guess been inside me, the frustration of standin at that fork in the road and wantin to choose one thing for my life, like goin' away to school, studyin' somethin', that'll give me the life I see up on the movie screens an' then the other fork that says I'm a second class citizen, the fork of survival, that path I hopped on at a young age an' never could git off, even if that other fork presented itself, just briefly, at times...it was that frustration that come up in me at this moment.

"We don't need to look up to a white Jesus but look to the strength of who we are as a people. We're strong men, we can take these white men. We don't need to listen to words put to us in a book by white people. Hell we know what's right and wrong. We do wrong because for us to make it by doin right, that just gets us hangin' from a rope, our women raped and a bes' friend shot dead between the eyes. All these crooked ass preachers want one thing: for you to pass that plate. Pass that plate. You all walkin' an the Reverend he ridin in a new shiny black Cadillac. Ask yourselves. When has the Reverend ask you if you need a ride? Passed you on that dirt road, seein' you walk miles home an' stopped his car an said, "brother, sister come on in." When?" You know what Tigner and I come for?

Tigner go to pullin' on my suit.

"Foots, sit down niggah!"

I turned to the window and point to the women at that fire pit. Smoke just flowin' up the sky.

"Y'all smell that? That chicken? That's what Tigner and me come for. The barbecue. As soon as I get my barbecue sandwich, y'all will never see me again."

The PREACHER raise up, "SHAME ON YOU!"

Now I stood up an made my way to the pulpit.

"Shame on you preacher for chargin' one dollar for a barbecue chicken sandwich and a bottle of pop."

A young woman started to cry an' run out the church. The gals next to her were giving Tigner the look of death. He looked at me. Shrugged his shoulders.

"Hand me the plate nigga'."

Tigner got his ten-dollar bill out of the plate.

"Foots less go! Yo' yerlla ass done put the plug in the dam."

"What the hell does that mean?'

"She done run out the chuuch man, no point in me stayin'."

"You mean you came..?"

"Shut up niggah an' less go git the car." Tigner lit up outta the church. Red-hot.

Now I understood why we was here. This man dragged me here for this little ol' gal. Tigner gon' pay for my sandwich. What am I doin' here again?

The Preacher cued the organ, the Deacons eased on back to their seats near the pulpit! The preacher hollared out, "LESS PRAY FOR THESE BOYS LET US PRAY."

I walked down the aisle. Clappin' all the way. The church people, even the ones that were beyond Jesus touchin' me in kindness. The preacher's wife threw her fan at me and one of those crooked niggars screamed out that I need to git right with the Lawd! That young boy that was starin' at me slowly got to his feet.

The music got me all the way to the door, I spun around on my heels.

HEY!!! I SAID HEY!!!!

The preacher stopped the organ. I dipped back in.

"Y'ALL WANNA BE FREE? GIT THE HELL OUTTA THIS PLACE!"

Silence. Everyone was lookin' at me. Even the guy who was with Ms. Pitts was lookin' at me funny. The young boy walked toward me, kicked me in the leg an' took off runnin' outta the church.

The Preacher saw this as an opportune time to strike it up for the Lawd!

"YOU GOOD PEOPLE DON'T NEED TO HEAR THE WORDS OF THE DEVIL'S PROPHET."

He raised his hands like a conductor conductin' a orchestra. The people rose up as one. He took that white handkerchief and wiped his sweaty brow.

"Congregation y'all got your work cut out for you."

He snapped his fingers at the organist, a three hundred pound, biscuit, pork chop eatin mutha fucker. Lookin' like Fats Waller. Oh he was sharp and could play like him too. He struck his hands on the keys and the organ seem to take life on its own. The pipes blew out sound only the heavens and his angels could summon up. He snapped his fingers at the choir who stood to attention. The one three beat notes moved the people, the buildin' heaven an' earth. The LAWD had stepped in his house. The congregation swayin' back and forth singin' Give Me That Old Time Religion. The end of each chorus the brother on the organ ripped his fingers against the black and white keys movin' forth another verse. It was loud overwhelming, my heart was jumpin to the two four syncopated, holy roller sound. They unleashed their prayer dance, hoppin up and down, swayin' side to side, stompin' feet. The holy holy in their voices, ridin' notes, pushin' me outta the church.

I tumbled outside into some dark woods. The music stopped. I turned over to look behind me and there was no church. Just pitch black forest. My body tumbled into the dirty ground. The damp wet mud soilin' my trousers suckin' me into the earth. Thick leaves blanketin' my body formin' the top of ma grave as I sunk deeper and deeper into the earth. The damp mud pushin' me down deeper an' the last thing I see is a white man with a beard and long hair, smilin'. He took my hand, his hand was the color of mine but it was too late. The last light disappeared as I sunk, deeper, settlin' further into the earth, the damp mud sealin' my corpse.

My eyes open. I jump. Look about me ta' see my car rammed up against a tree. It was quiet. Look down at my guns gripped tight in my hands. The butt imprinted in the lines of my flesh. I shake the nightmare off. Light breaks through the many leaves; now I can see more of what happened to me. The sheriff and his boys tried to kill me. Shot at me. The little boy, ridin' with me took my barbecue sandwich an' run off. Hell maybe Jesus was on my side last night. Just a little bit. Trouble is Sheriff Fountain an' his boys believe in Jesus too…Wonder whose side he gon' be on today?

Hunger gripped my stomach. I raised up off the ground, gave my body a good stretch, folded the flaps of my collar down.

"Well I gotta long long walk ahead."

TWIST

: to bend or turn (something) in order to change
its shape: to bend or turn (something) into a
shape or position that is not normal or natural:

A plot twist is a radical change in the expected direction or
outcome of the plot of a novel, film, television
series, comic, video game, or other work of narrative.[1] It is
a common practice in narration used to keep the interest of
an audience, usually surprising them with a revelation.
Some "twists" are foreshadowed.

A method used to undermine the expectations of the
audience is the false protagonist. It involves presenting a
character at the start of the film as the main character, but
then disposing of this character, usually killing them – a
device known as a red herring.

THE PIG
Roald Dahl

In England once there lived a big
And wonderfully clever pig.
To everybody it was plain
That Piggy had a massive brain.
He worked out sums inside his head,
There was no book he hadn't read.
He knew what made an airplane fly,
He knew how engines worked and why.
He knew all this, but in the end
One question drove him round the bend:
He simply couldn't puzzle out
What LIFE was really all about.
What was the reason for his birth?
Why was he placed upon this earth?
His giant brain went round and round.
Alas, no answer could be found.
Till suddenly one wondrous night.
All in a flash he saw the light.
He jumped up like a ballet dancer
And yelled, "By gum, I've got the answer!"
"They want my bacon slice by slice
"To sell at a tremendous price!
"They want my tender juicy chops
"To put in all the butcher's shops!
"They want my pork to make a roast
"And that's the part'll cost the most!
"They want my sausages in strings!
"They even want my chitterlings!
"The butcher's shop! The carving knife!
"That is the reason for my life!"
Such thoughts as these are not designed

To give a pig great piece of mind.
Next morning, in comes Farmer Bland,
A pail of pigswill in his hand,
And piggy with a mighty roar,
Bashes the farmer to the floor…
Now comes the rather grizzly bit
So let's not make too much of it,
Except that you must understand
That Piggy did eat Farmer Bland,
He ate him up from head to toe,
Chewing the pieces nice and slow.
It took an hour to reach the feet,
Because there was so much to eat,
And when he finished, Pig, of course,
Felt absolutely no remorse.
Slowly he scratched his brainy head
And with a little smile he said,
"I had a fairly powerful hunch
"That he might have me for his lunch.
"And so, because I feared the worst,
"I thought I'd better eat him first."

THE LOTTERY
Shirley Jackson

The morning of June 27th was clear and sunny, with the fresh warmth of a full-summer day; the flowers were blossoming profusely and the grass was richly green. The people of the village began to gather in the square, between the post office and the bank, around ten o'clock; in some towns there were so many people that the lottery took two days and had to be started on June 2th. but in this village, where there were only about three hundred people, the whole lottery took less than two hours, so it could begin at ten o'clock in the morning and still be through in time to allow the villagers to get home for noon dinner.

The children assembled first, of course. School was recently over for the summer, and the feeling of liberty sat uneasily on most of them; they tended to gather together quietly for a while before they broke into boisterous play. and their talk was still of the classroom and the teacher, of books and reprimands. Bobby Martin had already stuffed his pockets full of stones, and the other boys soon followed his example, selecting the smoothest and roundest stones; Bobby and Harry Jones and Dickie Delacroix-- the villagers pronounced this name "Dellacroy"-- eventually made a great pile of stones in one corner of the square and guarded it against the raids of the other boys. The girls stood aside, talking among themselves, looking over their shoulders at the boys. and the very small children rolled in the dust or clung to the hands of their older brothers or sisters.

Soon the men began to gather. surveying their own children, speaking of planting and rain, tractors and taxes. They stood together, away from the pile of stones in the corner, and their jokes were quiet and they smiled rather than laughed. The women, wearing faded house dresses and sweaters, came shortly after their menfolk. They greeted one another and exchanged bits of gossip as they went to join their husbands. Soon the women, standing by their husbands, began to call to their children, and the children came reluctantly, having to be called four or five times. Bobby Martin ducked under his mother's grasping hand

and ran, laughing, back to the pile of stones. His father spoke up sharply, and Bobby came quickly and took his place between his father and his oldest brother.

The lottery was conducted--as were the square dances, the teen club, the Halloween program--by Mr. Summers. who had time and energy to devote to civic activities. He was a round-faced, jovial man and he ran the coal business, and people were sorry for him. because he had no children and his wife was a scold. When he arrived in the square, carrying the black wooden box, there was a murmur of conversation among the villagers, and he waved and called. "Little late today, folks." The postmaster, Mr. Graves, followed him, carrying a three- legged stool, and the stool was put in the center of the square and Mr. Summers set the black box down on it. The villagers kept their distance, leaving a space between themselves and the stool. and when Mr. Summers said, "Some of you fellows want to give me a hand?" there was a hesitation before two men. Mr. Martin and his oldest son, Baxter. came forward to hold the box steady on the stool while Mr. Summers stirred up the papers inside it.

The original paraphernalia for the lottery had been lost long ago, and the black box now resting on the stool had been put into use even before Old Man Warner, the oldest man in town, was born. Mr. Summers spoke frequently to the villagers about making a new box, but no one liked to upset even as much tradition as was represented by the black box. There was a story that the present box had been made with some pieces of the box that had preceded it, the one that had been constructed when the first people settled down to make a village here. Every year, after the lottery, Mr. Summers began talking again about a new box, but every year the subject was allowed to fade off without anything's being done. The black box grew shabbier each year: by now it was no longer completely black but splintered badly along one side to show the original wood color, and in some places faded or stained.

Mr. Martin and his oldest son, Baxter, held the black box securely on the stool until Mr. Summers had stirred the papers thoroughly with his hand. Because so much of the ritual had been forgotten or discarded, Mr. Summers had been successful in having slips of paper substituted for the chips of wood that had been used for generations. Chips of wood, Mr. Summers had argued. had been all very well when the village was tiny, but now that the population was more than three hundred and likely to keep on growing, it was necessary to use something that would fit more easily into he black box. The night before the lottery, Mr. Summers and Mr. Graves made up the slips of paper and put them in the box, and it was then taken to the safe of Mr. Summers' coal company and locked up until Mr. Summers was ready to take it to the square next morning. The rest of the year, the box was put way, sometimes one place, sometimes another; it had spent one year in Mr. Graves's barn and another year underfoot in the post office. and sometimes it was set on a shelf in the Martin grocery and left there.

There was a great deal of fussing to be done before Mr. Summers declared the lottery open. There were the lists to make up--of heads of families. heads of households in each family. members of each household in each family. There was the proper swearing-in of Mr. Summers by the postmaster, as the official of the lottery; at one time, some people remembered, there had been a recital of some sort, performed by the official of the lottery, a perfunctory. tuneless chant that had been rattled off duly each year; some people believed that the official of the lottery used to stand just so when he said or sang it, others believed that he was supposed to walk among the people, but years and years ago this p3rt of the ritual had been allowed to lapse. There had been, also, a ritual salute, which the official of the lottery had had to use in addressing each person who came up to draw from the box, but this also had changed with time, until now it was felt necessary only for the official to speak to each person approaching. Mr. Summers was very good at all this; in his clean white shirt and blue jeans. with one hand resting carelessly on the black box. he seemed very proper and important as he talked interminably to Mr. Graves and the Martins.

Just as Mr. Summers finally left off talking and turned to the assembled villagers, Mrs. Hutchinson came hurriedly along the path to the square, her sweater thrown over her shoulders, and slid into place in the back of the crowd. "Clean forgot what day it was," she said to Mrs. Delacroix, who stood next to her, and they both laughed softly. "Thought my old man was out back stacking wood," Mrs. Hutchinson went on. "and then I looked out the window and the kids was gone, and then I remembered it was the twenty-seventh and came a-running." She dried her hands on her apron, and Mrs. Delacroix said, "You're in time, though. They're still talking away up there."

Mrs. Hutchinson craned her neck to see through the crowd and found her husband and children standing near the front. She tapped Mrs. Delacroix on the arm as a farewell and began to make her way through the crowd. The people separated good-humoredly to let her through: two or three people said. in voices just loud enough to be heard across the crowd, "Here comes your, Missus, Hutchinson," and "Bill, she made it after all." Mrs. Hutchinson reached her husband, and Mr. Summers, who had been waiting, said cheerfully. "Thought we were going to have to get on without you, Tessie." Mrs. Hutchinson said. grinning, "Wouldn't have me leave m'dishes in the sink, now, would you. Joe?," and soft laughter ran through the crowd as the people stirred back into position after Mrs. Hutchinson's arrival.

"Well, now." Mr. Summers said soberly, "guess we better get started, get this over with, so's we can go back to work. Anybody ain't here?"

"Dunbar." several people said. "Dunbar. Dunbar."

Mr. Summers consulted his list. "Clyde Dunbar." he said. "That's right. He's broke his leg, hasn't he? Who's drawing for him?"

"Me. I guess," a woman said. and Mr. Summers turned to look at her. "Wife draws for her husband." Mr. Summers said. "Don't you have a grown boy to do it for you, Janey?" Although Mr. Summers and everyone else in the village knew the answer perfectly well, it was the business of the official of the lottery to ask such questions formally. Mr. Summers waited with an expression of polite interest while Mrs. Dunbar answered.

"Horace's not but sixteen yet." Mrs. Dunbar said regretfully. "Guess I gotta fill in for the old man this year."

"Right." Sr. Summers said. He made a note on the list he was holding. Then he asked, "Watson boy drawing this year?"

A tall boy in the crowd raised his hand. "Here," he said. "I m drawing for my mother and me." He blinked his eyes nervously and ducked his head as several voices in the crowd said thin#s like "Good fellow, lack." and "Glad to see your mother's got a man to do it."

"Well," Mr. Summers said, "guess that's everyone. Old Man Warner make it?"

"Here," a voice said. and Mr. Summers nodded.

A sudden hush fell on the crowd as Mr. Summers cleared his throat and looked at the list. "All ready?" he called. "Now, I'll read the names--heads of families first--and the men come up and take a paper out of the box. Keep the paper folded in your hand without looking at it until everyone has had a turn. Everything clear?"

The people had done it so many times that they only half listened to the directions: most of them were quiet. wetting their lips. not looking around. Then Mr. Summers raised one hand high and said, "Adams." A man disengaged himself from the crowd and came forward. "Hi. Steve." Mr. Summers said. and Mr. Adams said. "Hi. Joe." They grinned at one another humorlessly and nervously. Then Mr. Adams reached into the black box and took out a folded paper. He held it firmly by one corner as he turned and went hastily back to his place in the crowd. where he stood a little apart from his family. not looking down at his hand.

"Allen." Mr. Summers said. "Anderson.... Bentham."

"Seems like there's no time at all between lotteries any more." Mrs. Delacroix said to Mrs. Graves in the back row.

"Seems like we got through with the last one only last week."

"Time sure goes fast.-- Mrs. Graves said.

"Clark.... Delacroix"

"There goes my old man." Mrs. Delacroix said. She held her breath while her husband went forward.

"Dunbar," Mr. Summers said, and Mrs. Dunbar went steadily to the box while one of the women said. "Go on. Janey," and another said, "There she goes."

"We're next." Mrs. Graves said. She watched while Mr. Graves came around from the side of the box, greeted Mr. Summers gravely and selected a slip of paper from the box. By now, all through the crowd there were men holding the small folded papers in their large hand. turning them over and over nervously Mrs. Dunbar and her two sons stood together, Mrs. Dunbar holding the slip of paper.

"Harburt.... Hutchinson."

"Get up there, Bill," Mrs. Hutchinson said. and the people near her laughed.

"Jones."

"They do say," Mr. Adams said to Old Man Warner, who stood next to him, "that over in the north village they're talking of giving up the lottery."

Old Man Warner snorted. "Pack of crazy fools," he said. "Listening to the young folks, nothing's good enough for them. Next thing you know, they'll be wanting to go back to living in caves, nobody work any more, live hat way for a while. Used to be a saying about 'Lottery in June, corn be heavy soon.' First thing you know, we'd all be eating stewed chickweed and acorns. There's always been a lottery," he added petulantly. "Bad enough to see young Joe Summers up there joking with everybody."

"Some places have already quit lotteries." Mrs. Adams said.

"Nothing but trouble in that," Old Man Warner said stoutly. "Pack of young fools."

"Martin." And Bobby Martin watched his father go forward.

"Overdyke.... Percy."

"I wish they'd hurry," Mrs. Dunbar said to her older son. "I wish they'd hurry."

"They're almost through," her son said.

"You get ready to run tell Dad," Mrs. Dunbar said.

Mr. Summers called his own name and then stepped forward precisely and selected a slip from the box. Then he called, "Warner."

"Seventy-seventh year I been in the lottery," Old Man Warner said as he went through the crowd. "Seventy-seventh time."

"Watson" The tall boy came awkwardly through the crowd. Someone said, "Don't be nervous, Jack," and Mr. Summers said, "Take your time, son."

"Zanini."

After that, there was a long pause, a breathless pause, until Mr. Summers. holding his slip of paper in the air, said, "All right, fellows." For a minute, no one moved, and then all the slips of paper were opened. Suddenly, all the women began to speak at once, saving. "Who is it?," "Who's got it," "Is it the Dunbars?,"

"Is it the Watsons?" Then the voices began to say, "It's Hutchinson. It's Bill," "Bill Hutchinson's got it."

"Go tell your father," Mrs. Dunbar said to her older son.

People began to look around to see the Hutchinsons. Bill Hutchinson was standing quiet, staring down at the paper in his hand. Suddenly. Tessie Hutchinson shouted to Mr. Summers. "You didn't give him time enough to take any paper he wanted. I saw you. It wasn't fair!"

"Be a good sport, Tessie." Mrs. Delacroix called, and Mrs. Graves said, "All of us took the same chance."

"Shut up, Tessie," Bill Hutchinson said.

"Well, everyone," Mr. Summers said, "that was done pretty fast, and now we've got to be hurrying a little more to get done in time." He consulted his next list. "Bill," he said, "you draw for the Hutchinson family. You got any other households in the Hutchinsons?"

"There's Don and Eva," Mrs. Hutchinson yelled. "Make them take their chance!"

"Daughters draw with their husbands' families, Tessie," Mr. Summers said gently. "You know that as well as anyone else."

"It wasn't fair," Tessie said.

"I guess not, Joe." Bill Hutchinson said regretfully. "My daughter draws with her husband's family; that's only fair. And I've got no other family except the kids."

"Then, as far as drawing for families is concerned, it's you," Mr. Summers said in explanation, "and as far as drawing for households is concerned, that's you, too. Right?"

"Right," Bill Hutchinson said.

"How many kids, Bill?" Mr. Summers asked formally.

"Three," Bill Hutchinson said.

"There's Bill, Jr., and Nancy, and little Dave. And Tessie and me."

"All right, then," Mr. Summers said. "Harry, you got their tickets back?"

Mr. Graves nodded and held up the slips of paper. "Put them in the box, then," Mr. Summers directed. "Take Bill's and put it in."

"I think we ought to start over," Mrs. Hutchinson said, as quietly as she could. "I tell you it wasn't fair. You didn't give him time enough to choose. Everybody saw that."

Mr. Graves had selected the five slips and put them in the box. and he dropped all the papers but those onto the ground. where the breeze caught them and lifted them off.

"Listen, everybody," Mrs. Hutchinson was saying to the people around her.

"Ready, Bill?" Mr. Summers asked. and Bill Hutchinson, with one quick glance around at his wife and children. nodded.

"Remember," Mr. Summers said. "take the slips and keep them folded until each person has taken one. Harry, you help little Dave." Mr. Graves took the hand of the little boy, who came willingly with him up to the box. "Take a paper out of the box, Davy." Mr. Summers said. Davy put his hand into the box and laughed. "Take just one paper." Mr. Summers said. "Harry, you hold it for him." Mr. Graves took the child's hand and removed the folded paper from the tight fist and held it while little Dave stood next to him and looked up at him wonderingly.

"Nancy next," Mr. Summers said. Nancy was twelve, and her school friends breathed heavily as she went forward switching her skirt, and took a slip daintily from the box "Bill, Jr.," Mr. Summers said, and Billy, his face red and his feet overlarge, near knocked the box over as he got a paper out. "Tessie," Mr. Summers said. She hesitated for a minute, looking around defiantly. and then set her lips and went up to the box. She snatched a paper out and held it behind her.

"Bill," Mr. Summers said, and Bill Hutchinson reached into the box and felt around, bringing his hand out at last with the slip of paper in it.

The crowd was quiet. A girl whispered, "I hope it's not Nancy," and the sound of the whisper reached the edges of the crowd.

"It's not the way it used to be." Old Man Warner said clearly. "People ain't the way they used to be."

"All right," Mr. Summers said. "Open the papers. Harry, you open little Dave's."

Mr. Graves opened the slip of paper and there was a general sigh through the crowd as he held it up and everyone could see that it was blank. Nancy and Bill. Jr.. opened theirs at the same time. and both beamed and laughed. turning around to the crowd and holding their slips of paper above their heads.

"Tessie," Mr. Summers said. There was a pause, and then Mr. Summers looked at Bill Hutchinson, and Bill unfolded his paper and showed it. It was blank.

"It's Tessie," Mr. Summers said, and his voice was hushed. "Show us her paper. Bill."

Bill Hutchinson went over to his wife and forced the slip of paper out of her hand. It had a black spot on it, the black spot Mr. Summers had made the night before with the heavy pencil in the coal company office. Bill Hutchinson held it up, and there was a stir in the crowd.

"All right, folks." Mr. Summers said. "Let's finish quickly." Although the villagers had forgotten the ritual and lost the original black box, they still remembered to use stones. The pile of stones the boys had made earlier was ready; there were stones on the ground with the blowing scraps of paper that had come out of the box Delacroix selected a stone so large she had to pick it up with both hands and turned to Mrs. Dunbar. "Come on," she said. "Hurry up."

Mr. Dunbar had small stones in both hands, and she said. gasping for breath. "I can't run at all. You'll have to go ahead and I'll catch up with you."

The children had stones already. And someone gave little Davy Hutchinson few pebbles.

Tessie Hutchinson was in the center of a cleared space by now, and she held her hands out desperately as the villagers moved in on her. "It isn't fair," she said. A stone hit her on the side of the head. Old Man Warner was saying, "Come on, come on, everyone." Steve Adams was in the front of the crowd of villagers, with Mrs. Graves beside him.

"It isn't fair, it isn't right," Mrs. Hutchinson screamed, and then they were upon her.

FRIENDS
Jaha Zainabu

Me and him never was really all that close
Guess cos I never was really all that cute
But Talanda
She was more
Been friends sixty years now and I won't try to explain her
kinda special
But that what I called her
More

She was more than the better what thought they was
somethin' round there
Only thang
She thought bein' more meant she had to put up with
bottom
So quite natural like she married the biggest asshole she
could find
Who confused real life with bulllshit on the daily
I guess on the other side of thangs he was more too
He was the most

Yeah I did everything I could to stop that wedding
Cos I just knew
A monkey knew
I was one playerhatin'
Cock blockin'
Jealous at the same time
Protectin'
Best friend

I know what you thankin'
Here another story about another brotha don don anotha
sista wrong
Not this time
Not from me

Yeah he had everything to do with the technical parts of
her death
But dammit now she did it to herself
May as well gon call a lie a lie and let the livin' live
What I always says

I told Talanda time over time
Talanda
A woman's got to lover herself enough to love herself all
by herself if she got to
You gotta go
You's a dead woman in this house
Every time I tell her she just look at me cross
Tell me shame on me for not showin' family respect
I never did tell nobody but Talanda
But me and him is first cousins on my daddy side
But that don't never no mind to me

Woman is thicker than blood
Always has been
Besides
Talanda was my friend
My very good friend

Now I need y'all to excuse me
But I had to tell y'all that before I could begin this story
right

I saw her blood all over me before he ever shot her

For years she put up with senseless beatins and name
callins
Some stabbins and gamblins
Cheatins was a given cos it was the time we lived in
Time we livin' in now
So quite right he was a liar too
To this day I'll never know why he bothered with that
The truth was right there in his draws
And she washed them out every night for forty and nine
years
But habit is habit

I was sittin' right there where you are
He was over there about ten feet from us
And Talanda was standin' above me to my left
Course the room was facin' a different way

She and I had been in the house alone at first
She was still prancin' around in the dress she bought that
day
I didn't too much care for it
But I was glad to see her proud
With her head up finally
Some strength about herself

Talanda was a tall woman about 5'9"
Thin too
About 125
Cute little shape though
Lil ole waist and ok breasts and hips for a woman our age
Course she never did have no kids she was allowed to
keep

The dress was red
Not really blood red
But I bet it used to be when it was new

In good shape though
It has small small blue and yellow flowers or somethin' all
over it
A long dress
With red buttons goin' all the way down
'Cept the one at the waist didn't match
Not by design though
Like somebody did best they could to replace it before they
passed it on
It had short sleeves
A swoop neck collar
An elastic band on the back
Rayon?
Yes rayon

Yes indeed
She was somebody new in that dress
Somebody I didn't even know
And I knowed her a long time

She bought the dress from a secondhand store
And I like to believe that the woman who owned it first
Was some kinda kin to her
Was sendin' her some kinda message
Some kinda strength through the dress

Me
I was just sittin' there drinkin' wine
I keeps me a short dog in my purse you know
Then he comes in pushin' right past us like he high offa
somethin'
Walk straight to the room mumblin' somethin' loud don't
nobody know
The woman I useta know would be shakin' in her slippers
by now
But this new Talanda with the dress

Shiiiiiiiiiiit
Didn't pay him a bit a mind
And I told you
I had a little ripple in me

I starts laughin' at him
What I do that for
I shol wish she left him like I told her
Like she knew she wanted to
Just scared is all

Once I even offered her five thousand dollars of my own
funeral money
I will have me a very nice funeral with a fine cherry wood
casket and plenty of expensive wine to go around

I offered her the money to just go
Go somewhere far away
Somewhere and have a better life for the both of us
I shol wish she took it
He came home marchin' in the room with all his man on
Goes over and slaps Talanda in the face
Real hard too
I have told her
Talanda was my very good friend
But I spent almost my whole life in the middle of her and
him

You can't see it
But right here under my right breast where he cut me once
Tryin' to kill her
For a while I thought I had some something honorable like
Ain't no honor in riskin' yo own life for a woman lookin'
to get on the death train anyway
Leastways ain't lookin' to stop it from comin
And I gots kids!

Un ummmmmmmmmm

I told her after that
That was the last time
And like my daddy says
I keeps my word like I keeps my money
I kept right on laughin' too

He slapped her again
This time she look at me like I'm the one crazy
Like I'm the one spent my life up under somebody call me
ugly and do me wrong
Come to think of it
I kinda got mad at her for lookin' at me that way
I started to getup and get in both they faces
But I didn't
I sat right down there and didn't say a word

You would think that would be enough
Then from nowhere he is holdin' a gun to her head
Lookin' straight at me and said
Laugh again and I'll kill yo friend
Dancin' wit it too
Like it's some kind of jump rope song
I just didn't know which to do

Until I looked at Talanda in that dress
I thought about the woman who was her great
grandmother
Who maybe useta own the dress
Holdin' her real strong and real proud
I thought
One day he is gonna die
And it will shol be nice if he meets her in that other world
While she is wearin' that dress
So she could whip his natural ass good

I looks up at him
And I laughs the meanest, coldbloodnest laugh I could
muster
I laughed for what she was gon do to him one day
If she was gonna die
Cos everybody is
She was gonna die in that dress
I would see to it

Like I have already told you
Talanda was my very good friend
So I laughed and laughed
Laughed right through the gunshot
Laughed while she fell slow in my lap

I didn't stop laughin'
I laughed when he walked out the house
I carried her bloody body and drove her to my house
And buried her in my own backyard

Now every year on September the 23rd
I sit on his porch with a candle all lits up
And every year when his new wife asks what I'm doin'
I looks up at the sky and says sadly and happy at the same
time
I'm laughin

SOCIAL JUSTICE

Social of or relating to people or society in general
Justice *a* : the maintenance or administration of what is just : the administration of law; *especially* : the establishment or determination of rights according to the rules of law or equity : the quality of being just, ;impartial, or fair *(1)* : the principle or ideal of just dealing or right action *(2)* : conformity to truth, fact, or reason : correctness

Social justice is defined as "... promoting a just society by challenging injustice and valuing diversity." It exists when "all people share a common humanity and therefore have a right to equitable treatment, support for their human rights, and a fair allocation of community resources." In conditions of social justice, people are "not to be discriminated against, nor their welfare and well-being constrained or prejudiced on the basis of gender, sexuality, religion, political affiliations, age, race, belief, disability, location, social class, socioeconomic circumstances, or other characteristic of background or group membership" (Toowoomba Catholic Education, 2006). Social justice is generally equated with the notion of equality or equal opportunity in society.

POEM ABOUT POLICE VIOLENCE
June Jordan

`Tell me something
what you think would happen if
everytime they kill a black boy
then we kill a cop
everytime they kill a black man
then we kill a cop

you think the accident rate would lower subsequently?
sometimes the feeling like amaze me baby
comes back to my mouth and I am quiet
like Olympian pools from the running
mountainous snows under the sun

sometimes thinking about the 12th House of the Cosmos
or the way your ear ensnares the tip
of my tongue or signs that I have never seen
like DANGER WOMEN WORKING

I lose consciousness of ugly bestial rapid
and repetitive affront as when they tell me
18 cops in order to subdue one man
18 strangled him to death in the ensuing scuffle
(don't you idolize the diction of the powerful: *subdue*
and *scuffle* my oh my) and that the murder
that the killing of Arthur Miller on a Brooklyn
street was just a "justifiable accident" again
(Again)

People been having accidents all over the globe

so long like that I reckon that the only
suitable insurance is a gun
I'm saying war is not to understand or rerun
war is to be fought and won

sometimes the feeling like amaze me baby
blots it out/the bestial but
not too often tell me something
what you think would happen if
everytime they kill a black boy
then we kill a cop
everytime they kill a black man
then we kill a cop

you think the accident rate would lower subsequently

i'm raising CHILDREN
V. Kali

i'm raising CHILDREN
i'm NOT the farmer's daughter
raising CHICKENS
to be slaughtered
not the sharecropper's child
raising CANE to be
CUT DOWN
i'm raising CHILDREN here
RAISING
not california singing dried fruit
raisinettes
not raising STRANGE FRUIT
to hang from some oppressors's tree
i'm raising PRECIOUS fruits
to grow HIGH on the vine
PRECIOUS FRUITS reaching toward
the sunshine
raising the fruits of my womb
to multiply   by fives
to stay alive
i'm raising CHILDREN here.
no little bo peep
leading her sheep to be slaughtered
these are my daughters
these are my sons
i'm raising CHILDREN y'all
raising them UP
ABOVE the flood waters
i AM the crossing guard
cross me and YOU'LL be sorry

'cause i'm raising CHILDREN here
between rock and hard place
betwixt slim and none
'tween fatback and no slack
i'm raising CHILDREN y'all
the instructions are included
DON'T FOLD SPINDLE OR MUTILATE
the instructions are included
DON'T FOLD SPINDLE OR MUTILATE
the instructions BEEN included

DO NOT FOLD SPINDLE MUTILATE
NEGLECT MISUSE OR ABUSE

just follow the instructions
like you do OGUN OSUN and the MOON

just follow the instructions

cause i'm raising CHILDREN here

i'm raising CHILDREN y'all

i'm raising CHILDREN here.

YOU ARE NOT FORGOTTEN
Akoldpeice

They call you an irritant
A nuisance
Irrelevant
A burden
You are not forgotten
Over looked
See thru
Invisible
You are not the disease
Plaguing the city
Eye See You
Abuela
Grandfather
Mother
Baba
Brother
Sister
Sun
Daughter
It doesn't matter how you got here?
You are our past
Our future
Living in the present
A gift
Eye see you
We are spirits
Going through a human experience
In Lost Angeles
Angels we see you
Eye see you

We hear you
We are not better than you
Some of us are lost angels too
254,000 in this city are homeless
Men, women & children
They sleep on the street,
shelters,
cars,
parks
bus stops
abandon houses
& Rose gardens
Rose Garden
701 State Dr. Los Angeles, Ca. 90037
Exposition Park Rose Garden
My home for close to a year
When the sun set and the garden closed
Forgotten
6'4, 255lbs and invisible
Visible is the Sky
Staring past the street lights
Even the stars shine brighter
When you sleep outside
No need for alarm clock when you have the sunrise
Hungry
Starving
Forgotten
7 out of 10 Americans are 1 paycheck away from being
homeless, hungry
starving
Its been days and I need to eat
Fatigue
I need to eat
Headache
I need to eat
Sir, ma'am I don't want any money

I'm hungry
Please can you help me
Excuse me, excuse me, hello, ma'am, sir, please can you
help me
I just need to eat

Excerpt from A Lesson Before Dying
Ernest Gaines

Paul was in the office when the sheriff and the executioner came in, followed by the two special deputies, Claude and Oscar Guerin. The sheriff sat behind his desk and motioned for the executioner, whose name was Henry Vincent, to have a seat. Vincent took off his cowboy hat and hung it on the rack beside the sheriff's cowboy hat. Paul noticed that the hair on top of Vincent's head was not as gray as the sideburns were. The sheriff asked Vincent if he wanted some coffee, and Vincent said yes. The sheriff told Oscar to go down the hall and get that pot of coffee and bring back some cups. Vincent asked the sheriff if the prisoner had been shaved. The sheriff said no. Vincent asked the sheriff if he didn't think it was about time. The sheriff looked at Paul standing by the window. He told Paul where the things were; he should get Murphy out of the cell and have him do it. Vincent instructed Paul to make sure Murphy did it right, shaved him close. He pointed to areas on the leg and wrist. He said electrodes had to be attached there as well as to the head, and all that had to be shaved very clean. The sheriff told the executioner that the prisoner had hardly any hair on his body other than on his head. Vincent told Paul that Murphy must shave the prisoner everywhere he told him to; electricity sometimes found hair that the naked eye would never see. He said that this was an execution, not torture, that he had seen enough of that for a lifetime. Paul asked the sheriff if someone else couldn't do this. The sheriff told him that Clark would not be there until later, and that he had to do it. Paul nodded for Claude Guerin to come with him, and they went into the next room. He could hear Vincent asking the sheriff if he thought Paul was all right, and the sheriff saying that he was, but this was his first

385

time. Vincent told the sheriff that all they needed was for one of their own men to come apart. The sheriff assured him that Paul was okay, but that this was his first time, that's all. Vincent told the sheriff he hoped he knew his men. Paul and Claude left through another door, Claude carrying a washbasin, clippers, scissors, and a safety razor. People came out of their offices to ask Paul if it was time yet. The special deputy told them that it was only hair-cutting time. A man standing at one of the office doors said oh, yes, he had heard that they got a haircut first. Someone else said what an experience, what an experience, you didn't get to witness this every day. Paul and Claude went up to the cellblock, and unlocked Murphy's cell and told him they had a job for him to do. Murphy looked at the things in Claude's hands and asked why him. Because the sheriff said so, Paul told him. Murphy came out, and the three of them went down to the last cell. Jefferson had been lying on his back, but he sat up and looked at them when they came in. He didn't seem frightened; he appeared tired. Paul could see how red his eyes were and knew that he had not slept at all. Paul asked him how he felt, and he said he was all right. He wore a blue denim shirt and denim trousers. His laceless shoes were halfway under the bunk. The radio and the notebook were on the floor beside the wall. The radio was silent. A bird sang in the sycamore tree outside the window. Paul told Jefferson that he had to have his hair shaved. He sent Murphy to get warm water and a piece of soap from the shower room. While Murphy was gone, Paul and the other deputy stood near the unlocked cell door. Jefferson sat on the bunk, leaning forward and staring down at the floor. The two deputies watched him, but no one said anything. The bird continued its chirping in the tree outside the window. Jefferson turned to look at the deputy standing beside Paul and asked him how was Miss Bernice. Claude didn't know whether he should answer, until Paul nodded, and Claude told him that his wife was

386

okay. And little Roy? Jefferson wanted to know. Claude looked at Paul, and Paul nodded again. Little Roy was all right, too; he was at school. Jefferson looked down at the floor. Murphy came back with a washbasin of warm water and a piece of white soap. He set the basin of water on the floor at the foot of the bunk and took the clippers from Claude Guerin. Claude tried not to meet Jefferson's eyes when Jefferson looked up at him. The two deputies stood back by the door and watched as the layers of hair fell to the floor. When Murphy had finished with the clippers, he dipped his hand into the basin of warm water and started rubbing Jefferson's head with the piece of white soap. Claude handed him the safety razor. When the head was shaved, black and shining, Paul instructed Murphy to take the scissors and cut Jefferson's trouser legs and shirt sleeves. He stood over Murphy and pointed out the areas around the ankles and wrists where he wanted him to shave. All this time, Jefferson obeyed as if he were in a trance, as if he felt nothing. When Murphy was finished, he stood back and examined his work, but Jefferson was looking down at the floor. Paul asked him if he needed anything, and when he did not answer, the deputy motioned for Claude and Murphy to leave. He followed and locked the cell door. As he was about to walk away, Jefferson raised his head and looked at him. He told Paul that he wanted him to bring me the notebook and that he wanted Paul to have the radio. Paul told him he couldn't take the radio, but he would give it to the other inmates, for use in the dayroom, if Jefferson didn't mind. Jefferson asked Paul if he wanted the marble that Bok had given him, and Paul told him he would accept the marble. He told Paul to be sure that Mr. Henri got the pocket knife and the little gold chain. Paul said he would see to that. Jefferson continued to look at Paul, a long, deep look, and the deputy felt that there was something else he wanted to say. Murphy and the other deputy were still waiting. "Well," Paul said, and started to walk away. "Paul?" Jefferson said quietly. And his eyes were speaking, even more than his mouth. The deputy looked back at him. Murphy and Claude did too. "You go'n be there, Paul?" Jefferson asked, his eyes asked. Paul nodded. "Yes, Jefferson. I'll be there."

RESEARCH

noun re·search \ri-ˈsərch, ˈrē-ˌ\
: careful study that is done to find and report new knowledge about something: the activity of getting information about a subject: careful or diligent search: studious inquiry or examination; *especially* : investigation or experimentation aimed at the discovery and interpretation of facts, revision of accepted theories or laws in the light of new facts, or practical application of such new or revised theories or laws

Research comprises "creative work undertaken on a systematic basis in order to increase the stock of knowledge, including knowledge of humans, culture and society, and the use of this stock of knowledge to devise new applications."[1] It is used to establish or confirm facts, reaffirm the results of previous work, solve new or existing problems, support theorems, or develop new theories. A research project may also be an expansion on past work in the field. To test the validity of instruments, procedures, or experiments, research may replicate elements of prior projects, or the project as a whole. The primary purposes of basic research (as opposed to applied research) are documentation, discovery, interpretation, or the research and development (R&D) of methods and systems for the advancement of human knowledge. Approaches to research depend on epistemologies, which vary considerably both within and between humanities and sciences.

1830
Hiram Sims

They used to kill us for this
Gave us death sentences just for writing sentences
Penned down and murdered for the right to write on pen
and paper
Lined up on a firing wall for these fractions
Subject to the pulling of triggers for learning trigonometry
My grandmothers perished for paragraphs
Indented on indentured servitude in this peculiar institution

They used to kill us for this
My grandfathers pronounced dead for hiding pronouns
under their pillows
Vocabulary pouring out with the blood, forbidden ink
oozing out of their pores
Mutilated for our metaphors
Decapitated for Capital letters
Killed for the curiosity of quadratic equations
my kinfolk slaughtered for synonyms
killed for these commas
lynched for their lexicon
knocked off for these nouns
run down for these run-ons
my mothers massacred for writing their monikers
just for writing their names
beautiful brown leaves hanging from the branches of my
family tree
terminated for their terminology

We used to die for this
America's southern graves are filled with students

Who looked like us, walked like us, wanted to learn
Like us And when they speak to me at night
From their shallow graves in Arkansas
As I contemplate the thought of being furious
They say, do not be Angry for Me
 Read for Me, Write for Me, Count for Me
Spell for me, study for me, learn for me, speak for me
Read for Me, Write for Me,
Read for Me, Write for Me
And live

Comfort Woman
Tanya Hyonhye Ko

1943, Shanghai, China

One night
a soldier asked all the girls

Who can do one hundred men?
I raised my hand

Soonja did not.

The soldiers put her in boiling water
alive

and fed us.

What is living?

Is Soonja living in me?

1946, Chinju, Korea

One year after
liberation
I came home.

Short hair
not wearing hanbok
not speaking clearly.

Mother hid me

in the back room.

At night she took me to the well.
Scars seared with hot steel
like burnt bark
like tree roots
all over my body.

Under the crescent glow
she smiled when she washed me.
My baby! Your skin
is like white jade, dazzling.

She made white rice and seaweed soup
put my favorite fish on top.
But Mother, I can't eat flesh.

That night in the granary
she hanged herself
left a little bag for me
my dowry, with a rice ball.

Father threw it at me
waved his hand toward the door.

I left at dusk.

Struggle to Smuggle
Matt Dlouhly

A green neon Heineken beer sign blinked every two seconds. The room smelled like stale cigarettes. He heavily perspired through his blue t-shirt. It felt close to 100 degrees inside. He glanced down at his twenty dollar Rolex knockoff. It was 2:15 in the morning. He was supposed to leave with his friends in a little over 4 hours. He and his friends were going to fly directly on flight 345 from Bogotá to Los Angeles. He raised his index finger. The bartender poured him another shot of rum. He took out 5 thousand pesos from his wallet and slid it toward the bartender. The bartender held the bill up to a light bulb and checked for a watermark.

"Gracias." The bartender said.

He grabbed his face with his palms and shook his head. He was going to be used as a mule. He felt naïve; he had fallen into a trap that required him to smuggle cocaine out of Columbia. His cell phone vibrated. He took out his iphone and swiped his screen. The DJ darkened the lights as the song came to an end. He squinted his eyes and tried to read the message he had just received.

"Ey, Jeff, meet me @ da corner. I wnt 2 tlk to u." The text message incoherently read.

The message was from Jeff's friend, Dave. Dave was the planner and leader of the entire trip. Dave was an outgoing guy, but he had a slimy personality. Dave introduced Jeff to binge drinking, gambling, and cocaine. Jeff stood up from the barstool and chugged the rest of the rum. He placed the ice filled glass on the counter and maneuvered his way through the crowded club. The DJ cranked up the bass and began playing "Strobe lights," from the dubstep artist,

Krewella. The audience cheered. Red, blue, and green strobe lights distorted the color of the brown brick room. All he could hear being yelled across the club was Portuguese, French, and German. Jeff figured at least 20% of these tourists were also smugglers. He opened the door and inhaled the fresh air. A cool breeze swooshed against his face. It was a sweltering 90 degrees outside, but it felt cooler than inside. He snapped his fingers next to his ringing eardrums. His cochlea could barely detect a vibration. He could see Dave leaning against the side of a parked Bimbo truck, under a streetlight. Dave wore a blue LA Dodgers baseball cap and a Viva Columbia T shirt. Dave could not have looked any more like a tourist. Dave spotted Jeff. Jeff staggered down the littered sidewalk.

"Wow, we have to fly out of the country in four hours with coke taped around us, and this jerk's already plastered! Are you kidding me?" Dave thought.

Dave nodded his head as Jeff approached him. Jeff looked haggard. His eyes were blood shot red. A police car crept past them. A shiver ran down Jeff's spine. He worried that the plan had already fallen through. Jeff placed his right hand over his chest and tried to catch his breath. The driver turned on the emergency lights and made a sharp turn around the corner. The siren screamed down the narrow brick street. Jeff assumed he was going to see police all throughout the airport. He figured the police were trained to search more thoroughly for foreigners.

"Where the hell have you been?" Dave asked.

Jeff scratched the back of his head. Despite Jeff's appearance, Jeff was sober enough to follow what Dave had asked him. Jeff did not know how to respond to Dave without insulting him. He stared at Dave's shadowed face. Dave was not a fun friend when he discussed business.

"I've been thinking…..and….uh…well……I don't want to do it." Jeff said.

"What? What are you talking about? Dude, we're gonna' make some money. Then we can keep coming back here. It'll be like a series of vacations." Jeff said encouragingly.

"I don't wanna' come back here. Plus, they're gonna' catch on if we do this again. I mean, it's not like a lot of people from America want to come to Bogotá; Cartagena maybe, but there's not much to do here. We're not even Columbian. I'm not coming back here and I'm not smuggling the load. You keep the money you make; I don't want any part of it." Jeff protested.

"Unbelievable. I come with you all the way down here, ask you to do one small favor for me, and you do *this* to me. What the hell? What did I ever do to you?" Dave shouted.

"No it's not that. We're still friends. I just…..I just don't want to get caught." Jeff said.

"You won't. Trust me. I know what I'm doing. Trust me….you won't get caught." Dave said.

"You don't know that. Haven't you seen the show, Locked Up Abroad? I don't want to go to jail here!" Jeff shouted frantically."

"Shhhhh! Shut up you're gonna' blow our cover. Listen to me. I've done this before with other people. The security at the El Dorado Airport is beyond embarrassing. I mean, I don't even know if they have metal detectors for Christ's sake." Dave said jokingly.

"You've done this before?" Jeff shouted.

Dave swore under his breath. The truth accidentally slipped out. Dave wondered when the three mules he dragged along were going to realize that he was an experienced smuggler. Dave removed his hat and wiped his sweaty brown hair. Nobody had ever wimped out on his other trips. Jeff sighed. He had no choice but to resort to hostility to protect himself, his identity, and his side business.

"You used me. I thought I was your friend." Jeff said angrily.

"You are a friend. We all need to do this together. It'll be a team effort." Dave said.

"I'm not taping that…. *you know what*, to my ribs and legs, okay? That wasn't part of the trip's itinerary. None of this shit was! The five hour hike in the mountains to get the packages, the army helicopters flying over us through that mosquito infested rainforest, the scary interrogation from the cartel; all of this wasn't supposed to happen!" Jeff spitefully shouted.

Dave rolled his eyes-he did not care. He always made a habit of persuading other suckers to travel with him on his smuggling trips. Dave usually found new people, so it never became a problem if friends like Jeff decided not to come back with him. Controlling a mule's behavior was sometimes a challenge for Dave. He never used to worry about his selected friends, but he was now concerned. He had almost been ratted out by a friend earlier in the morning. He began to worry that Jeff was going to rat him out next. Dave placed his arm around Jeff's shoulder. He knew he needed to do something *for*, or *to* Jeff before things got out of hand. Jeff shoved Dave's arm off.

"Keep the drugs; you can keep my damn plane ticket too." Jeff muttered.

Jeff ignored Dave and continued walking down the street. Dave desperately followed after him. Dave was not sure what Jeff was capable of doing. The fear of getting caught plagued Dave's mind. The road on the side of the street was under construction. Three shovels and a pick axe lay beside a pile of loose gravel. Dave grabbed a rusty pick-axe and raised it into the air. He rushed up behind Jeff and swung the blade into Jeff's neck.

"Ahhhhh!" Jeff screamed as he fell.

Jeff's left side struck the ground. He defenselessly stared up into Dave's wild wandering brown eyes. Jeff cuffed his right hand around his wound. Warm sticky blood seeped between Jeff's fingers and ran down his arm. Jeff's vision became distorted and his hearing deafened.

"Ahhhhh….Don't kill me. {Gasp}….Don't kill me…..{Gasp}…Don't kill me." Jeff wailed.

Dave raised the pick-axe and struck the tip between Jeff's eyes. The axe penetrated through Jeff's skull and struck the concrete sidewalk. The crunching thud startled a flock of parrots. Five parrots squawked and flew off of an overhanging roof. A loose tile fell off the roof and shattered inches away from Jeff's cracked skull. Dave glanced over his shoulders. His muscles twitched. Lights in surrounding buildings began to turn on.

"I gotta' get the hell out of here." Dave fearfully muttered.

***

"Hurry up Roger, we're gonna' miss a taxi." Dave scolded.

"I'm taping as fast as I can. Where the hell is everybody? Where's Jake and Jeff?" Roger asked.

"That's their problem if they don't come. They can't make us late. If we miss our flight we're shit out of luck." Dave grumbled.

Roger was another mule that was duped into coming on the trip. Roger and Dave were old acquaintances from high school. Dave ripped off a piece of duct tape and strapped a wrapped lump of cocaine to the left side of his ribs. Roger tore off a roll of tape and fastened a package around his abdomen. Roger crept into the bathroom and stared at his reflection. He had gained no tan on this disappointing tropical vacation. He was wearing a black 5 o'clock shadow; he looked paler than when he left. He did not know what to expect on their ordeal back to LA. He shook his head as he placed a light jacket over his shirt. Dave stood beside the door.

"Come on, let's go." Dave nagged.

"Is it really worth it? I mean yeah, it should be easy getting through this airport, but what about LAX. What if those TSA Nazis find our stashes on us? I mean, they have X-rays. I don't know about this. Damn. Where the hell is Jeff and Jake? I'm gonna' look next door." Roger said.

Dave's eyes widened. Roger unlocked the connecting door and walked inside.

"Hey are you guys up? Where are they? Pugh. It smells like an ashtray in here." Roger said.

Dave had smoked half a pack of Marlboro to mask the scent of what silently lurked in the closet. Roger plugged his nostrils shut and shrugged his shoulders.

"I guess they're out partying." Dave suggested.

"Yeah, I guess so. They're gonna' have a rough day ahead of them. They're so stupid to.......what's that thumping noise?" Roger asked.

Dave's heartbeat jolted each time he took a breath. Sweat drops fell down his forehead. The room seemed like it had gotten twenty degrees hotter. He was worried that his plan had backfired. Dave also heard the thumping noise, and it sounded like it originated from the closet.

"That noise? Uh....what noise? I don't hear any noise." Dave said quickly.

"It sounds like it's coming from the closet." Roger muttered.

Roger crept toward the closet which stood next to the front door. Dave quickly pulled out his phone from his pocket and waved it in front of Roger's perplexed face.

"Jeff sent me a text! He sent a text! They're already waiting for us at the airport. Can you believe that? Hahaha....They had the nerve to scare us like that." Dave said chaotically.

"Hmmm. Alright, we'll, let's go get a taxi." Roger suggested.

Roger went back into his room. Dave eased open the closet door. The door squeaked. Jake's body swayed in the closet. His shoes clanked against the wooden door. Jake's neck was supported by a nylon rope that Dave had coincidently purchased at a vendor near the hotel. Jake's face was pale.

His eyes and mouth hung open in a silent scream. Dave closed the door. The nauseating odor of death was seeping back into the room. Jake was the third mule and acquaintance that Dave had dragged along. Jake refused to smuggle his share of cocaine suddenly after Jeff unexpectedly departed to the night club. Jake panicked and attempted to warn the police about Dave's devious plan. Unfortunately, Dave had disabled the phone in Jake's room long before Jake tried to warn the police. Jake tried to escape to the front desk, but he was confronted by Dave. Dave brought Jake back to Jake's empty room, and murdered him.

"Where'd you go?" Roger asked.

"Coming." Dave said quickly.

They rolled their suitcases down the stairwell. The elevator was broken, along with the pool, ice machine, and most of the light bulbs in the hallway. The hotel had seen better days.

"This place must have had a quarter of a star. This dump really makes Motel 6 look like a Marriott." Roger thought.

They stood beside the sidewalk and waited for a taxi. Rows of police cars rushed through the street. The cars drove in the direction that Jeff had been murdered.

"Hey. Let's check out what happened." Roger said.

"No!" Dave shouted.

"What? What's the problem?" Roger asked.

"It's too dangerous. This is Columbia. It's probably some shooting with a cartel. You don't want to die do you? The whole point of this trip was for all of us to make it out alive." Dave said. Roger nodded.

***

They walked out of the airport check-in line and headed toward the security checkpoint. Roger was convinced by Dave that Jeff and Jake were still waiting by the gate. Dave stopped walking. Policemen in blue uniforms stood beside work dogs. Dave's chest pounded.

"What's going on? They never had drug dogs here before. How did they know I'd be here today? Do they know I'm coming? Jeff was right......maybe they did catch on to me." Dave thought.

"I gotta' go to the bathroom. I'll be right back." Dave said.

Dave barged open the bathroom door and rushed into a stall. He slammed the door shut.

Dave took off his jacket and shirt. He grabbed a loose end of tape and braced for the sting. His fingertips were bright white from tugging. The sound of sticky duct tape echoed throughout the tile room. He squinted his eyes and clenched his teeth to relieve the pain. He tugged on the silver tape until the packs loosened. The packs of cocaine plopped onto the ground. He picked up the packs and dropped them into the toilet bowl. He checked his watch. He had left Roger waiting for seven minutes. He flushed the toilet and rushed to the sink. He was out of breath. He glanced behind him. Water seeped out from the toilet he had just clogged. Packs of white powder surfaced onto the floor.

"Oh...... shit." He muttered.

Dave yanked his suitcase forward and rushed out of the bathroom. Roger stood beside the checkpoint line with his arms crossed. He raised his hands. Dave's face was bright red.

"We're losing time. Did you fall in or something?" Roger scowled.

"I'm sorry. I had diarrhea. Don't worry it all came out......at least I think it did." Dave said.

Roger feared that Dave was coming down with the flu. He distanced himself from Dave. Dave took this as an advantage. A disturbing grin came to Dave's face. He was just five people away from crossing the checkpoint. Dave's arms shook. He was excited. The ordeal was almost over. His daring plans had worked. He had unfortunately murdered two people in the process, but he had gotten away with it. He held his head up high as he yanked his suitcase forward.

"A paid vacation, some quick cash, and a mule to do my dirty work; what more could I ask for? I should ask those other suckers from the bar to go with me next month. Calvin and….Jack…or…..I don't know their names, but who cares? They're dumb enough to fall for this scam. Hahaha. Roger's next. I can't wait. LA here I come." Dave thought.

A work dog sat in front of Roger and stared up at the policeman. Dave's victory smile swiftly disappeared. He became sweatier and his muscles became more agitated. Roger stared back at Dave. Roger's face was blank. The policeman and security guard argued back and forth in Spanish. The German Sheppard barked. Dave swore under his breath.

"Sir, come wit' me." The policeman said to Roger.

Dave stepped back from Roger. Roger turned around and pointed at Dave. Roger looked like he had lost his mind. His body quivered and his eyes enlarged. Terror struck his face.

"He's smuggling coke too! Check him! Pat him down!" Roger screamed.

Dave looked down at his suitcase. He pretended he had never met Roger.

"Dave! You son of a bitch! You set me up! He's guilty too! I swear! Pat him down!" Roger shouted.

The policeman raised Roger's jacket and shirt. The packs were clearly visible.

"Cocaína." The guard and policeman simultaneously said. Three policemen handcuffed Roger and guided him to the side of the checkpoint. Dave stood next to the security guard. He raised his arms and separated his legs. Dave fearfully closed his eyes. Roger was now a dangerous liability. The guard waved Dave through. A policeman waved his index finger. Dave ignored the policeman. Dave pretended he had not seen him.

"Señor, ey,' you. Sir, cahm' wit' me." The policeman said in a thick accent.

The policeman guided Dave to an inspection area. A policeman took Dave's suitcase and unzipped it. Dave was anxious to escape the room. He was tempted to run out of the airport and flee the city.

"I need to escape the country. I can escape to the Peruvian Andes, or hide out in the Brazilian Amazon. Nobody will ever know who I am, or what I'm doing there. This is bad….this is really bad. Wait a minute. I dumped the cocaine. I'm clean. I don't have anything on me. I shouldn't have to worry about a thing. Wow, I got all worked up for nothing. What are they gonna' find? I'm innocent." Dave thought.

Two policemen placed a portable x-ray machine against Dave's abdomen. The two men nodded at one another. They had seen other smugglers do what Dave had tried to get away with.

"Oh shit! I swallowed those condoms." Dave thought.

A policeman raised a pair of handcuffs from his belt. The couplings clicked once they fastened around Dave's wrists. Dave lowered his head. The game was over. His mission was failed, and his life as he once knew it was about to be changed for the worse.

"Okay, sir. You swallow….eh….de' cocaine condom….and eh…..that's….a crime in Columbia. You go to jail now….and eh…..get…..eh…. lawyer tomorrow, okay?" The policeman said.

"I was forced to swallow coke! They made me be a drug mule! Let me go!" Dave screamed.

"Okay….okay. De' judge…eh….say what he wan' you to do tomorrow, okay?"

"It wasn't me. I swear! I swear to God, I was forced to swallow it." Dave pleaded.

"Okay…okay….cam' down. Ey, man, I ave' to do my job, okay? You hide …..eh…cocaine….eh….it's a-legal, okay? You try to smuggle…..you get consequence."

Dave swore as the policemen escorted him out of the room.

"You don't expect drug dog, eh? Dog….he sniff everyone…..now everyone struggle to smuggle. Hope your embassy save you, man. Dey' cartel gonna' kill you in jail." A security guard said.

PERSONIFICATION

: the practice of representing a thing or idea as a person in art, literature, etc.: attribution of personal qualities; especially : representation of a thing or abstraction as a person or by the human form

Personification is one of the most commonly used and recognized literary devices. As a literary device, personification is the projection of characteristics that normally belong only to humans onto inanimate objects, animals, deities, or forces of nature. These characteristics can include verbs of actions that only humans do or adjectives that describe a human condition. The characteristics can also be emotions, feelings, or motives given to objects incapable of thought. For example, if someone said, "the trees whispered their discontent," this would personify the trees both as able to whisper and of feeling unhappy. Personification is also sometimes referred to as anthropomorphism when it is used to give human feelings and actions to animals.

Personification can also mean the embodiment of an abstract idea or quality. This definition of personification can extend even to humans. For example, a person can be said to personify the patriotism of his country or the ambition of her company. We could say, "She is the personification of the grit and determination needed to make this start-up work."

Purposéx

405

hip-hop is HIV positive
Conney Williams

always on stage massaging its
infection at some awards show
applying for Section 8 housing
I regularly witness hip-hop
panhandling for an I.V. of respect
and a few cc's of validity
hip-hop once seized the neck of rhythm
gave it a gut check, unharnessed
the libido of street speak
it's breath was like eucalyptus oil
poured from a warrior's horn
hip-hop dismantled fear
embedded beneath the beat
"I said hip-hop, you don't stop"
like the reign of Fidel, it didn't
the onslaught of scratches and pentameter
street terrorists patois braggadocio
that rebelled the vocabulary
recreating dialect for the disaffected
disoriented since leaving the 90's
 "and what you hear is not a test"
inspiration now asleep at the turntable
it's no more than a contagion
spreading lyrical disease through
the constipation of thought
hip-hop is HIV positive
full blown and in need of AIDS

MONEY
Poetri

My money has been acting funny, lately
Tripping.
This ain't the first time.
Every now and then, I can expect money to disappear for
awhile,
watch me smile when I see her back in my hands.
My money's been acting funny, lately,
and I don't mean ha ha funny.
No, I'm talking strange wierd, different type funny.
This time money's gone all out,
leaving me, showing up and then leaving as quickly as she
came,
ignoring me, treating me like a poor man,
What I do boo?
All I ever did was love you!
Maybe too much, cause now it's like we ain't cool no
more.
We use to be ro-dogs, inseparable,
but lately my money's been acting funny and I haven't
seen money in months.
I have more than a hunch that she's playing me, trying to
make me jaelous,
hanging out with other fellas,
always in some other brother's pocket.
I try and tell her that those other guys are just using her.
"They just using you, ☐money!!"
She don't wanna hear me.
She doesn't even return my phone calls.
She won't go to the movies with me.
She won't even go with me to get nothing to eat.
And you know a brother can't eat, without money!

Don't you know I miss you? I want you!
Okay, I need you to survive, my life evolves around you.
I can't replace you money, believe me I've tried.
There's only so much bread and water I can take.
Call me spoiled, but I remember the days when people
used to see at the hottest clubs,
the expensive restaurants,
all the high-priced stores. I made sure
I looked good with money.
I treated you right! I never abused you...did I?
Money, did I abuse you? Did I love you too much?
Did I get used to you hanging around
and now you're giving me a taste of what it feels like to
live without you?
People still think we're tight!
They still ask about you.
I don't like them all in my business,
so I just reply, money and I,
aren't as close as we used to be.
My money's been acting funny, lately.
I can't even call out her name when I'm playing ball.
I saw her the other day in Beverly Hills. She didn't even
acknowledge me.
She looked at me like
"...what are you doing in Beverly Hills?
Ever since money hasn't been around, I feel like I'm losing
my other friends, too!
American Express, Visa, Discover, now they starting to act
shady.
I think she's spreading lies on me!
I tell you, I don't know what I did, but my money's been
acting real funny, lately.
And I don't know her anymore and my life ain't same.
Never will be the same, until money comes back into my
life.
So, if you see her, or any of her family,

she has a whole bunch of cousins running around,
let her know that I miss her,
I love her,
and I want her to come home.

Gary and Ray
Wendy Rainey

For thirty years I was glued to a plastic crucifix on the top of Ethel's T.V. set in a trailer park in El Monte. Bitch croaked about a month ago and I ended up on sale for five dollars at a junk shop off of Magnolia. Rubbing shoulders with an Elvis whiskey decanter is not how I had dreamed of spending my twilight years. Besides, every time I tried to talk to him he just stared off into space with that Elvis sneer. I thought he was a stuck-up little turd who thought he was too good to give me the time of day. But when he turned around to swat a fly buzzing behind his head, I could see the crack in his skull, which explained why he never spoke. After that I felt awful for ever having thought anything bad about him. Anyway, I had gotten real sick of having to hear Ethel's soap operas all the time after she got laid off from the plant. And when she finally got another job, as soon as she'd come home from work every night, she'd turn on American Idol, Dancing With The Stars, or The Home Shopping Network. There's so much desperation in those shows that sometimes it would make my stigmata bleed. And it was a big pain in the ass because Ethel would have all of her little friends over to her trailer so they could watch me bleed during The Bachelor. They would just sit there gawking at me and taking photos while my blood collected into an empty Hungry Man T.V. Dinner tray.

It was about a year ago that I lost my best friend, Ray. Ethel bought Ray after she saw The Story Of The Bible on The History Channel. Turns out that Jesus didn't have blue eyes and fair skin like me. He was brown-eyed and dark. So Ethel ordered an "Authentic Nazarene Jesus" from The Home Shopping Network. When Ethel took him out of the

410

box I was impressed by his long white linen gown. It had intricate gold stitching and a gold belt. He was wearing sandals made out of real leather. Even his hair looked better than mine. I had strawberry blond hair that was thinning at my temples. My skin was grey from the residue of the smoke that Ethel blew at me while she watched television. My white robe had been stained by the wine Ethel had sloshed on me one night as she adjusted her T.V. set. She cackled as she ripped off my wet robe and replaced it with a floral nightie she swiped from one of her baby dolls she collected. I felt like a slob next to the new guy who had skin that glowed, brown eyes that caught the light, and thick dark hair that fell to his shoulders. When he moved it was as if his feet were on fire. He came with a hand carved wooden cross that Ethel positioned him on next to me on the T.V. I was pretty leery of him at first. I mean I had already been living on Ethel's Sony Trinitron for fifteen years, so I wasn't exactly in the mood to share the spotlight with another Jesus. Much less one about a thousand times better looking than me. But nevertheless, I knew I had to get along with him if we were both to live atop Ethel's Sony, so I said, "Welcome to the trailer park, Jesus." He laughed, and told me his name was Ray. He asked me what my name was and I told him, "Jesus." "Bullshit!" he laughed again. "You look like a Gary. I'm gonna call you Gary." He asked me what I did for fun. I told him the truth, "Nothing, Man. I just stand here and watch Ethel drink and smoke. I can see the reflection of the T.V. screen in the microwave in front of me, so sometimes I watch the shows, but I try not to because they make me bleed." He looked into my eyes and said, "Stick with me, brother. It's the only way we're gonna make it."

That night, after Ethel had passed out drunk, Ray jumped off his cross and leapt over the set to where she was reclining on her Lay-Z-Boy. He took her bottle of Scotch, and drank a third of it. He lit up one of her Pall

411

Malls and smoked it, flicking the ashes into her Stardust Casino ashtray. Then he jumped up to the knick-knack shelf and started ogling the water nymphs in their pool. Ethel had a set of ten porcelain nymphs in a glass bowl designed to look like a pond for bathing. She had filled the glass pond with real water and had fresh cut lilies floating on the surface of the water. She had arranged the naked nymphs in seductive poses. It had never occurred to me that I could move around Ethel's trailer after she passed out every night, but Ray took it as a given that we had free reign of the place. He got ahold of the remote and turned the channel to the adult station. "Come on, Gary. Get your goddamned ass off that T.V. Come on down here and live a little, motherfucker!"

Every night was a new adventure with Ray. Sometimes we'd sneak out of Ethel's trailer and lay on our backs on the grass and look up at the stars in the sky. Ray would talk about what he had read that day from the set of Britannica Encyclopedias that Ethel's husband had left on her shelf after he split with her. The Cretaceous- Tertiary extinction event was always on his mind. Ray would go on for hours about why the dinosaurs died out. After Ethel bought her first computer Ray would get on the web and spend hours in video chat rooms while Ethel was at work. Sometimes after Ethel fell asleep in her chair at night Ray would turn the camera on her and live stream her snoring, farting and talking in her sleep. I don't know how he managed it, but he was able to get ahold of Ethel's PIN number and purchase his own iPhone on the internet. He opened up a Facebook page from his phone. He had over 4,000 friends from all over the world. He loved to take selfies of us swimming and drinking beer in Ethel's fiberglass pool. Sometimes Ray would snag a joint from Ethel's neighbor and we'd float on the inner tube getting high and eating the leftover Hamburger Helper in Ethel's refrigerator.

I had fourteen of the best years of my life with Ray. But one night, about a year ago Ethel came home from work shit-faced and grumbling about the extra charges on her credit card. Apparently she had caught on to Ray's activities. She picked him up and looked into his eyes, "You are the one who has been using my credit card, drinking my liquor, smoking my cigarettes, eating my food, and playing fast and loose with my nymphs. God only knows what else you're up to, you sonofabitch!" Ray roared his baritone laugh in Ethel's face. Ethel lost it. "You sound just like my ex-husband!" she screamed, hurling him against the wall, smashing him to bits. That night I never bled so hard in my life. And it wasn't just blood. I started crying all the time too. Of course Ethel had to put me on display for the whole park to see every time I bled and cried. I really despised her. So when the old biddy finally bit the dust, I was happy as hell. I don't think I'll ever find another friend like Ray. I think about him all the time. And when I see guys like Elvis next to me with the cracked skull and empty eyes, well, I just want to throw myself off the highest shelf of this junk store and feel myself smash into a thousand tiny pieces and have it done with for once and for all. It's a strange feeling to know that the best years of my life are already behind me.

RESEARCH METHODS

WHY DO WE RESEARCH?

- To give the book a sense of authenticity
- To give credibility to yourself as an author, so that the reader stays in the story and trusts what you are telling them. Something too off or obviously under-researched will jar a careful reader out of the story
- To better create a strong sense of time and place
- To provide story inspiration and ideas
- To accurately convey actions, for example if characters are doing something like churning butter while having a conversation, it's good to know how much effort and time something like that takes
- To find details to use in your description that are true to the time and place
- To be able to tell stories not only reliant on your experience and current knowledge
- To better characterize your characters, for example researching astrology, birth order, psychological disorders, trauma effects to help make your people layered, flawed, and real

Primary Sources: maps, photos, artwork, letters, personal papers, etc., periodicals from the time period/location, items from the period, obituaries, interviews. Can be located in archives, libraries, thrift stores, personal collections, online, etc.

Secondary Sources: books, films, or articles about the time period/location/subject matter, etc. Can be located in libraries, university journal databases.

TIPS:

- Specificity: Don't be afraid to use reality to make your locations, events, etc. plausible. Lots of great fiction starts from looking at something very real. For example, if you have a scene about a slave auction, look at handbills for or accounts of real slave auctions and put your characters at one of them. If your story is set in a city you have access to, drive neighborhoods and find the house in which your character lives. You can always change what you want, but starting with the real world will help you to get specificity.
- Thoroughness: Consult a variety of sources: primary, secondary, textual, human, visual, etc. Take or save pictures of items, take thorough notes from books, film or transcribe interviews. You never know what you might be able to use. When you find a good book, scan or photocopy and keep their endnotes or bibliography; it will contain other possible sources. Try to get a well-rounded picture of the time period/location, subject matter, etc. Cast a wide net.
- Creativity: Be creative about how you use sources to get more information about a certain time, topic. For example, I looked at Urban dictionary entries online and listened to albums from the very early nineties to get the slang right. I looked at album covers of popular R&B and hip hop acts and movies from those years to get a sense of the fashion. I looked at homicide and police reports from the days

of the riots to get a better sense of what was going on in the city.

- Immersion: Use your research to immerse yourself in the time/location/topic. Find music from the time/place/cultural context of your setting and play it while you write. Find clothes from the time in a thrift store (if you can't make it or find specific items in one Etsy a great source for vintage items) and try them on to see how they work, fasten, etc. If you can get to a place, go there, if note use tools like Google maps, property records, etc. If your character has a hobby or something they like to do (woodworking for example) take it up yourself. Interview someone who has your character's career.

Don't get too bogged down by research. It should be fun, and provide you with a wealth of material that you'll probably end up not using most of. But, like character mapping, research is important to make sure you have an arsenal of material culture, details, information at your disposal.

417

WRITING ACTION IN PROSE

It can be difficult to depict things actually happening in prose. Many writers are more comfortable with dialogue, description, or showing things in flashback than they are writing real-time physical action. Some tips:

- Use the space, take your time. It's ok for the characters to move more slowly than reality.
- Research or try the kinds of actions you are depicting—make sure they are accurate (in how long they take, the force required to do certain things, etc.)
- Use active verbs. Get out your thesaurus. Use active, interesting verbs rather than rely on adverbs to convey the nature of an action. For example, "she stalked away" rather than "she stomped angrily away." Maybe "His fingertips nibbled her elbow as he steered her into the room" rather than "He softly touched her elbow as he steered her into the room"
- Use active voice
- It doesn't have to be all action. Intersperse with dialogue, description, flashback, thoughts, memory, reactions. Things can speed up, slow down, speed up again as needed. Put flesh on the skeleton of what is happening.
- Think honestly about human reactions and make sure the action gives space to depict and absorb honest reactions.

FIGURATIVE LANGUAGE FOR FICTION

- Avoid clichés. Make sure that your language is original without being so clever that it is unclear or slows the reader down.
- Metaphors and other uses of figurative language will be more seamless and powerful if they fit into the "world" of the novel. For example, a novel set in an urban area might not have as many agrarian, nature type metaphors, language. In my novel, a coming of age story about a young girl in an urban area, I tried to make sure all of my figurative language fit the world, that it reflected the point of view of a young girl…for example in one scene Tanis compares the flowers in someone's yard to a lady's fingernails.
- Restate each of these clichés in your own original language, using at least one image and making sure that the images used fit the world of your novel.

1. She fell in love with him.
2. Her heart was broken.
3. It's raining cats and dogs.
4. There were butterflies in her stomach.

CHAPTER CONSTRUCTION

Each chapter should somehow move your story forward. When writing your chapters, think about the things below that they should contain. It is possible for these elements to overlap.

Function-What functionally, needs to happen at this point in the story? Is there exposition that needs to be done, characters that need to meet, a location that needs to be established, something that needs to be set up for the future?

Event-Something has to happen in a chapter, in real time. It doesn't have to be big, but there does need to be something that somehow advances the story.

Character Shift-Something needs to happen with your protagonist, or another major character. The major characters should somehow change, or learn over the course of a story. Every chapter should be a small step in the major character/s' transformation, or should impart to them some kind of knowledge. This can be subtle, and the change your character undergoes doesn't have to be linear, only forward moving. But something, however subtle should happen internally with major character/s.

NARRATIVE PERSPECTIVE

Know who is telling the story, who your reader is supposed to align themselves with in the scene. In revision, make a clear and specific choice about your narrative perspective, and understand what it allows for and what it forecloses.

- First person-"I" narration. Is very useful for maintaining a very clear narrative perspective, aligning reader firmly with a point of view character, being able to get into one characters reactions, thoughts, emotions. Sometimes characterizing the I of a first person narration can be challenging, as so much is coming from their observation of others. your story is limited to what this character can know, observe, and participate in

- second person-"You" narration, addressing a presumed or actual reader. Common in epistolary, but otherwise fairly rare, hard to sustain in long fiction

- third person camera-"He" "She" "They" but still firmly in one character's point of view, as if the camera is on their shoulder. A lot of the same limitations and advantages of first person, though characterization and description of this character might be easier, and point of view slips might be more common. Commit to one person's point of view in a scene, keep the camera on that person's shoulder

- ○ third person omniscient-"He" She" They" godlike perspective, the narrator is looking down on everything, sees and knows anything, but maintains equal distance and/or intimacy with the characters

- ○ third person ensemble cast-an omniscient narrator that transitions between different characters' point of view, moving the camera from shoulder to shoulder—this gives advantages of access to more knowledge and interiority, but has to be done very skillfully ...If you do choose to move back and forth within the scene, you have to take your time in the movement, and you have to signal properly and at consistent intervals so that readers have clarity and expectations of who they are with

ABOUT
THE EDITOR

Hiram Sims is a poet, essayist, short fiction writer, and Creative Writing Professor at The Los Angeles Film School. He is also the Founding Director of The Community Literature Initiative. In addition to being a great fan of every writer in this book, he is also incredibly handsome. Visit Hiramsims.com